WOMEN IN AMERICAN HISTORY

*Series Editors*
MARI JO BUHLE
JACQUELYN D. HALL
ANNE FIROR SCOTT

*Private Matters*

# PRIVATE MATTERS

## American Attitudes toward Childbearing and Infant Nurture in the Urban North, 1800–1860

### SYLVIA D. HOFFERT

UNIVERSITY OF ILLINOIS PRESS

URBANA AND CHICAGO

Publication of this work was supported in part
by a grant from the Andrew W. Mellon Foundation

*This book is printed on acid-free paper.*

LIBRARY OF CONGRESS CATALOGING-IN-PUBLICATION DATA

Hoffert, Sylvia D.
   Private matters : American attitudes toward childbearing and
infant nurture in the urban North, 1800–1860 / Sylvia D. Hoffert.
      p. cm. —(Women in American history)
   Bibliography: p.
   Includes index.
   ISBN 0–252–01547–9 (alk. paper)
   1. Motherhood—United States—History—19th century. 2. Mother
and child—United States—History—19th century. 3. Privacy—United
States—History—19th century. 4. Women—United States—Attitudes—
History—19th century. I. Title. II. Series.
HQ759.H69 1989
306.8'743—dc19                                          88–3766
                                                              CIP

*To Dick*
*Whose love and support made this book possible*
*and*
*to Kristi and Mindy*
*Who taught me how to be a mother*

# *Contents*

# Illustrations

# Acknowledgments

I wish to express my thanks to Lewis Perry, M. Jeanne Peterson, Jan Shipps, and Irene Neu, who read early versions of this manuscript, and to Stephen Stein, George Alter, Ellen K. Rothman, Philip Greven, Susan Hartmann, Anne Firor Scott, Mari Jo Buhle, Sally McMillen, and Elson Harmon, who conscientiously critiqued all or part of later drafts of this book. Their attention to detail, careful criticism, probing questions, and helpful suggestions made the writing process both stimulating and challenging. I would also like to thank the archivists at the Arthur and Elizabeth Schlesinger Library at Radcliffe College, the Houghton Library at Harvard University, the Longfellow National Historic Site, the Stowe-Day Foundation, the New-York Historical Society, the New York Public Library, the Maine Historical Society, the Chester County Historical Society, the New York Hospital–Cornell Medical Center, the Historical Society of Pennsylvania, Pennsylvania Hospital, and the Washington University Medical School Archives for their help. Audrey Berkley and Elizabeth Mueth at the St. Louis Medical Society Library were particularly generous with their time and expertise. Finally, I would like to thank Barbara Bush Wells, Alfred D. Chandler, Jr., Natalie Cabot Neagle, and Thomas A. Dana for permission to use their family papers.

Sylvia D. Hoffert
St. Louis, Missouri

Ah me! conceiv'd in sin, and born in sorrow,
A nothing, here to day, but gone to morrow.
Whose mean beginning, blushing cann't reveale,
But night and darkenesse, must with shame conceal.
My mothers breeding sicknes, I will spare;
Her nine months weary burden not declare.
To shew her bearing pangs, I should do wrong,
To tel that paine, which cann't be told by tongue;
With tears into this world I did arrive;
My mother stil did waste, as I did thrive;
Who yet with love, and all alacrity,
Spending was willing, to be spent for me;
With wayward cryes, I did disturbe her rest;
Who sought stil to appease me, with her brest,
With weary armes, she danc'd, and *By, By*, sung,
When wretched I (ungrate) had done the wrong.

—Anne Bradstreet, "The Four Ages of Man"

# Introduction

DESPITE periodic and sometimes even dramatic changes in the birthrate, bearing and nurturing children has been central to the female experience. For many women the biological and social activities associated with maternity have served as the basis for female consciousness. The experience of becoming and being mothers has dominated their thoughts, determined their behavior, helped to establish their place in society, and defined their relationships with others. The biological process of birthing and nurturing has remained essentially the same over time. But the way women have experienced and perceived those processes has depended on such variables as when they lived, where they lived, what socioeconomic positions they found themselves in, and what kind of health care was available to them.

American women in the first half of the nineteenth century would have found that many aspects of their maternal experience were similar to those of their grandmothers and great-grandmothers. The need for assistance during labor, delivery, and the postpartum period remained essentially the same. Despite advances in medical knowledge and technology, childbearing women continued to express anxiety about the risks that pregnancy and birth posed both to their health and to that of their children and to fear the pain that often accompanied the birth process. After birth they stressed the pleasure they felt in the presence of their babies and deemphasized the pain they had suffered only a short time before. Concern about the ability to provide adequate and nourishing food for their babies remained, and mothers continued to worry about the risks that teething, weaning, and disease posed to their infants' comfort and well-being. When their children died in infancy, they, like many who had suffered such losses before, felt a sense of emptiness and grief and sought to find some meaning in the tragedy. Some things did not change.

Between 1800 and 1860, however, a number of powerful influences combined to alter the context in which some American men and women carried out the private function of bearing and rearing children. Responding to the increasing heterogeneity and complexity of the urban environment in early nineteenth-century America, many middle- and upper-class families living in the towns and cities of the North began to hold society at a distance, to withdraw from the community. For them the family became a refuge from an alien, impersonal, and threatening outside world[1] and took on a new importance as a source of emotional security and comfort as well as the primary agent of early socialization. One result of this move toward privacy was that some aspects of the conduct of major life events such as birth, marriage, and death were increasingly removed from the public sphere.

A clearly articulated ideology of motherhood, corollary to the cult of domesticity,[2] placed the primary responsibility for the physical and moral nurture of children on mothers and required that they maintain harmony in the household by ensuring that family members were bound together by strong ties of affection. It demanded dedication and self-sacrifice as it encouraged childbearing women to take a greater interest in their maternal responsibilities. It assured them that having children could fulfill both private and public needs. Bearing children, it promised, was certain to guarantee personal happiness because it renewed the bonds of intimacy that served as the basis for stable marriages. Popular authors described infants as pledges of mutual love that could strengthen the "cords of affection . . . between husband and wife."[3] Domestic bliss, they suggested, was a condition made possible only by the presence of a child, whose birth was guaranteed to enhance the affection that husband and wife felt for each other. The ideology of motherhood also offered childbearing women the opportunity to demonstrate their patriotism by rearing paragons of civic virtue. It was by developing moral sentiments in children, shaping their temperaments, and preparing them to fulfill the responsibilities of citizenship that mothers could ultimately, if indirectly, fulfill an important public and political role that would allow them to "hold the reigns of government" and shape "the destiny of our great nation."[4] According to Linda Kerber, fulfilling this mission of Republican Motherhood provided women a way of integrating the ideas of the American Revolution into their domestic lives. It gave them a political role in the new republic that was in harmony with their domestic function.[5] It also gave those who presumed to speak in the public interest the opportunity to attempt to maintain control over the private matters of family formation and the nurture of children.

The increasing availability of information on family limitation provided women of childbearing age with the chance to control the size of their families, space their pregnancies, and invest more physical and emotional energy in each individual child.[6] Increased investment in children encouraged them to reassess the meaning of both the lives and the premature deaths of infants.

Geographic mobility combined with the slow but steady growth of towns and cities tended to depersonalize the environment in which the private lives of young couples were conducted. The act of moving away from friends and family meant that conventional wisdom concerning the conduct of pregnancy, childbirth, and child rearing was not always immediately available. Letters and visits helped to maintain traditional ways of dealing with such matters, but living in the midst of relative strangers induced some to look for other sources of assistance, information, and advice about childbearing and infant nurture.[7] The rise of the publishing industry in the early decades of the nineteenth century as well as the availability of public lectures gave literate and interested women separated from their mothers and the friends of their childhood alternative sources of advice on family matters.[8] Doctors, health reformers, editors, novelists, and ministers intruded on the private matters of family formation and the conduct of family life by creating a body of publicly available literature that both reflected the attitudes of their authors and attempted to influence the reading public's behavior.

The anonymity of urban life combined with the possibilities for social mobility engendered by a rapidly expanding economy made it difficult for people who lived in the city to determine immediately where those who were strangers to them belonged in the social structure. This difficulty together with the opportunity to improve one's social status made ambitious, urban, middle-class families receptive to demands of fashion as a way of demonstrating their position in the social structure and encouraged them to modify the rituals of birth and recovery in order to establish or maintain their reputation as genteel and respectable.[9]

Advances in technology and medical knowledge, the determination of doctors to build their practices by attending women in childbirth, and the availability of private nurses allowed urban women to alter traditional birthing practices.[10] At the same time, the availability of obstetric forceps, ergot, and anesthesia forced doctors to define their professional goals, reassess their attitudes toward the birth process and their female patients, and struggle to establish meaningful standards of medical ethics regarding the application of medical technology to obstetrics.

These factors—by offering some women the opportunity to make previously unavailable choices regarding the conduct of their maternal responsibilities—had a disordering, unsettling effect on traditional assumptions, attitudes, and unwritten codes of behavior that had once determined how pregnancy, childbirth, recovery, and infant nurture had been conducted and how infant death had been understood. Thus, the choices that women made posed a challenge to the continuity of tradition and the ability of the community to monitor maternal behavior. In an attempt to maintain or reimpose community authority over such matters, neighbors, friends, and relatives as well as authors, editors, and publishers bombarded mothers with advice about the conduct of childbearing and child rearing. In the sense that the advice they offered was informative, their efforts were altruistic. It was helpful for young mothers to know, for example, that there were ways to limit the size of their families, that doctors had knowledge of the use of forceps and anesthesia, and there were ways of making a child more comfortable during the teething process. It was comforting to be assured that when children died prematurely, their deaths were not meaningless. At another level, however, the advice was manipulative. It was designed to mold the attitudes of mothers and control the decisions they made by establishing ideal standards for judging maternal performance.

The influences I have outlined eventually affected attitudes toward childbearing in all parts of the country, but before the Civil War they had their most immediate impact in the towns and cities of the North among the middle and upper classes.[11] The period between 1800 and 1860 was clearly a transitional one during which the way people responded to the experience of becoming and being parents and the way they perceived and described their responses to those experiences were changing. It was a period that allowed women unprecedented opportunities to modify or discard traditional customs and practices associated with bearing and rearing children. After the Civil War many of the practices they adopted spread across the country and became conventional.

Thus, studying the attitudes of middle- and upper-class men and women toward pregnancy, childbirth, recovery, infant nurture, and infant death during the first sixty years of the nineteenth century can serve as the basis for analyzing the always complex and often subtle relationship between the individual and society and for refining our understanding of the effect that extrapersonal influences had on private attitudes and behavior patterns. The response of some urban couples to these influences also reveals a great deal about the values of the emerging middle class in the early nineteenth century. Their desire to control their lives, their willingness to adapt to change and take advantage of opportunities, their interest in comfort and safety, the value that they placed on the presence of children in the family, their assumption that mothers rather than fathers should bear the primary responsibility for child rearing, and their desire to distinguish themselves from the masses are reflected in their attitudes toward childbearing and infant nurture and their response to infant death.

To study these attitudes I have relied on the private writings of childbearing women and their friends and relatives as well as on representative published works such as obstetrics manuals, popular health manuals, medical journals, novels, ladies' magazines, and religious periodicals. The private sources allow us to piece together some idea of what it meant to native, white, Protestant, middle- and upper-class women living in northern towns and cities to bear children and assume primary responsibility for the physical, emotional, and spiritual well-being of infants during the first sixty years of the nineteenth century.[12] The public sources provide the kind of information we need to re-create the cultural environment in which their childbearing and child rearing took place.

As one might expect, some private papers provide more intimate detail about the attitudes and behavior patterns associated with childbirth and infant nurture than others. Nearly all the letters or diaries written by a woman during her childbearing years contain some comment about her experiences as a mother or the experiences of her relatives, friends, or neighbors. Some diaries like that of Sarah Snell Bryant of Cummington, Massachusetts, for example, were written in small volumes in which only a few lines were reserved for daily entries.[13] Such diaries provide little room for introspective remarks. Nevertheless, their brief entries allow us to trace the activities that a woman pursued during her pregnancies and child-nurturing years. Of more value are diaries like that of Mary Rodman Fisher Fox of Philadelphia.[14] Fox did not always write regularly in her diary, but some of her sporadic entries provide a detailed description of her feelings about the prospect of becoming a mother.

Letters written during the first six decades of the nineteenth century vary as much as the diaries. Elizabeth Dwight Cabot of Brookline, Massachusetts, for example, regularly wrote long, newsy, candid letters to her sister in England, letters in which she described her emotional and physical responses to the prospect of bearing a child and the frustrations that accompanied her efforts to care for her young family.[15] Other women, less committed to correspondence or less inclined to frankness about such intimate matters, wrote in more general terms about the birth of children and the problems they confronted in caring for them.

These individual diaries and letters are not uniform in either the quantity or the quality of the information they provide. Nevertheless, they do describe the attitudes and experiences of respectably genteel women who had the education, leisure, and introspective inclination to leave a record of their thoughts and feelings about the experience of childbearing and child rearing.

The lives of these women followed a fairly consistent pattern. Born between the last decades of the eighteenth century and the 1830s, most of them were married in their mid-twenties. They came from somewhere in the middle or upper classes and married men whose occupations as doctors, lawyers, ministers, teachers, merchants, reformers, or military officers allowed them to consider themselves a cut above the ordinary. Generally, their social status tended to reflect a consistent mental attitude rather than a specific or secure economic or social position. They thought of themselves as at least middle class—sometimes because of their economic positions and sometimes despite it. Geographically mobile, these women typically moved away from their families to establish households with their husbands. Often they found themselves pregnant by the end of their first year of marriage. After the birth of the first baby, they commonly gave birth at two or three year intervals, eventually assuming responsibility for rearing from four to seven children. During their early married lives they spent most of their time running their households and caring for their children. Domestic obligations made it difficult for many of them to take an active role in community affairs. Their diaries and letters are filled with private rather than public matters. They took their maternal responsibilities very seriously.

The public sources that I have used illustrate the ways in which those who presumed to speak in the public interest attempted to influence the conduct of maternity. The information and advice that doctors offered was directed toward two different audiences. By 1800 American physicians, trained in Europe or in the newly founded American medical schools in Boston and Philadelphia, began to write midwifery texts and journal articles to supplement the texts that had been imported from abroad. In general agreement with their European counterparts that the childbearing process was potentially pathological and was, therefore, a legitimate concern for the medical community, these so-called regular doctors intended to influence the way their students and colleagues clinically treated the obstetrical patients they attended. By the 1830s a few physicians were attempting to convince the medical community that the treatment of children deserved special attention.[16]

During the first decades of the nineteenth century, however, the authoritative position that regular doctors hoped to establish for themselves in such matters was being challenged by a wide variety of health practitioners in what was called sectarian medicine. Sectarian health care regimens tended to be cheaper, more accessible, and more convenient than those offered by the regular medical community. By the 1840s and 1850s the American public could choose from a number of medical systems, including botanic medicine, homeopathy, eclecticism, hydropathy (water cure), phrenology, and the popular health movement.[17]

All of these sects, represented by irregular doctors or health reformers, viewed childbearing as a natural rather than as a pathological condition. They recognized, however, that childbirth was fraught with potential complications. Bypassing the regular medical community, these enterprising sectarians wrote health manuals intended for popular rather than professional consumption. By providing the sort of information and advice they thought married women needed in order to understand the process, discomforts, and dangers of childbirth and the responsibilities of infant nurture, they hoped to improve health care delivery and at the same time to undercut the credibility and position of regular practitioners and to establish a strong base of support for themselves.

To recognize that the interest of doctors and health reformers in obstetrics and infant care was self-serving, however, is not to deny that some were genuinely concerned about providing childbearing women and their children with the best medical care available. These men and women were, after all, members of families who had a personal stake in the outcome of childbirth and infant nurture. Their professional interests were congruent with their personal concerns in the sense that their stature as health care authorities and their happiness as family members were both served by doing their best to assure the survival of childbearing women and their children.

While doctors and health reformers of various persuasions attempted to influence the conduct of pregnancy and childbirth and the physical care of infants, the editors of ladies' magazines and theological periodicals as well as domestic novelists and the writers of sentimental poetry generally ignored the birth process and confined themselves to discussions of the social significance of familial relationships and the moral nurture of children. Sensitive to the tension that could exist between private interests and public responsibilities, they were primarily concerned about the breakdown of family relationships, the abuse of maternal power, and maintenance of social and political order. Ignoring or minimizing the influence of fathers, the editors of ladies' magazines published stories, articles, and poems that described and prescribed the most effective way for mothers to rear the kind of citizens that they considered necessary for perpetuating a strong American republic. Domestic novelists in turn tended to write about the ways in which a woman committed herself emotionally to her new infant, the effect that the assumption of the responsibilities of motherhood had on her life, and the role that an infant might play in the family.[18] The ministers who served as editors of both popular and professional religious periodicals were also more interested in the living child than the unborn one. They limited their concern about babies to redefining attitudes toward the state of the infant soul, explaining the role that infants were supposed to play in the family, and suggesting ways of preparing the young to take their place in the Christian community both on earth and in heaven. Collectively, they were more interested in what it meant to be a mother than in what it meant to become one.

We know that all of these sources were available to the medical and lay public, but we cannot be sure what their precise influence was.[19] It seems apparent that conscientious, regularly trained doctors read obstetrics texts and heard lectures based on their content.[20] It remains uncertain, however, how physicians translated what they read or heard into the actual practice of obstetrics and family medicine. Popular health manuals proliferated as the century progressed, but only rarely did women and their friends or relatives mention reading them.[21] The market for novels expanded between 1800 and 1860 to the point where it is possible to identify best-sellers.[22] Since we know that novels were popular, we can assume that women with the money to buy them and the time to read them did so. The same can be said of ladies' magazines and religious periodicals.[23]

Whether or not the specific suggestions this literature offered were widely read and followed is not as relevant to our purposes as the fact that the private choices women made became the focus of public concern, that authors, editors, and publishers thought it was necessary and lucrative to provide advice. By going to the trouble and expense of writing and publishing such literature, they made common assumptions about the needs, attitudes, and interests of both their audience and society. They clearly believed that motherhood had taken on increased significance for the family, the community, and the nation. They assumed that social and technological changes were undermining traditional ways of dealing with the problems associated with pregnancy, childbirth, and child rearing and were convinced that some of the conventional ways of dealing with these problems were no longer adequate or appropriate. They assumed that traditional community influences over private matters relating to family formation and child care were declining and that they as authors and editors could and should intervene in the conduct of family life by attempting to provide women with informed and thoughtful advice about the ideal conduct of their maternal role. It was also assumed that responsible married women recognized that the knowledge required to carry out their maternal obligations was not instinctive, that they were willing to acknowledge their inadequacies, and that they would enthusiastically consume advice and information directly by buying and reading books and magazines and attending lectures or indirectly through the ministrations of doctors and clergymen. The private conduct of motherhood was on its way to becoming the concern of big business.

The intensity of their concern and the occasional shrillness of their admonitions about inadequately fulfilled maternal responsibilities and unsatisfactory familial relationships indicate that they also believed there was an inherent conflict between private needs and public responsibilities. Their collective rhetoric testifies eloquently to their fear that somehow the choices that childbearing couples in general and mothers in particular had the opportunity to make were potentially subversive, a threat to a social and political system that demanded self-sacrifice. Therefore, this literature performed a function that extended beyond a mere attempt to accommodate social change, to serve the public interest by establishing ideal standards for judging maternal behavior, or to make money. It also provided a platform for contemporary observers and commentators to express and attempt to relieve their conscious and unconcious anxieties about the ability and willingness of American women to carry out their social and political obligations. For them motherhood was as much a public as it was a private matter.

## Notes

1. Mary P. Ryan, *Cradle of the Middle Class: The Family in Oneida County, New York, 1790–1865* (Cambridge: Cambridge University Press, 1981), 145–85. For general discussions of the privatization of family life, see Philippe Aries, *Centuries of Childhood: A Social History of Family Life*, trans. Robert Baldick (New York: Vintage, 1962); Lawrence Stone, *The Family, Sex, and Marriage in England, 1500–1800* (New York: Harper and Row, 1977); Christopher Lasch, *Haven in a Heartless World: The Family Besieged* (New York: Basic, 1977); and Edward Shorter, *The Making of the Modern Family* (New York: Basic, 1975).

2. Barbara Welter, "The Cult of True Womanhood, 1820–1860," *American Quarterly* 18 (Summer 1966): 151–74; Mary P. Ryan, "American Society and the Cult of Domesticity, 1830–1860" (Ph.D. diss., University of California–Santa Barbara, 1971); Nancy F. Cott, *The Bonds of Womanhood: "Woman's Sphere" in New England, 1780–1835* (New Haven: Yale University Press, 1977), 63–100.

3. For expressions of these ideas in popular literature published between 1800 and 1860, see Lydia H. Sigourney, *Letters to Mothers* (New York: Harper and Bros., 1840), 9; William Buchan, *Advice to Mothers on the Subject of Their Own Health* (Philadelphia: John Bioren, 1804), 23; Timothy Shay Arthur, *Our Children: How Shall We Save Them?* (New York: Brognard, 1850), 20; J. Thayer, *The Drunkard's Daughter* (Boston: William S. Damrell, 1842), 6; quotation from *Reproductive Control; or, A Rational Guide to Matrimonial Happiness* (Cincinnati: n.p., 1855), 64.

4. "Influence of Mothers," *Christian Review* 5 (Sept. 1840): 447; Rev. William Lyman in 1802, as quoted in Ruth H. Bloch, "American Feminine Ideals in Transition: The Rise of the Moral Mother, 1785–1815," *Feminist Studies* 4 (June 1978): 115; Mary J. Hasper, "Woman's Mission," *Ladies' Wreath* 12 ([1859]): 81.

5. Linda Kerber, *Women of the Republic: Intellect and Ideology in Revolutionary America* (Chapel Hill: University of North Carolina Press, 1980), xii, 11, 227–31, 283. See also Mary Beth Norton, *Liberty's Daughters: The Revolutionary Experience of American Women, 1750–1800* (Boston: Little, Brown, 1980), 247–49.

6. Between the 1830s and 1860 contraceptive information and abortion became more readily available. For discussions of birth control and abortion during this period, see James Reed, *From Private Vice to Public Virtue: The Birth Control Movement and American Society since 1830* (New York: Basic, 1978); James C. Mohr, *Abortion in America: The Origins and Evolution of a National Policy, 1800–1890* (New York: Oxford University Press, 1978).

7. Support from other women remained important, however, during pregnancy, childbirth, and recovery. See Judith Walzer Leavitt and Whitney Walton, "Down to Death's Door: Women's Perceptions of Childbirth," in *Proceedings of the Second Motherhood Symposium: Childbirth, the Beginning of Motherhood*, ed. Sophie Colleau (Madison, Wis.: Women's Studies Research Center, 1982), 116–18.

8. Carl Bode, *The Anatomy of American Popular Culture, 1840–1861* (Berkeley: University of California Press, 1960), 109–16.

9. The use of the term *middle class* is problematic for historians. It is both descriptive and imprecise. The perspectives that are most useful for this study are those offered by Peter Gay and Stuart M. Blumin. Gay described the nineteenth-century European and American middle classes as respectable, relatively prosperous, and cultivated groups of businessmen and professionals (including lawyers, churchmen, teachers, and doctors) who occupied a social and economic position somewhere between the very rich and the laboring poor (*The Education of the Senses* [New York: Oxford University Press, 1984], 17–44). Blumin argued that what most characterized the middle class in America was that it comprised people who were aware that they shared similar attitudes, beliefs, and experiences in the areas of work, consumption, residential location, membership in formal and informal groups, and family organization and child-rearing strategies ("The Hypothesis of Middle-Class Formation in Nineteenth-Century America: A Critique and Some Proposals," *American Historical Review* 90 [Apr. 1985]: 299–338).

10. For a general discussion of the relationship between advances in medical technology and the choices that women made in response to them, see Judith Walzer Leavitt, "'Science' Enters the Birthing Room: Obstetrics in America since the Eighteenth Century," *Journal of American History* 70 (Sept. 1983): 281–304; Judith Walzer Leavitt, *Brought to Bed: Childbearing in America, 1750 to 1950* (New York: Oxford University Press, 1986).

11. Factors such as region, ethnicity, class, and race were significant in determining the degree to which these influences affected attitudes and practices associated with childbearing and child rearing. For a discussion of childbearing among white Southern women, see Sally McMillen, "Their Sacred Occupation: Pregnancy, Childbirth and Early Infant Rearing in the Antebellum South" (Ph.D. diss., Duke University, 1985); for a discussion of childbearing among poor women in New York City, see Virginia Metaxas Quiroga, "Poor Mothers and Babies: A Social History of Childbirth and Child Care Institutions in Nineteenth Century New York City" (Ph.D. diss., State University of New York at Stony Brook, 1984).

12. In the early nineteenth century the term *infant* might be used to describe a newborn child as well as a child of three or four. Under normal

circumstances most of the mothers in this study weaned their babies sometime during the child's second year. By that time most parents also had begun
to shift from a willingness to tolerate the demands of their babies to a desire
for that child to begin submitting to the will of the parents. Therefore, I will
confine the use of the term to children of not more than two years of age. In
gathering evidence for this study, I consulted more than seventy diaries,
memoirs, and letter collections of women who lived in New England, the
middle Atlantic states, and the Midwest. The women whom I will be discussing include those listed in the Appendix as well as others about whom
much less is known.

13. Sarah Snell Bryant diary, Houghton Library, Harvard University, Cambridge, Mass.

14. Mary Rodman Fisher Fox diary, box 13, folder 30, Logan–Fisher-Fox
Papers, Historical Society of Pennsylvania, Philadelphia.

15. Elizabeth Dwight Cabot Letters, Hugh Cabot Family Collection,
Schlesinger Library, Radcliffe College, Cambridge, Mass.

16. Ideas in American midwifery texts generally paralleled those in British
and European texts, and American authors did not hesitate to refer to British
and European authorities. For discussions of the practice of regular medicine
in early nineteenth-century America, see Joseph Kett, *The Formation of the
American Medical Profession: The Role of Institutions, 1780–1860* (New Haven:
Yale University Press, 1968); William G. Rothstein, *American Physicians in
the Nineteenth Century: From Sects to Science* (Baltimore: Johns Hopkins, 1972);
Henry Burnell Shafer, *The American Medical Profession, 1783–1850* (New
York: Columbia University Press, 1936); and Richard Harrison Shryock,
*Medicine and Society in America, 1660–1860* (New York: New York University
Press, 1960). The first pediatrics manual written by a regular physician in
America was William P. Dewees, *Treatise on the Physical and Medical Treatment
of Children* (Philadelphia: Carey and Lea, 1825).

17. For discussions of sectarian medicine and home health care, see the
essays in Guenter B. Risse, Ronald L. Numbers, and Judith Walzer Leavitt,
eds., *Medicine without Doctors: Home Health Care in American History* (New York:
Science History Publications, 1977). For discussions of Thomsonianism (botanic medicine), see James Harvey Young, *The Toadstool Millionaires: A Social
History of Patent Medicines in America before Federal Regulation* (Princeton, N.J.:
Princeton University Press, 1961), 44–57; Kett, *Formation*, 100–131; Rothstein, *American Physicians*, 125–51. For discussions of homeopathy, see Kett,
*Formation*, 132–64; Rothstein, *American Physicians*, 152–74; Martin Kauf-
man, *Homeopathy in America: The Rise and Fall of a Medical Heresy* (Baltimore:
Johns Hopkins, 1971). For discussions of eclecticism, see Rothstein, *Ameri-
can Physicians*, 217–29; Kett, *Formation*, 105–7. For a discussion of hydrop-

athy, see Harry B. Weiss and Howard R. Kemble, *The Great American Water-Cure Craze: A History of Hydropathy in the United States* (Trenton, N.J.: Past Times, 1967). For discussions of phrenology, see John D. Davies, *Phrenology, Fad and Science: A 19th-Century American Crusade* (New Haven: Yale University Press, 1955); Madeleine B. Stern, *Heads and Headlines: The Phrenological Fowlers* (Norman: University of Oklahoma Press, 1971). Joseph Kett takes phrenology less seriously and tends to view the Fowlers as quacks (*Formation*, 146). For a discussion of Sylvester Graham and the popular health movement, see Stephen Nissenbaum, *Sex, Diet, and Debility in Jacksonian America: Sylvester Graham and Health Reform* (Westport, Conn.: Greenwood Press, 1980).

18. While they were concerned with social relations, it was unusual for domestic novelists to address the issue of motherhood. See Nina Baym, *Woman's Fiction: A Guide to Novels by and about Women in America, 1820–1870* (Ithaca, N.Y.: Cornell University Press, 1978), 26, 38.

19. Jay E. Mechling, "Advice to Historians on Advice to Mothers," *Journal of Social History* 9 (Fall 1975): 44–63.

20. For an example of the assignments and lectures used in an obstetrics class, see "Notes on the Lectures on Midwifery in the University of Pa. Delivered by Doctors [Thomas Chalkey] James and [William Potts] Dewees," 1826, Historical Collections, College of Physicians of Philadelphia.

21. Elizabeth Drinker of Philadelphia and her daughters used William Buchan's *Domestic Medicine* (Cecil K. Drinker, *Not So Long Ago: A Chronicle of Medicine and Doctors in Colonial Philadelphia* [New York: Oxford University Press, 1937], 65). Eliza Fenwick also used Buchan's manual (A. F. Wedd, ed., *The Fate of the Fenwicks: Letters to Mary Hays* [London: Methuen, 1927], 159).

22. Frank Luther Mott, *Golden Multitudes: The Story of Best Sellers in the United States* (New York: R. R. Bowker, 1947).

23. The circulation of American magazines increased dramatically over the period in question. By 1860 the average circulation of monthly magazines was about 12,000. See Frank Luther Mott, *A History of American Magazines, 1741–1850* (New York: Appleton, 1930), 199–200, 514; Frank Luther Mott, *A History of American Magazines, 1850–1865* (Cambridge: Harvard University Press, 1938), 10.

# To "Abide the Appointed Hour": Attitudes toward Childbearing and Pregnancy

Six months after her marriage Fanny Appleton Longfellow of Cambridge, Massachusetts, wrote to her sister-in-law: "Somewhere between May and June I hope to give you a little nephew or niece. . . . You can read our hearts . . . and therefore need not to be told how grateful we feel to God for this promised addition to our happiness." Longfellow's pregnancy was uneventful. As the birth of her child approached, she wrote to her mother-in-law, "I patiently abide the appointed hour although I must confess to a good deal of curiosity and anxiety to behold the expected stranger." Her curiosity was satisfied and her anxiety calmed when the next day she safely gave birth to a little boy.[1]

Longfellow began to fulfill her destiny as a mother during a period in which the meaning of pregnancy was changing. The increasing accessibility of birth control information encouraged some couples to be more deliberate about matters involving the size of their families and the spacing and timing of pregnancy. For those who began to gain control over their fertility, family formation increasingly became a matter of choice and not chance. At the same time, the ideology of motherhood increased the political and social stakes involved in bearing children and sent women conflicting messages regarding their behavior. On the one hand it encouraged them to regard the sacrifice of good health and personal comfort as the price that had to be paid to attain the honorable and powerful position of mother. On the other hand it suggested that failure to do whatever was necessary to assure their own health and that of their unborn child was to be negligent. Encouraged to be both passive and active, childbearing women found themselves making choices regarding their public and private behavior in a social milieu that sometimes blurred the line between self-indulgence and social responsibility. In addition, some physicians and health reformers were beginning to define the whole process of childbearing as an illness and to encourage childbearing women to view their condition as one deserving medical attention. They focused attention not only on the physical changes, discomforts, and mental stress that frequently accompanied pregnancy but also on the clothing and activities of pregnant women. Their concerns only aggravated the anxieties that childbearing women had about the process of bearing children. Eventually, the view that pregnancy was an illness led to attempts to redefine what constituted appropriate behavior during pregnancy and encouraged women to use the way they conducted themselves before the birth of their children as a way of testifying to their position in society.

While it is clear that Longfellow's first pregnancy was welcome, it is not clear that it was planned. Indeed, it probably was not. There is nothing in the Longfellow papers to indicate that Fanny and her husband made any attempt to limit the size of their family. But the falling birthrate indicates that others did. Demographers have found that despite the fact that 90 percent of all women married, their fertility measured by the ratio of young children to women of childbearing age in the United States as a whole fell almost 30 percent between 1800 and 1860.[2]

Typically, however, couples chose to limit the size of their families only after they had borne what they considered to be an appropriate number of children. This was not a new behavior pattern. Late in the eighteenth century Margaret Shippen Arnold had written to her married sister, "It gives me great pleasure to hear of your prudent resolution of not increasing your family; as I can never do better than to follow your example, I have determined upon the same plan; and when our Sisters have had five or six, we will likewise recommend it to them."[3]

Arnold considered five or six the ideal number of children. During the first part of the nineteenth century, the size of the model family remained a matter of opinion. In 1826 Sarah Hill Fletcher of Indianapolis wrote that she and her husband were "blessed with the trouble of only two children." Her husband, Calvin, however, wanted a large family, and in the course of twenty-five years Sarah bore eleven children. After the birth of their seventh child in 1835, Calvin noted in his diary, "Must acknowledge (tho' it is not fashionable to be the parents of many childrin [sic]) that I am more gratified than at any time heretofore on a similar occasion." Two years later, after the birth of their eighth child, he again noted that he continued to differ from most in his desire for many children. "I would here again remark," he wrote, "that the number of children is a matter of different concern to me to what it is to most persons. The generality of the world are opposed to having large families."[4] While Fletcher did not find his large family burdensome, William Lloyd Garrison did. After the birth of his sixth child in 1846, he began to feel that his parental responsibilities restricted his ability to travel and lecture as much as he wished. "I would not have the number of our children less," he wrote, "but it is difficult to look after so many, and at the same [time] to discharge the duties of my position as a 'leading' abolitionist."[5] Others were less concerned about the effect that a large family would have on their ability to carry out their public duties than they were about preserving their private pleasures. In her advice book, *The Mother and Her Work*, Helen E. Brown described a woman who was perfectly satisfied as the mother of an only child. "I did not marry to be a slave to maternity," the woman wrote,

> to spend my best years in worse than a nursery maid's occupation. My husband does not wish it either. We want to ride, journey, visit, enjoy *ourselves*—and we will not be hindered at every turn by the needs and cries of helpless infancy. We do not wish, either, to spend all our resources in supporting and educating a large family. One is quite enough for us to maintain and care for. So, for economy's sake, as well as our personal convenience and enjoyment, we prefer our condition.[6]

Family size was clearly a matter of concern to northern middle- or upper-class couples. But the decisions they made or did not make about trying to control their fertility rarely had anything to do with the desire for a male heir. This is not to say that they had no sexual preferences but rather that their predilections were not dictated by dynastic considerations. Some hoped that their firstborn might be a boy and apologized when the baby turned out to be a girl. Others were so concerned about bearing a healthy child that its sex was irrelevant. Men sometimes but not always hoped for sons. Women often wished for daughters who might give them companionship. Both men and women expressed a desire that they might have children of both sexes. Others hoped for children of the same sex so that they might provide companionship for each other.[7]

Middle-class men and women also held a variety of attitudes toward spacing children and timing pregnancy. Despite the increasing availability of information on birth control and access to abortion, some, like Richard Henry Dana, Jr., continued to believe that "the having children or not . . . seem[s] to be placed quite beyond the sphere of our determining." It, like the sex of a child, he believed, was "[so] much a matter of direct Providence" that he felt little concern about it.[8]

Others, however, were much more willing to try to control their fertility and plan their families or to pass judgment on those who appeared to be breeding indiscriminately. One woman wrote a friend in 1839 that having gone through the strain of childbirth and nursing, she preferred to put off future pregnancies for three or four years. (She did not mention how she proposed to do so.)[9] The comments of other women indicate that they were as concerned about their friends as they were about themselves. "It is sad slavery," wrote Abigail Adams of a young relative who in 1800 had just had a miscarriage, "to have children as fast as she has."[10] Elizabeth Dwight Cabot of Brookline, Massachusetts, also showed concern for a friend who had found herself pregnant five times in rapid succession and had already suffered two miscarriages when she wrote to her sister: "Mary Guild . . . is just beginning on number three, number two being seven months old. Don't you call this severe? . . . She seems perfectly cheerful about it, rather proud of it, I should say." Cabot could not understand Guild's cheerfulness or pride and indicated that she worried about the effects of rapid childbearing on the health of her friend.[11]

Other women were concerned about the timing of pregnancy.

Eleanor Parke Custis Lewis, writing of her daughter, prayed that she might be spared the danger of bearing children soon after marriage.[12] But Lewis's hopes differed from others who felt that the early years of marriage were the best time to have children. Laura Stone Poor, in a letter to her sister-in-law, wrote that babies were a great blessing, but that they were more of a blessing "when we are *young* and *strong*, and hopeful. . . . I have often thought what a wise and beneficent arrangement it is, that we have our children when we are younger, for many reasons."[13] Adams wrote of a friend who found herself pregnant after having had a reprieve from childbearing for some years. "It is really a foolish Business to begin after so many years, a second crop."[14]

The experience of Maria D. Brown might have confirmed the observations of Poor and Adams. Married at the age of eighteen in 1845, she spent the next twenty-five years bearing two "crops" of children. She gave birth to four between 1846 and 1854 in Ohio and then four more between 1860 and 1870 in Iowa. In her memoirs she reflected on the birth of her last child, born in 1870 when she was almost forty-three. This "baby was not desired by anyone," she recalled. Brown had lost her seventh child the year before; and as she remembered it, everyone in the family understood that the seventh baby "had been born to a mother who was too tired to nourish her offspring properly. They naturally did not want to see a repetition of that experience. I felt that they regarded the last baby as an unwelcome addition to the family circle." Weakened by hard work and childbearing, Brown spent much of her last pregnancy in ill health. She remembered the birth of her last child only in terms of the suffering it had caused her.[15]

It appears that Brown made no effort to prevent conception after the birth of her first four children. Others were not as willing to let nature take its course. Sometimes women took the responsibility for initiating attempts to limit the size of their families. But the most successful efforts to avoid conception were likely to have been those that resulted from close cooperation between husband and wife, as was true for Thomas and Hannah Myers Longshore. The Longshores married in 1841. Their first child was born in 1842 and their second in 1845. There were no more. Years later in his autobiography Longshore explained, "We had resolved in the beginning that we were not strong and healthy enough to raise a large family, and without the necessary supplies that two children might be more than we could give good constitutions and proper training and educate." [16]

The Longshores were not alone in their willingness to share responsibility for family limitation and to communicate openly about it. In 1848 Anna Colton Clayton of West Chester, Pennsylvania, wrote to her husband John: "I am still in hopes to greet 'old Granny' [a euphemism for menstruation] but if I don't I will consider things and let you know. . . . I can't believe but what nature will bring back my healthful symptoms and I will wait patiently perhaps she [nature] is debating don't be scard dear naughty, it ain't your fault . . . I can safely vouchsafe that." Later in the same letter she wrote: "Whew!! what's this. I am *all straight* congratulate me." [17] A farm wife from upstate New York wrote similarly to her husband in 1849: "The old maid [another euphemism] came at the appointed time. I do think you are a very *careful* man." [18]

All of these people had decided at some point in their courtships or marriages that they should limit the size of their families. They had presumed to attempt to control this particular aspect of their lives. The statistics on fertility indicate that they were not alone.

Once they became pregnant, women like Longfellow did not await the births of their children in blissful serenity. They had to deal with attempts on the part of the medical community to define their condition as an illness and to influence the way they conducted themselves. They had to cope with the physical and emotional strains that pregnancy placed on them. And during the last months of pregnancy, they had to adjust their wardrobes, prepare layettes, and make sure arrangements were made for someone to care for them during their confinements.

By the early 1800s regular doctors trained in Europe or in the newly founded American medical schools were claiming a place for themselves as midwives in middle- and upper-class lying-in chambers. [19] In an effort to increase the market for their services, a few of them also began to argue that the complaints associated with pregnancy were an appropriate concern for the medical profession.

In an article published in 1803, the dean of early American medicine, Benjamin Rush, advised his colleagues to bleed parturient women in order to relieve the symptoms of their "disease."[20] Despite their respect for his reputation, however, most of Rush's medical brethren in England and America remained unconvinced that pregnancy was a pathological condition. Like Dr. William Buchan, author of a popular health manual, or Dr. Thomas Denman, a prominent British obstetrician, they were more inclined to believe that pregnancy was a condition of "increased sensibility," or that pregnancy produced "an altered, but not a morbid state" in women.[21] Nevertheless, they did recognize that there were complaints that accompanied pregnancy which, according to Buchan, "merit attention and which sometimes require assistance of medicine."[22] Consequently, midwifery texts and popular health manuals devoted to concerns about women's health contained chapters on the "Diseases of Pregnancy" in which the authors identified such harrassing discomforts as vomiting, heartburn, constipation, swollen feet and legs, and hemorrhoids as diseases and suggested treatment for their relief.[23]

Rush was not totally off the mark when he called pregnancy a disease. For doctors who wished to treat the symptoms of pregnancy, using the term was a convenient classification that patients could be expected to understand. As Denman explained in his midwifery text, applying the term *disease* to the "temporary complaints" of pregnant women allowed the doctor to explain them to her intelligibly.[24] Since pregnancy frequently produced annoying discomfort, a doctor could use the word as a means of subtly attempting to inspire his patients' confidence in him by implying that he understood the complex nature of their condition and was therefore particularly well suited to treat the discomforts that it produced.[25]

Inspiring confidence was important since the willingness of some physicians to treat the complaints of pregnancy did not parallel a similar willingness on the part of pregnant women to seek prenatal medical care.[26] In their diaries and letters, women rarely mentioned consulting a doctor during pregnancy. Some, of course, had no reason to. Even though they may have anticipated ill health, there were those who found that pregnancy did not produce the discomforts they had expected, and they mentioned feeling well with a sense of surprise at somehow having escaped anticipated misery. "I am so well," wrote Elizabeth Dwight Cabot during her first pregnancy in 1858, "that I think I ought to be described in the medical journals, as an encouraging case for instead of feeling disabled & uncomfortable all the time, as I expected, by this time, I . . . often feel better than ever before in my life."[27]

Others found the discomforts they were experiencing interesting rather than irritating or worrisome. Describing fetal movement that was at times distracting as well as uncomfortable, Anna Colton Clayton complained to her husband, "Little naughty is as refractory as ever and thumps all the time, well, pretty soon it will be my turn to *thump*." A few weeks later she again mentioned the activities of the fetus in her womb: "Little naughty cuts up such capers that he wearies me. I wonder if he will be lively; and fond of music." Ten days after that she said of her continuing discomfort, "Little naughty is as wicked as ever and sometimes he and the mosquitoes wont let me sleep much."[28] Women like Clayton were clearly uncomfortable, but they did not think of themselves in need of medical advice. Most simply dealt with their discomforts stoically or treated themselves. When they suffered from nausea or constipation, they rarely mentioned it.

When women did consult a physician, it was either because they were frightened or because they wished to avoid some anticipated difficulty. Mary Rodman Fisher Fox, for example, suffered from a serious fall in the last months of her pregnancy and called in a doctor to reassure her that she had done no real damage to herself or to her baby.[29] Elizabeth Dwight Cabot consulted two doctors, one of them her brother-in-law, about the advisability of moving into a new house only a short time before her first confinement because she feared that the move might be dangerous for a woman in her condition.[30] Late in her second pregnancy she again consulted her brother-in-law, this time hoping to avoid a problem that she had experienced previously in nursing. His treatment, however, proved to be almost as uncomfortable as the problem she had hoped to avoid. After applying a "wash" he had prescribed for her breasts, she broke out in a rash that tormented her so much she "had to be poulticed & anointed & nursed just like a baby & when all was done probably had three or four good crys in the course of the day."[31]

A number of factors may have discouraged pregnant women from routinely seeking the advice of doctors about the physical symptoms and discomforts of pregnancy. There were no doubt some over-worked or unsympathetic physicians who resisted the increasing pressure to expand the field of obstetrics into prenatal care. Hester Pendleton, the author of a hydropathic manual on pregnancy and childbirth, noted that physicians were "not as frequently consulted" about the regimen of pregnant women as they might have been because when they were consulted they would commonly "*make light of it.*"[32] Some women simply could not convince their doctors to take their complaints seriously.

It is also possible that women did not consult regularly with physicians during the normal course of pregnancy because they were not convinced that doctors could prescribe treatments any more effective than those they could prescribe for themselves. Certainly Cabot was dissatisfied with the unpleasant effects of the wash that her brother-in-law prescribed. She was only one of many in the nineteenth century who found regular medical therapy objectionable.[33] An example of early nineteenth-century humor that appeared in 1806 in a ladies' magazine reflected the belief that medical treatment by a doctor might be as likely to kill as it was to cure: "A physician who lived in N——, visited a lady who lived in E——. After continuing his visits for some time, the lady expressed an apprehension that it might be inconvenient for him to come so far on her account. 'Oh! madam!' replied the doctor, 'I have another patient in this neighborhood, and by that means, you know, *I kill two birds with one stone.*'"[34]

Ordinary people were simply skeptical of the benefits of regular medical treatment. In a sketch appearing in the *Ladies' Literary Cabinet* in 1822, a wife sent for a doctor to see her husband. The husband responded to her wifely concern by assuming that she wanted to see him dead. "Here doctor," he said, "take your fee . . . when I am weary of my life, I'll send for you."[35] Given such disdain for regular medical therapy and a strong tradition of self-help, it is not surprising to find that pregnant women sometimes simply prescribed for themselves.[36] Anna Colton Clayton, for example, was convinced that substances like rhubarb pills or patent medicine were superior to medically prescribed oil and magnesia for treating constipation during pregnancy.[37]

Rigid standards of modesty also prevented some women from

consulting male physicians during their pregnancies. Convinced that male midwives should be called in all cases of difficult childbirth, Valentine Seaman nevertheless recognized that some women absolutely refused to hire a man to deliver their babies, and he argued in the introduction to his midwifery manual that improved training for female midwives was "indispensable."[38] Writing in support of medical education for women in 1853, William Cornell testified that women continued to find it embarrassing to discuss their medical problems with male doctors.[39]

Traditionally women had turned to the female community for information and advice on the conduct of pregnancy. One could always ask friends and family members to share their experiences. But when pregnant women were not satisfied with the information they received from friends and relatives and were unwilling to ask their doctors about their condition, they could turn to popular health manuals. These books served as sources of "private consultation and reference," according to one manual writer, and freed women from the need to consult with a regular doctor with all its "attending indelicacy."[40] A woman, wrote H. B. Skinner, the author of another manual, "will find no difficulty in *reading* information upon some delicate subjects, upon which she can never feel to freely express herself" and which she might therefore feel unable to discuss with a physician.[41] By billing their books as "confidential" friends to married ladies,[42] the authors of popular health manuals attempted to diffuse female anxiety about publicly seeking specialized and authoritative advice by emphasizing the impersonal and private nature of the source.

By the 1850s women living in or near major metropolitan areas could also attend public lectures offered by health reformers or newly trained female physicians. In 1852 Mary Pierce Poor attended the lectures of Elizabeth Blackwell in New York.[43] During the early months of her second pregnancy in 1861, Elizabeth Dwight Cabot drove into Boston from Brookline to attend lectures on female anatomy, physiology, and hygiene given by Marie Zakrzewska. She found them "sensible and suggestive" as well as thorough. "She has gone elaborately into the process of having babies from the beginning to the end," she wrote to her sister in England,

"& I have liked very much her perfectly decent way of speaking of things that are generally left in silence."[44]

Sarah Josepha Hale, the editor of *Godey's Lady's Book*, supported such lectures. Because women were "ignorant of their own constitutions," she complained in one editorial, they brought "wretchedness and misery upon themselves, discomfort and suffering upon their families, and worst of all," entailed "enfeebled constitutions and diseases upon their offspring."[45] In the interests of improved health and happiness for American families, the editorial policy of the magazine clearly supported efforts to improve women's knowledge of their bodies.

Health lecturers were happy to oblige. In 1838, for example, Mary Gove, who as Mary Gove Nichols eventually established herself as a leading water cure advocate, began giving public lectures on the subject of women's health in Boston. By the end of the year, she had scheduled similar lectures in Lynn, Haverhill, Providence, and New York. Attendance at her lectures is estimated to have ranged from 400 to as many as 2,000.[46] Organizations such as the Ladies' Physiological Institute of Boston and Vicinity sponsored similar lectures for their members and occasionally for the general public, charging ten to fifteen cents per person.[47] By 1854, according to *Godey's*, graduates of the Female Medical College of Pennsylvania could earn the considerable sum of $50 to $100 a week by giving public lectures to classes of ladies on physiology and health.[48]

The efforts of doctors and health reformers gave concerned women access to the information and the assurance that they needed to make their months of waiting less tedious and anxious. When women purchased health manuals and attended health lectures, they indicated their willingness to combine conventional wisdom with medical advice and use both as guides for evaluating and dealing with the physical and emotional stresses they were experiencing.

Despite the physical changes and discomforts that accompanied pregnancy, women who had already borne children typically did not dwell on their condition in their private writings. Busy mothers had little time to spend thinking and writing about themselves, their feelings, and the changes that were occurring in their bodies. Sarah Ripley Stearns, mother of three young children, wrote in her diary in 1815, "I do not find so much time to write in my journal as formerly when I lived in my father's house—the cares of a rising family and a feeble state of health, take up much time and day after day, month after month passes away."[49] Having gone through the experience before, women like Stearns knew what to expect.

The uninitiated, however, were sensitive to what was happening to their bodies. "I am growing quite big," Clayton wrote, "because I cant hold my appetite enough. I try to restrain myself and do succeed in the midst of many temptations."[50] Sometimes women noted that the size of their bodies bore little relationship to the amount of food they were able to keep down. Miriam Whitcher reported to her family that she was growing big despite recurring bouts of nausea.[51] In the absence of irritating symptoms, however, it was ultimately the change in the proportions of a woman's body that served as proof of her condition and approaching motherhood. "I often think," mused Cabot during her second pregnancy, "that if I did not *see* myself, I should not know that anything was going on, except by queer motions in my interiors, which do not amount to anything to be complained of."[52]

Despite their self-consciousness, there is no evidence to justify the assumption by historians that, throughout the entire nineteenth century, women in the middle and upper classes restricted their public activities, separated themselves from polite society, and confined themselves to their homes during the last months of pregnancy because they believed that their appearance might offend the genteel sensibilities of their friends and neighbors.[53] Before the Civil War there was a wide range of respectable behavior patterns available to pregnant women who lived in towns and cities, and they were still able to decide for themselves whether they would continue to engage in their normal activities or whether they would restrict those activities because of personal inclination or ill health.

Those expecting their first child frequently kept up their usual activities when their health permitted and they were so inclined. In their last three months of pregnancy, they continued to do such normal things as take walks and carriage rides, make and receive calls, and attend church services as well as an occasional theater production or musical concert. Activity served to pass the time and relieve the tedium of waiting for the onset of labor. Ellen Strong of New York, for example, attended the opera with her husband during the eighth month of pregnancy in 1851. During a subsequent pregnancy she accompanied him to a concert rehearsal only days before delivery.[54] The diaries of Mary Harris Lester of New York and Harriet Hanson Robinson of the Boston area show that they did not hesitate to appear in public during their last months of pregnancy. Lester continued to take rides and singing lessons, went to the dressmaker, made and received calls, and attended church, Sabbath school, and the theater.[55] Robinson also continued her usual social activities, including three trips into Boston, during her last months of pregnancy.[56]

Women who were obviously pregnant also appeared at special social events in metropolitan areas like Boston and New York. Six months pregnant, Fanny Appleton Longfellow accepted an invitation to a fancy dress ball given by her mother. Dressed in her altered wedding gown with her hair fashionably coiffed, she took a cab into Boston, where she dined on capons at dinner, sat with the lieutenant governor at supper, and socialized with the hundreds of guests who apparently were quite unscandalized by her appearance. During the same pregnancy she attended a concert two and one-half weeks before the birth of her child.[57]

Elizabeth Dwight Cabot attended a similar social event when she was eight months pregnant. Invited to a series of theatricals, she wrote to her sister that special arrangements had been made to make her comfortable and accommodate her delicate condition: "I am to be allowed a seat where I can creep in and out easily & keep myself out of harm's way. I am not a pretty figure for company, but I hope to manage so as not to be obnoxious, & couldn't refuse such kindness & amusement too."[58] Cabot's sense of vanity caused her to consider carefully whether she wanted to appear in public but did not prevent her from amusing herself.

While women like Cabot did not feel a social obligation to withdraw from society, they did consider it their right to do so. Shortly before the birth of her second child, Cabot visited members of her family in Beverly, Massachusetts, thus relieving herself of the need to keep up the social demands that might have been made on her had she remained at home. She continued to be physically active by taking morning walks and driving out in the afternoons but gave herself a vacation from what she considered to be taxing social activities. "No calls to make, none to receive, no one to be asked to dinner, & no one staying in the house take a large & time consuming set of occupations out of one's life," she wrote as she relished her freedom from social obligations in her "oasis of leisure."[59] Bessie Huntting Rudd escaped to her mother's house in Sag Harbor, Long Island, during her first pregnancy. There she spent her days sewing, visiting, walking, and missing her husband, who remained behind in New York City and visited her whenever he could on weekends. Country living was more agreeable to her than living in the city particularly since she felt no desire to be sociable.[60]

One did not necessarily have to leave town to escape the demands of society. Awaiting the birth of her fourth child in as many years, Elizabeth Sedgwick chose to retreat into her home in New York City as she lost interest in social activities. "My home was so happy a one," she wrote, "that I found my interest in general society constantly lessening." She simply used her home like a cocoon and waited for her baby to be born.[61] Fictional mothers-to-be also chose to limit their social lives by staying at home. Mrs. Richman, a character portrayed in Hannah Foster's *Coquette*, began to appear less and less at parties as her fondness for retirement increased in proportion to the advancement of her pregnancy.[62]

Fear that overexertion might endanger the well-being of either mother or child also encouraged some pregnant women to limit their activities. Women like Julia Ann Hartness Lay of New York were reluctant to give up public obligations as their confinement approached. Extremely active in the distribution of religious tracts and in poor relief, Lay continued her philanthropic endeavors throughout the first six months of her pregnancy. At the end of her sixth month, however, she began to consider giving them up, not because she felt conspicuous but because she was concerned about the effect of such activities on her health and that of her unborn child. A few days after Christmas she wrote in her diary, "Now I think it will be unsafe for me to continue the distribution any longer at present as every time I go out I am putting my health in jeapardy [*sic*] as it is so near my confinement and I have so many stairs to ascend." Carefully she balanced concern for her health with her sense of usefulness and the pleasure she got from her work. "How hard it is," she wrote as she considered her problem, "for me to give it up as I am feeling such an interest in many of the people and they appear so pleased to see me. I never had a district where I think I could be so useful as in this." It was not until nearly a month later that she finally did give up her work.[63]

The behavior of the women in Elmira, New York, in the 1840s provides an interesting example of the way in which popular assumptions about pregnancy were translated into behavioral patterns that encouraged women to restrict their normal social and domestic activities. In 1848 Frances Miriam Berry Whitcher, the new wife of Elmira's Episcopalian minister, wrote to her sister describing the behavior of pregnant women in Elmira: "It is the *custom of women here* to shut themselves up for about three or four months, & groan with back-ache & '*such* a pain in the side, & *such* distr*essed* feelings in the head, it seems as if they *should* die.'"[64]

The behavior of Whitcher, even in the eighth month of her first pregnancy, did not conform to local custom. She not only continued to feel perfectly well but insisted upon taking long walks and performing her normal domestic duties. Subtly at first and later more directly, local matrons attempted to impress upon her the importance of conformity to local custom. When they came to visit, for example, they would ask the maid at the door, "Is Mrs Whitcher up?" [implying that while they may have expected her to be in, they did not expect her to be up]. "I do'nt [*sic*] want to disturb her if she's lying down" [implying that in her condition she should be]. To such inquiries the maid replied, "Up? She's never anything else—you could'nt [*sic*] coax her to go to bed in the day time." They found that Whitcher stubbornly refused to limit her activities. "I have no back ache, no pain in the side, nor any where else," she wrote, "& I see no use in pretending to have any."[65]

Whitcher's behavior and her maid's comments implied that local custom could easily be used as an excuse for self-indulgent malingering.[66] To justify their behavior local matrons became more explicit in their attempts to impress upon her the need to protect herself from the difficulties and dangers they believed to be inherent in childbearing. One female caller, who had recently borne a child, felt it necessary to provide Whitcher with a graphic, detailed description of the misery that she had endured during pregnancy. Whitcher made the mistake of remarking that she was grateful for her "freedom from the sufferings that seemed to be the portion of most ladies *beforehand.*" "O," said the visitor, "I've heard of such cases before, but they're always the *sickest* in the end—they seldom *live.*" The very same day another visitor was equally encouraging. "How wonderfully you keep up Mrs Whitcher," she remarked. "Well—you're having an easy time now—you're just the *build* to be awful sick."[67]

As it turned out, Whitcher was indeed "awful sick" during her confinement. She delivered a stillborn child and almost died in the process.[68] Knowledge of her unfortunate experience could well have been used by Elmira matrons to confirm their belief that pregnant women should remove themselves from the social mainstream and limit their domestic activities in order to preserve their health and that of their unborn children. Their belief was in conformity with that held by many orthodox and sectarian physicians. Only water cure doctors like Mary Gove Nichols and Rachel Gleason were consistent in encouraging women not to pamper themselves either before or after delivery.

Although before 1860 some women did abdicate their social and domestic responsibilities during their last months of pregnancy because they found them tiresome or because they were worried about their health, they did not yet consider it their social obligation to do so. Nevertheless, the process of change that would eventually lead to seclusion had begun. The stress that the ideology of motherhood placed on the importance of maternal responsibilities and the increasing concern of the medical community about their condition encouraged women to be particularly sensitive to the need to protect their own health and that of their unborn infants. To maintain a public life that might place the health of an unborn child at risk or reduce a woman's ability to care for it properly was to suggest that she did not regard her nurturing role as one of primary importance. Moreover, as gentility came to be associated with delicate health and difficulty in childbirth, it became equally important to testify to one's respectability by taking appropriate precautions. In addition, the declining birthrate made confinement during the last trimester more practical because a woman did not have to restrict her public activities very often. By the latter part of the nineteenth century, these factors served as the basis for expanding the meaning of confinement to include the period before as well as the period after birth.

Whether a pregnant woman appeared in public or stayed at home, she had to make adjustments in her wardrobe. Since colonial times American women had adapted their dresses to accommodate pregnancy by constructing their clothes with drawstrings, pleats, and darts.[69] Claudia Kidwell has suggested that the short gown, a blouselike garment worn over a full petticoat by ordinary women from the seventeenth century through the first decades of the nineteenth, was ideally suited to accommodate childbearing. It did not fit tightly around the waist, and the front of the dress was often held in place by a pin or an apron, thus making it easy to nurse a child during the day.[70] Women who did not have the means to accumulate an extensive wardrobe could adjust their one or two dresses to the demands of maternity.

Maternity wear for middle-and upper-class women in the first half of the nineteenth century illustrates the degree to which their lives were divided between public and private spheres. In the privacy of their homes, pregnant women wore housedresses, wrappers, and dressing gowns.[71] But if they intended to appear in public in fashionable dress during the last months preceding their actual confinement, they had to adapt their clothes to accommodate the changing proportions of their bodies. Seven and one-half months pregnant, Cabot wrote to her sister about the changes she had made in her wardrobe: "I live now in a black velvet jacket made on the pattern of my Minalaga and trimmed with the Guipure lace off my mantilla, and the skirt of the silk I bought in Paris. I think the effect is decent, & it is very comfortable. I shall wear the same rig to the Theatricals only putting on the blue silk skirt I wore in house last winter, & with lace collar and sleeves."[72] The costume described by Cabot was both fashionable and functional for a woman of her class in her condition. Established as an alternative to the back fastening bodice, the jacket-style bodice was introduced in 1851 and remained popular throughout the decade.[73] Its advantages for the pregnant women were that it fastened in the front and hid a waistline no longer fashionably small.

Women like Fanny Longfellow had their dresses altered when, as she put it, they could "no longer cover one beating heart only."[74] Other women, who could afford it, apparently made or had the dressmaker sew maternity dresses specifically designed as such. These dresses differed from regular dresses by closing down the front with hooks and eyes, rather than down the back, and often had ties to allow for necessary adjustments around the abdomen. Complete with trains and worn over crinolines, their quite fashionable appearance and elegant fabric indicate that they could easily have been worn in society.[75]

For women expecting their first child, a modification of their clothing served as an important "prop," a kind of "ceremonial dress" that acted in a nonverbal way to prepare them and those around them for their initiation into motherhood.[76] It served as public testimony to their imminent change in status. At the same time, wearing clothes that deemphasized their pregnancies and conformed as closely as possible to the prevailing standards of fashion allowed them to minimize the changes in their appearance caused by their advancing pregnancies. Despite the glorification of motherhood, they did not think pregnancy made them more attractive. Cabot did not consider herself "a pretty figure for company" despite her efforts to maintain a fashionable appearance.[77] And Bessie Huntting Rudd, awaiting the birth of her first child in 1862, wrote that she hoped her friends would wait for a few months to come for a visit since she was "not a very *elegant looking* body."[78] Ambivalence rather than pride characterized their attitude toward their appearance during the last stages of pregnancy.

It is unclear what sort of undergarments women wore during pregnancy. Throughout the period from 1800 to 1860, popular health and medical manual writers objected to the custom of wearing corsets and the practice of tight lacing during the last stages of gestation. There appear to have been various reasons why middle- and upper-class women persisted in wearing tight corsets during this time. According to Valentine Seaman, a New York physician trained by Benjamin Rush, it was popularly held around 1800 that

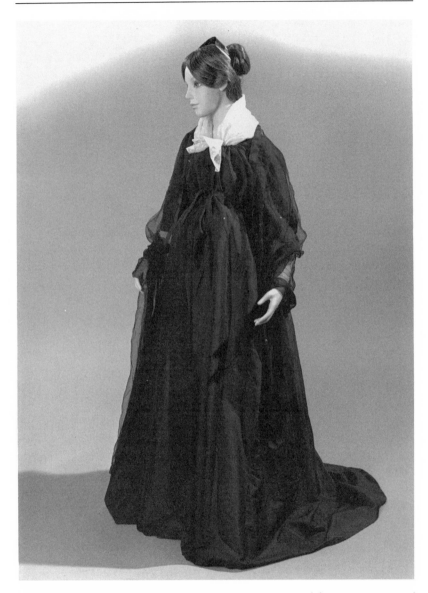

*Figure 1.* This maternity dress dating from the period between 1795 and 1800 is made of black silk and was suitable for wear by a woman in mourning. It was worn by Betsey Rogers Barker of Maine (1765–1812). Courtesy of Old Sturbridge Village, Sturbridge, Massachusetts. Photo by Henry E. Peach.

*Figure 2.* This dimity dressing gown dates from the period 1848 to 1850 and was appropriate for wear in the home during pregnancy. The four drawstrings attached to the inside of the bodice made the waistline adjustable. Courtesy of the Metropolitan Museum of Art, New York. Gift of Mrs. Harold Blake, 1945. (CI 45.97.3)

34

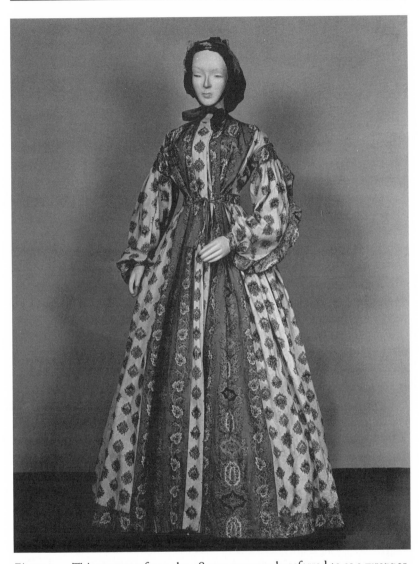

*Figure 3.*  This garment from the 1840s, commonly referred to as a wrapper, was intended to be worn in the privacy of the home. The front panels hang straight from two deep pleats at the shoulder seams. The narrow belt is set in at the back but left loose at the side seams and tied in a bow at the front, enabling a pregnant woman to adjust it to accommodate the changes in her body. Courtesy of the Metropolitan Museum of Art, New York. Gift of Bianca Louise Raetzer. (CI 44.35)

35

wearing corsets during pregnancy would ensure the mother an easier delivery by artificially pushing the fetus down in the womb. Charging that such notions were wrong as well as dangerous, Seaman recommended wearing loose jumpers that fell from the shoulders and placed no pressure whatever on the abdomen.[79]

Concern for fashion was undoubtedly another consideration. In an urban society increasingly characterized by social mobility, adherence to popularly determined standards of fashion was a way of establishing one's position in society. In 1838 Sarah Josepha Hale admitted in an editorial that "to be out of fashion" was generally thought to be an indication that a person was "wanting in spirit or purse" and marked that individual as socially insignificant.[80]

Anxiety that fashion dictated the unhealthy wearing of tight corsets brought the demand that expectant mothers forgo fashion and protect their own lives and those of their unborn children by resisting the temptation to lace during pregnancy. "It is highly probable," wrote one dress reformer in 1838, "that no small portion of the deaths of children and of mothers that take place in this delicate process of nature, arises from this cause."[81] Doctors, reflecting their concern for the health of both mother and fetus, joined health reformers in trying to discourage lacing during pregnancy.[82] But most felt it was useless to demand that pregnant women give up wearing corsets altogether. The next best thing, then, was to offer advice designed to minimize damage to the fetus particularly during the last few months of gestation. While some writers advised wearing the corset loosely, adjusting it for comfort,[83] others were more explicit: "The corsets worn during pregnancy should have lacings at each side, and over each bosom, so that they may be loosened or otherwise at pleasure; and as pregnancy advances, the unyielding steel blades so commonly used should be removed, and thin whalebone substituted. Due support will be thus obtained, and all mischievous compression avoided."[84]

By lacing during pregnancy and by attempting, however futilely, to perpetuate a physical shape that denied reality, some young married women may have been attempting to give themselves time to adjust to the rapid changes in their lives. H. B. Skinner observed in his 1849 health manual that such women "do not accommodate their dress to their new situation (from mistaken feelings of deli-

cacy) to conceal the fact from observation as long as possible."[85]
Pregnancy, which often came within the first year of marriage,
marked a dramatic change in a woman's psychological as well as
social life. It was a physical manifestation of a respectable woman's
change in status from a sexually naive virgin to a sexually experienced wife. It not only reflected that transformation but promised
a new one as well, the change from wife to mother with all its
accompanying responsibilities.

Some women were more serene than others in adapting themselves to these changes. As we saw earlier, Fanny Longfellow felt
very happy about the thought of bearing her first child. Writers of
advice literature might have regarded her casual acceptance of her
pregnancy so soon after her wedding as atypical. They were convinced that women were likely to have difficulty adjusting to the
transition from wife to mother. In 1853 Dr. Thomas Bull expressed
his concern about young married women who were, as he put it,
"so suddenly" after their marriages called upon to bear and nurture
a baby.[86] Reformer Henry C. Wright was similarly worried about a
woman's ability to make such rapid transitions early in her marriage. "Before she is aware," he dramatically wrote, "and before her
mind is prepared to meet them, the responsibilities, anxieties, and
sufferings of maternity are upon her. Grief, anguish, and a dread of
some unknown, but terrible suffering overwhelm her. Consterna-
tion seizes the heart, so recently buoyant with the hopes and joys of
a loving trusting bride."[87]

The case of Mary Rodman Fisher Fox of Philadelphia provides an
example of the very difficulty that Bull and Wright described. Married at the age of twenty-seven to Samuel Fox, Mary was not yet
secure in her new identity and role as a wife when she discovered
only six weeks after her wedding that she was already pregnant. In
her diary she clearly confessed that she was having great difficulty
in adjusting to the implications of her condition:

Within the last few days I have been agitated and disturbed
by feelings entirely new to me.—I am approaching an era in
my life—I shall be a mother. This should come to me as another blessing but I cannot receive it as such. My pride the
feelings of delicacy which I have cherished all my life—all are

37

outraged by any thing of this nature, following so soon after my marriage—(six weeks ago this night.) I never dreamed that I should be so "ungenteel" every feeling of my nature rises in rebellion against it.[88]

For three days her diary entries indicate that she struggled to exhibit the submission to circumstances that she felt to be appropriate in her situation. Letters from home aggravated her feelings of rebelliousness by reminding her of her previous untroubled single life and the warmth of relationships with family members left behind when she married. Those familiar relationships became increasingly appealing to her as her new position appeared threatening and objectionable, and she began to doubt the wisdom of marrying in the first place: "When I hear of Charley [probably her brother] being saddened in missing me, I think whether I should have married—and whether my position as Mary Fisher was not as likely to conduce to my happiness as any other."[89] Fox's feelings of violation and embarrassment as well as temporary doubts about the wisdom of marrying may have been extreme responses to the rapid changes in her life, but they nevertheless illustrate the difficulty some women faced in making the transitions demanded of them.

While some women adjusted more easily than Fox, few who recorded their thoughts about their approaching confinements failed to express negative feelings about the prospects of bearing a child. Emotions ranged from mere lack of enthusiasm at the inconvenience to anxiety or even depression caused by fear of the pain that was believed to be inherent in childbirth, fear of death in childbed, or concern about the physical, mental, and moral condition of the newborn. Millicent Hunt of Detroit was irritated about the inconvenience of bearing another child. She complained somewhat guiltily to her diary: "I find am pregnant again—yes even now, the frail foetus within me is the abode of an immortal spirit, and this has caused thoughts of discontent. I would it were not there, I love my liberty, my ease, my comfort, and do not willingly endure the inconveniences and sufferings of pregnancy and childbirth."[90] A friend of Elizabeth Cabot objected to pregnancy for similar reasons. "Lizzie B.," wrote Cabot, "feels rather down. She has gone the way of all flesh, expects her finale in August & doesn't like it *at all*. . . .

The fact is Lizzie wanted very much to go abroad & this puts a quietus on all such plans."[91]

Anxiety rather than irritation dominated the thoughts of most women, however, as they anticipated the pain of the birth process and the danger it posed to them and their babies. "O how happy I shall be if I become the *living mother* of a *living* and *perfect* child!" wrote Miriam Whitcher.[92] "I know," echoed Mary Lester in 1848, "that I soon shall be in pain and in peril and that perhaps the bed of pain may be the bed of death." She reported feeling "a fearful anticipation of the future at times . . . of pains that I never endured."[93]

When pregnant women expressed anxiety about dying in childbed, they showed more concern about separation from loved ones than they did about their eternal fate. "What anxious thots [*sic*] arise in my mind as the time draws near for fear it may be the day of our separation here. . . . Our dear little girl will be three years old next month and much does she need the protecting care of a Mother," wrote Mary Guion of Northcastle, New York, in her diary.[94] Clayton echoed such sentiments when she wrote during her first pregnancy, "Sometimes I am sad to think my time with one I love so dearly may be measured with a span."[95] Bessie Huntting Rudd wrote to her husband that if she died, she would regret it because she lived for her husband and wanted to help him "along life's pathways."[96]

Even those who held deep religious convictions expressed little concern about the state of their souls and were confident in their willingness to submit to a fate determined by a merciful God who they apparently believed was likely to reward an exemplary life on earth with eternal bliss in heaven. Mary Pierce Poor took comfort in reminding herself that "we are in the hands of One who doeth all things well."[97] Sarah Ripley Stearns prayed that "God in his infinite mercy" would admit her "to the Heavenly feast."[98] And Mary Harris Lester of New York hoped for "a free and quick admission" to the presence of God "and to Jerusalem my happy home." She was not afraid to die, she wrote, and "were death close upon" her, she would "not quail."[99] The use of biblical and hymnal phraseology gave these women the courage they needed to face whatever fate might befall them.

In their anxiety about death in childbed, some women could have found little comfort in their knowledge of the experiences of friends and relatives in a similar situation. "Poor Polly," lamented one woman, "she adds another to the list of our acquaintances who have died in the month within the last two years making 5. How strange for people to say there's little or no danger!"[100] Hunt also knew women who had died in childbed. Feeling particularly vulnerable with her husband away as her fourth confinement approached, she wrote, "My mind is filled with fearful forebodings—my memory too faithful reminds me that such and such of my acquaintances died in child-bed and in the absence of their husbands."[101] Even when they received the reassuring news that a friend had survived childbirth, that reassurance only served to remind them that childbirth could be fatal. "I congratulate Mrs. Adams upon being over such an awful time," wrote Jeannie McCall to her husband, "and only wish I was as safe—I am afraid to count months now—I feel as if I would almost rather bear the discomfort of this situation forever than come to the end of my time."[102]

Under the pressure of such anxieties, women found it difficult to maintain an optimistic attitude even though some tried valiantly to do so particularly when reassuring concerned friends and relatives. "I strive to drive away these [sad] thoughts and do often luxuriate in Hope," wrote Clayton to her husband, but she had to admit that sad thoughts did haunt her and left "a double pang" because she seldom had them.[103] Miriam Whitcher admitted to a friend, "I try to be patient but I cannot help feeling nervous and uneasy."[104] Mary Pierce Poor wrote as her confinement approached that she felt very well and that "there is no reason, as far as human forsight [sic] can go, to anticipate evil."[105]

In the privacy of their diaries, they freely expressed their fears. "I feel a strange presentiment of death," reported Millicent Hunt shortly before her third confinement. "The time for my confinement approaches—and the prospect fills me with gloomy forebodings."[106] Persis Sibley Black wrote in a similar vein, "My last stitch is taken & I am now ready for the event for w'h I am looking daily. . . . As the time draws near I fear & tremble. My feelings are peculiar . . . & often [I] find myself indulging in forbodings [sic] of evil."[107] While such entries were not intended for public scrutiny, the style in which they were written conformed to the kind of sentimental rhetoric often found in the consolation literature of the day.[108] These women prepared themselves for death in the privacy of their diaries by indulging in the drama of it. Their culture encouraged them to do so.

Even when pregnant women were not afraid, they sometimes thought they should be. In 1858 Elizabeth Dwight Cabot wrote to her sister about her continuing sense of well-being during her first pregnancy and her reservations about her anticipated labor: "You don't know how hard it is to realize that from a condition of vigorous health I am suddenly to drop into an illness. I think I must be very frivolous not to keep a steady eye on death & eternity all the time." She may have considered herself frivolous, but she took her condition seriously enough to write a will and "divide off" all of her personal possessions.[109] Bessie Huntting Rudd took the same precaution under similar circumstances. She informed her husband that she had arranged all of her accounts "should unforseen [sic] Summons come to me."[110]

All of these women could have identified with the concerns expressed by the anonymous author of an article, "A Mother's Trials," that appeared in the June 1857 edition of *Godey's Lady's Book*. The trials of a mother begin even before a child is born, the article read. A mother-to-be worries in

> most anxious solicitude, whether the being which, through her instrumentality . . . shall have a perfectly formed body, or be a cripple all its days, whether it shall be endowed with the gift of reason, or be hidden in an asylum; whether it shall be a blessing to parents, and an ornament in society, or the bane and curse of its species; whether it will go to heaven or hell.

In addition to concern about the physical, mental, and moral condition of her infant, continued the article, an expectant mother must face the "solemn thought that, in giving birth to the child, she may sacrifice her own life, and leave her babe in a cold world, deprived of the tenderness of a mother's care, in the helpless season of infancy."[111]

A sense of vulnerability and helplessness, anxiety about the outcome of labor, and fear of an "unforseen Summons" could easily lead to irritability and depression, particularly as the discomforts of advanced pregnancy imposed themselves on women awaiting the delivery of their child. "One or two nights lately," complained the normally cheerful Cabot, "I haven't slept perfectly well & then I have found myself appropriately gloomy in the course of the day."[112] The day before the delivery of her fifth child, Millicent Hunt described herself as "depressed in spirits" and in need of preparing her mind for her "approaching trial."[113] Even the usually optimistic Longfellow found that the prospect of her fifth confinement and the thought of the responsibilities that would result from it depressed her "a good deal."[114] Susan Mansfield Huntington expressed similar feelings: "The idea of soon giving birth to my 3d child & the consequent duties I shall be called to discharge distresses me so I feel as if I should sink."[115] Even a rare fictional reference to attitudes toward pregnancy described irritability and depression as the predominant emotional condition. Timothy Shay Arthur wrote of Anna Hartley in "The Wife" that "her spirits were often so depressed that it required her utmost effort to receive" her husband cheerfully when he returned home at the end of the day.[116]

But perhaps the most poignant comment describing the feelings of depression came from a friend of Sally Hughes. Expecting to add a child to a household plagued at the time by financial difficulties, she wrote: "I do not believe I shall ever have a living child while our family is in this situation. . . . No one knows what a constant state of depression and irritability I am constantly struggling with. It's wrong to give way to it but not wrong to feel so for I can no more help it than can a deranged person his unbalanced mind."[117] As helpless as she may have felt, it is unlikely that Hughes's friend sought professional help in an attempt to overcome the depression that plagued her.

Nevertheless, doctors were concerned about the emotional changes that accompanied pregnancy and attempted to explain and prescribe treatments for them. According to both British and American medical authors, it was as normal for pregnant women to exhibit nervous symptoms as physical ones. After conception, wrote one doctor, a woman may go through a "moral revolution" in which "without being considered insane," she is "in that state of mind which precedes if it does not in fact constitute the first state of mental derangement." [118] Some doctors blamed pregnancy for extraordinary changes in behavior. "Individuals who possess ordinarily the most agreeable tempers, and the most amiable dispositions," wrote Frederick Hollick in his popular health manual, "will become peevish and fretful, and often even violently passionate and malicious. Some have even been known to have a disposition to commit various crimes, of which they have the greatest horror in their natural state." [119] While most other doctors noted less extreme emotional reactions to the state of pregnancy, both regulars and sectarians were fairly consistent in recognizing that women could be expected to be restless, despondent, irritable, and capricious. [120] "All women, in the puerperal state," concluded John Burns, "are more irritable, and more easily affected both in body and mind, than at other times." [121]

Childbearing women admitted that their personalities changed during pregnancy. One woman complained that she became so irritable during pregnancy that "she was a perfect nuisance in the house." [122] Eliza Fenwick Rutherford, awaiting the birth of her first child, wrote to her mother in 1813 that her only complaint was that she had been "troubled with . . . *ill temper*, falling into violent fits of passion and petulance on the slightest contradiction." Her husband had borne the brunt of her bad temper, she reported, and she was glad that she was regaining her "original sweetness of disposition." [123] Elizabeth Parker was distressed by the unusual behavior of a pregnant friend: "Betsey has indulged such strong propensities lately and looks so weak and miserable, I dread to see the end thereof." Parker reported that when Betsey had taken tea with a mutual friend a short time before, she had embarrassed everyone by staring for an hour at one of the other guests. [124] Such propensities were disturbing to everyone concerned and tended to confirm the medical belief that women were likely to become emotionally unstable during pregnancy.

Doctors sought to explain such personality changes by viewing women as victims of both their cultural environment and their reproductive organs. They believed that middle- and upper-class women, who were likely to become their patients, were especially affected by the intellectual stresses and physical debilities that accompanied the shift from a rural-agrarian society to an urban one.

The complexities of modern life, they believed, predisposed women (as well as men) to mental maladjustment if not insanity.[125] Women were further jeopardized by their physiology and childbearing function. As early as 1812 Benjamin Rush wrote that women were susceptible to madness because of the physical demands made on them by menstruation, pregnancy, and parturition.[126]

While they may have agreed on which factors made women vulnerable to nervous afflictions during gestation, doctors could not explain precisely what caused such disorders. One physician attributed them to physical irritations in the body that simply spread to the brain.[127] Another speculated that a disturbance of the circulation caused emotional distress.[128] Whatever the specific physiological explanation, doctors accepted the traditional idea that the brain and uterus were closely connected and found it therefore unsurprising that pregnancy should be accompanied by disorders of the nervous system.[129]

Early nineteenth-century doctors did not restrict their search for causes of mental stress during pregnancy to physiology, however. They were perfectly willing to agree that even during a normal pregnancy women had legitimate reasons to be depressed and irritable. "It is very natural," wrote Fleetwood Churchill, "that with a known or unknown amount of suffering before them, and with a certain but unknown degree of danger connected with the termination of pregnancy, women should occasionally at least be subject to depression of spirits, and should take a gloomy view of their prospects."[130]

Since physicians recognized that depression was closely tied to fear, they objected to any practice that might result in alarming the expectant mother unnecessarily and threatening her emotional stability. They particularly protested the practice of relating to pregnant women "every accident that has ever been heard or known, to occur to a woman in her situation." "There [are] some women," wrote John Bright in his popular health manual,

> in the world that never can rest, when they hear of an accident happening to a woman in a state of pregnancy or in labour, till they go and tell it to some friend in a similar condition. And having related the case, and painted it in all the blackness of

colouring it admits of, they will say, I hope this will not be your case. . . . Such persons ought to have a patent right for killing their neighbors—through *kindness* as they call it—for in many cases it amounts to little less than murder.[131]

Bright was joined by some of the most prominent obstetricians in both Britain and the United States who sensed that inducing fear did nothing to improve the chances of survival for mother or child.[132]

Their concern was not ill founded. Certainly Miriam Whitcher in Elmira, New York, could not have found it very reassuring when, during her first pregnancy, local matrons warned that women who exhibited good health during pregnancy frequently had difficult deliveries and "seldom live." Eliza Rutherford reported to her mother a similar experience with well-meaning friends. As she awaited the imminent birth of her first child in 1813, Rutherford reported that she was not afraid of labor,

> tho' certainly that is no fault of the good Ladies I have happened to be in company with. From what principle of kindness and benevolence can it proceed, do you suppose,—the earnest desire which the Ladies I am acquainted with here have shewn to give me a full idea of the dangers and pains I have to encounter? They are determined I shall not be surprised at any suffering that may come.[133]

While Rutherford admitted that she had not been unduly alarmed by the stories, she nevertheless felt that her visitors were insensitive.

Because they believed that the predisposition of pregnant women to nervous disorders was enhanced by fear of the dangers that might accompany the birth process, doctors tended to define despondency as normal as long as it did not last too long or settle into "gloomy anticipation of evil," indifference, or apathy.[134] They were careful to advise their readers that under no circumstances should melancholy be dismissed since it could be an early indication of approaching madness. Unfortunately, however, they had no effective treatment for prenatal depression.[135] Parturient women were left to deal with their own feelings of anxiety and fear, and only a happy conclusion to the drama of birth could relieve their tension.

Making practical arrangements for the birth of a child may have helped to reduce the tension and tedium of awaiting the onset of labor. Preparing a wardrobe for an expected infant could consume a considerable amount of time since clothing was made by hand throughout most of the period. Contributions to an infant's wardrobe by friends and relatives relieved an expectant mother of a time-consuming responsibility. "Many thanks," wrote Fanny Longfellow to her sister-in-law, "for the kind 'pricking of your thumbs' in my behalf. My little wardrobe is filling up fast, but any additions your sisterly (or auntly) interest may suggest to your nimble fingers will have an honorable place therein above all other Lilliputian offerings." [136]

As confinement approached, someone also had to make the arrangements for lying-in attendants. By 1830 many middle- and upper-class women were hiring physicians rather than midwives to attend them during delivery. According to Charles Meigs they normally engaged a doctor sometime before the onset of labor. [137] Yet they were more likely to discuss in their diaries and letters the arrangements they had made for the attendance of a nurse than they were to comment upon the selection of a doctor. Only under special circumstances did they discuss their medical attendants. In 1853, for example, Mary Pierce Poor of New York reported to her sister that she had engaged Elizabeth Blackwell, one of the few woman doctors in the country, to deliver her baby. During the early months of her pregnancy, Poor had attended Blackwell's lectures and had been impressed by her professional approach to the subject of childbirth. In her letter she reassured her sister that she had "the greatest possible confidence" in Blackwell's "experience and skill." [138]

Unlike Poor, some women did not even make their own arrangements for a doctor to attend them. Parke Lewis Butler's mother-in-law engaged a doctor for her. [139] A friend might perform the same service. In 1834 Benjamin Drake, a New York physician, received a note from a colleague, a Dr. H. Hobart, asking him to attend an obstetrics patient if the need should arise in his absence. In the postscript of the letter, Hobart indicated that he could give Drake

no information about the patient since one of his female acquaintances had made the arrangements for her.[140]

It is not surprising to find that women expecting their first child
gave little more than passing notice to the doctor who would attend
them during childbirth. Any of them who had set up housekeeping
with their husbands some distance from their home towns would
have had little opportunity to develop more than a superficial ac-
quaintance with local physicians before they became pregnant.
Once they conceived a child, it is unlikely that they received regular
prenatal care. Thus their contact with a local physician before the
birth of their children would have been brief at best. Under normal
circumstances the doctor that delivered their babies would attend
them for only a few hours and then would leave them in the care of
their nurses. Doctors were technicians only. They were not central
to the birth experience itself. Consequently, women were not overly
concerned about ensuring the presence of a specific doctor at delivery. Their attitude was summed up by Jeannie McCall's mother,
who, in discussing a friend who had decided to have her baby away
from home, wrote, "Old Dr. Criss of Leesburg is said to be safe and
skillful in such matters but after all there is little for a Dr. to do—
[she] must do her own work."[141]

Practical arrangements made, it only remained for pregnant
women to wait for labor to begin. Feeling awkward and uncomfortable with few distractions to relieve the tedium, they did not always
find the wait easy. "I begin to feel like the old woman who had her
petticoats cast off & wonder whether 'I be I,'" wrote Elizabeth
Dwight Cabot as she waited for the birth of her second child. "My
calculations have proved so entirely at fault, that I feel in a blue
maze & find myself calculating on an indefinite length of days of
this sort, which I suppose must end finally, though I have no clue
to go by any longer."[142] Without the familiar comfort of thinking
that she knew when her baby would be born, Cabot felt adrift in a
sea of nervous anticipation.

While childbearing women awaited the imminent birth of their
children, the outside world continued to view pregnancy as a deeply
personal, insular experience. It remained throughout the period of
little interest to writers of prose and poetry, who made almost no

effort to probe deeply into the responses of women to the prospect of becoming mothers. T. S. Arthur summed up their attitude when he wrote in "The Wife" that, even though the first year of a woman's married life might be marked by the conception of a child, "her life is more strongly marked internally than externally. She feels much but the world sees little, and little can be brought forth to view." [143] Those close to a pregnant women also felt an inability to share her most intimate feelings. A. D. Mayo wrote of his wife during her first pregnancy, "If she had misgivings, or hours of despondency, they were concealed from every one." [144]

Writers like Arthur and husbands like Mayo may have been unwilling or unable to delve into the expectant mother's innermost thoughts and feelings. However, occasionally someone did try to describe what it meant for them. Bronson Alcott wrote of pregnancy that he believed it to be a "hard task" to wait with "patience and trust" for the birth of a child. [145] Nevertheless, that is precisely what women had to do. Pregnancy remained for them, as Fanny Longfellow described it, a period of patient, if anxious, waiting for the opportunity to give birth and for a new responsibility to be added to those they already bore.

## Notes

1. Edward Wagenknecht, ed., *Mrs. Longfellow: Selected Letters and Journals of Fanny Appleton Longfellow (1817–1861)* (New York: Longmans, Green, 1956), 103, 113.

2. Yasukichi Yasuba, *Birth Rates of the White Population in the United States, 1800–1860: An Economic Study* (Baltimore: Johns Hopkins, 1962), 49; Maris A. Vinovskis, "A Multivariate Regression Analysis of Fertility Differentials among Massachusetts Townships and Regions in 1860," in *Historical Studies of Changing Fertility*, ed. Charles Tilly (Princeton, N.J.: Princeton University Press, 1978), 230. An extensive debate has occurred over the role that urbanization may have played in the decline of fertility in the United States before 1860. The consensus seems to be that if it had any effect, it did so only at the end of the antebellum period. See Wilson H. Grabill, Clyde V. Kiser, and Pascal K. Whelpton, *The Fertility of American Women* (New York: John Wiley, 1958), 3, 15–16; Yasuba, *Birth Rates*, 22, 158, 187; Tamara K. Hareven and Maris A. Vinovskis, eds., *Family and Population in Nineteenth-Century America* (Princeton, N.J.: Princeton University Press, 1978), 4. Various ex-

planations have been offered concerning why married couples were willing to try to limit the size of their families. For discussions of this issue, see J. A. Banks, *Prosperity and Parenthood: A Study of Family Planning among the Victorian Middle Class* (London: Routledge and Kegan Paul, 1954); Grabill, Kiser, and Whelpton, *Fertility*, 3; Robert V. Wells, "Family History and Demographic Transition," *Journal of Social History* 9 (Fall 1975): 1–19; Nancy F. Cott, "Passionlessness: An Interpretation of Victorian Sexual Ideology, 1790–1850," *Signs* 4 (Winter 1978): 234; Daniel Scott Smith, "Family Limitation, Sexual Control, and Domestic Feminism in Victorian America," in *Clio's Consciousness Raised: New Perspectives on the History of Women*, ed. Mary S. Hartman and Lois Banner (New York: Harper and Row, 1974), 119–36.

3. Quoted in Randolph Shipley Klein, *Portrait of an Early American Family: The Shippens of Pennsylvania across Five Generations* (Philadelphia: University of Pennsylvania Press, 1975), 285 n.

4. Calvin Fletcher, *The Diary of Calvin Fletcher, 1817–1838, Including Letters of Calvin Fletcher and Diaries and Letters of His Wife Sarah Hill Fletcher*, ed. Gayle Thornbrough (Indianapolis: Indiana Historical Society, 1972), 138, 258, 453.

5. William Lloyd Garrison, *The Letters of William Lloyd Garrison: No Union with Slave-Holders, 1841–1849*, ed. Walter Merrill (Cambridge, Mass.: Belknap Press, 1973), 462.

6. Helen E. Brown, *The Mother and Her Work* (Boston: American Tract Society, 1862), 20–22. Italics appear in the original unless otherwise stated.

7. For references to such matters, see Elizabeth Ellery Sedgwick journal, 1824, 1825, Houghton Library, Harvard University, Cambridge, Mass.; Fanny Longfellow to Mary Appleton MacIntosh, Dec. 31, 1845, Frances Elizabeth Appleton Longfellow Papers, Longfellow National Historic Site, National Park Service, Cambridge, Mass.; Abigail Alcott to Samuel May, Mar. 27, 1831, box 1, folder 25, Abigail May Alcott Letters, Alcott Family Papers, Houghton Library; Kate Ross to Edward C. Ross, June 22, 1836, July 23, 1836, Aug. 9, 1836, Edward C. Ross Letters, Chrystie Family Papers, New-York Historical Society, N.Y.; Fletcher, *Diary*, ed. Thornbrough, 453; Mary Watson to Sarah Watson Dana, Sept. 8, 1848, box 15, folder 12, Sara Watson Dana Letters, Dana Family Papers, Schlesinger Library, Radcliffe College, Cambridge, Mass.; Mary Pierce Poor to Lucy Tappan Pierce, Nov. 26, 1842, box 6, folder 89; Mary Pierce Poor to Feroline Pierce Fox, May 12, 1844, July 13, 1844, box 12, folder 168; Mary Pierce Poor to John and Lucy Pierce, July 7, 1844, box 7, folder 91, Mary Pierce Poor Letters, Poor Family Collection, Schlesinger Library; Persis Sibley Andrews Black journal, May 9, 1847, in *Victorian Women: A Documentary Account of Women's Lives in Nineteenth-Century England, France, and the United States*, ed.

Erna Olafson Hellerstein, Leslie Parker Hume, and Karen M. Offen (Stanford: Stanford University Press, 1981), 219; Eleanor Parke Custis Lewis to Elizabeth Bordley Gibson, Jan. 22, 1829, Eleanor Parke Custis Lewis Letters, Historical Society of Pennsylvania, Philadelphia; Mary Rodman Fisher Fox diary, Sept. 28, 1851, box 13, folder 30, Logan-Fisher-Fox Papers, Historical Society of Pennsylvania; William Lloyd Garrison, *The Letters of William Lloyd Garrison: A House Divided against Itself, 1836–1840*, ed. Louis Ruchames (Cambridge, Mass.: Belknap Press, 1971), 659; Garrison, *Letters*, ed. Merrill, 276.

8. Richard Henry Dana, Jr., *The Journal of Richard Henry Dana, Jr.*, ed. Robert F. Lucid, 3 vols. (Cambridge, Mass.: Belknap Press, 1968), 1:267.

9. Elizabeth to Agnes Treat Lamb Richards, Dec. 9, 1839, Agnes Treat Lamb Letters, case 40, Lamb Papers, New-York Historical Society. Harriet Beecher Stowe showed similar determination. See Kathryn Kish Sklar, *Catharine Beecher: A Study in American Domesticity* (New York: W. W. Norton, 1973), 320 n.

10. Abigail Adams, *New Letters of Abigail Adams, 1788–1801*, ed. Stewart Mitchell (Boston: Houghton Mifflin, 1947), 244. See also Susan Osgood to Julian Osgood, May 25, 1819, Susan Kitteridge Osgood Field Papers, New-York Historical Society.

11. Elizabeth Dwight Cabot to Ellen Dwight Twistleton, Apr. 23, [1859 or 1860,] sec. 2, box 2, folder 18, Elizabeth Dwight Cabot Letters, Hugh Cabot Family Collection, Schlesinger Library.

12. Eleanor Parke Custis Lewis to Elizabeth Bordley Gibson, Apr. 5, 1825, Mar. 19, 1826, Eleanor Parke Custis Lewis Letters.

13. Laura Stone Poor to Mary Pierce Poor, Nov. 6, 1853, box 12, folder 183, Mary Pierce Poor Letters.

14. Adams, *New Letters*, ed. Mitchell, 41. ·

15. Harriet Conner Brown, *Grandmother Brown's Hundred Years, 1827–1927* (Boston: Little, Brown, 1929), 176, 178.

16. Quoted in James Reed, *From Private Vice to Public Virtue: The Birth Control Movement and American Society since 1830* (New York: Basic, 1978), 29. Since Hannah Longshore was a doctor, it may have been easier for the Longshores than for most to limit their childbearing.

17. Anna Colton Clayton to John Clayton, Aug. 3, 1848, Anna Colton Clayton Letters, John Clayton Papers, Historical Society of Pennsylvania.

18. Quoted in Carl N. Degler, *At Odds: Women and the Family in America from the Revolution to the Present* (New York: Oxford University Press, 1980), 211. Hannah Smith, the aunt of M. Carey Thomas, was unsuccessful in preventing pregnancy even with the agreement of her husband that they should try. See an excerpt from Smith's diary in *The Making of a Feminist: Early Jour-*

*nals and Letters of M. Carey Thomas*, ed. Marjorie Housepian Dobkin (Kent, Ohio: Kent State University Press, 1979), 149.

19. Catherine M. Scholten, "'On the Importance of the Obstetrick Art': Changing Customs of Childbirth in America, 1760–1825," *William and Mary Quarterly* 34 (July 1977): 434–38; Jane B. Donegan, "Man-Midwifery and the Delicacy of the Sexes," in *"Remember the Ladies": New Perspectives on Women in American History*, ed. Carol V. R. George (Syracuse: Syracuse University Press, 1975), 90–92; Jane B. Donegan, *Women and Men Midwives: Medicine, Morality, and Misogyny in Early America* (Westport, Conn.: Greenwood Press, 1978), 4–5.

20. Benjamin Rush, "On the Means of Lessening the Pains and Danger of Child-Bearing, and of Preventing Its Consequent Diseases," *Medical Repository* 6 (1803): 27–28. It should be noted that Benjamin Rush tended to greatly enlarge the number of things that could be regarded as disease by defining them as such. For a critical examination of this tendency, see Thomas S. Szasz, *The Manufacture of Madness: A Comparative Study of the Inquisition and the Mental Health Movement* (New York: Harper and Row, 1970), 137–39.

21. William Buchan, *Advice to Mothers on the Subject of Their Own Health* (Philadelphia: John Bioren, 1804), 29; Thomas Denman, *An Introduction to the Practice of Midwifery* (Brattleborough, Vt.: William Fessenden, 1807), 119, 401.

22. William Buchan, *Domestic Medicine; or, A Valuable Treatise on the Prevention and Cure of Diseases* (Leominster: Adams and Wilder, 1804), 324–25.

23. See, for example, Samuel Bard, *A Compendium of the Theory and Practice of Midwifery* (New York: Collins and Perkins, 1808), 69–72; John Burns, *The Principles of Midwifery, Including the Diseases of Women and Children* (Philadelphia: Hopkins and Earle, 1810), 170; James Blundell, *The Principles and Practice of Obstetricy* (Washington, D.C.: Duff Green, 1834), 121; Denman, *Introduction*, 118; Alexander H. McNair, *Suggestions to Parents and Others, on the Physical and Medical Treatment of Children; Also, Diseases of Females* (Philadelphia: McNair, 1842), 194, 199; John W. Bright, *The Mother's Medical Guide* (Louisville: A. S. Tilden, 1844), 47–52; H. B. Skinner, *The Female's Medical Guide and Married Woman's Advisor* (Boston: Skinner, 1849), 15–24, 84; A. M. Mauriceau, *The Married Woman's Private Medical Companion* (New York: Joseph Trow, 1847), 62–96.

24. Denman, *Introduction*, 119.

25. The role of therapeutics in the doctor-patient relationship is discussed in Charles E. Rosenberg, "The Therapeutic Revolution: Medicine, Meaning, and Social Change in Nineteenth-Century America," in *The Therapeutic Revolution: Essays in the Social History of Medicine*, ed. Morris J. Vogel and Charles E. Rosenberg (Philadelphia: University of Pennsylvania Press, 1979), 9.

26. It is not clear whether or not in earlier times women had consulted midwives throughout pregnancy. Catherine Scholten has written of midwives that "they advised the mother-to-be if troubles arose during pregnancy." However, she provides no specific evidence to substantiate her point. Nor does she specify what "troubles" might have induced a pregnant woman to consult with a midwife ("'On the Importance,'" 429). Obstetrics texts make it clear that although a physician might be engaged before the onset of labor, he could not necessarily expect to be well acquainted with his patient (Blundell, *Principles*, 143; Michael Ryan, *The Philosophy of Marriage and Its Social, Moral, and Physical Relations* [London: H. Bailliere, 1839], 282–83). Such observations suggest that even the most prominent of obstetricians could not expect to be called upon to offer prenatal care and that women continued to prescribe for themselves.

27. Elizabeth Dwight Cabot to Ellen Dwight Twistleton, Dec. 19, 1858, sec. 2, box 2, folder 17, Elizabeth Dwight Cabot Letters. See also Miriam Whitcher to her sister, Feb. 25, 1848, Frances Miriam Berry Whitcher Letters, Whitcher Collection, New-York Historical Society; Fanny Longfellow to Anne Longfellow Pierce, Jan. 17, 1844, Frances Elizabeth Appleton Longfellow Papers.

28. Anna Colton Clayton to John Clayton, July 16, 1847, Aug. 2, 12, 1847, Anna Colton Clayton Letters.

29. Fox diary, Aug. 16, 19, 24, 1851, box 13, folder 30, Logan-Fisher-Fox Papers. During her seventh month of pregnancy, Mary L. Ware sought the advice of a physician before she made plans to travel. See Mary L. Ware, *Memoir of Mary L. Ware, Wife of Henry Ware, Jr.*, ed. Edward B. Hall (Boston: Crosby, Nichols, 1853), 203.

30. Elizabeth Dwight Cabot to Ellen Dwight Twistleton, [Jan. 1859,] sec. 2, box 2, folder 18, Elizabeth Dwight Cabot Letters.

31. Elizabeth Dwight Cabot to Ellen Dwight Twistleton, Aug. 12, 1861, sec. 2, box 2, folder 20, Elizabeth Dwight Cabot Letters.

32. Hester Pendleton, *Parents' Guide for the Transmission of Desired Qualities to Offspring, and Childbirth Made Easy* (New York: Fowler and Wells, 1856), 176.

33. Catharine Beecher to the editor, *Boston Medical and Surgical Journal* 35 (Dec. 30, 1846): 449; Richard Harrison Shryock, "The American Physician in 1846 and 1946: A Study in Professional Contrasts," in *Medicine in America: Historical Essays* (Baltimore: Johns Hopkins, 1966), 150–51, 163.

34. *Weekly Visitor; or, Ladies' Miscellany* 4 (Aug. 30, 1806): 352.

35. "The Physician and Patient," *Ladies' Literary Cabinet* 5 (Feb. 2, 1822): 100–101. For another example, see Caroline Lee Hentz, "Neglecting a Fee;

or, The Young Physician and His Fortunes," in *Ugly Effie; or, The Neglected One and the Pet Beauty, and Other Tales* (Philadelphia: T. B. Peterson, [1850]), 275.

36. For a discussion of self-help and its relation to women, see Regina Markell Morantz, "Nineteenth Century Health Reform and Women: A Program of Self-Help," in *Medicine without Doctors: Home Health Care in American History*, ed. Guenter B. Risse, Ronald L. Numbers, and Judith Walzer Leavitt (New York: Science History Publications, 1977), 73–95.

37. Anna Colton Clayton to John Clayton, July 21, 1847, Anna Colton Clayton Letters.

38. Valentine Seaman, *The Midwives Monitor and Mothers Mirror* (New York: Isaac Collins, 1800), iii–iv.

39. William M. Cornell, "Woman the True Physician," *Godey's Lady's Book* 46 (Jan. 1853): 82. A number of scholars have described the threat that the practice of male midwifery was believed to pose to the maintenance of female modesty. See Jane B. Donegan, *Women and Men Midwives*, 141–236; Richard W. Wertz and Dorothy C. Wertz, *Lying-in: A History of Childbirth in America* (New York: Free Press, 1977), 77–108.

40. Horton Howard, *A Treatise on the Complaints Peculiar to Females: Embracing a System of Midwifery, the Whole in Conformity with the Improved System of Botanic Medicine* (Columbus, Ohio: Howard, 1832), v.

41. Skinner, *Female's Medical Guide*, 6.

42. A. Curtis, *Lectures on Midwifery and the Forms of Disease Peculiar to Women and Children* (Cincinnati: C. Nagle, 1846), 22. See also Frederick Hollick, *The Marriage Guide; or, Natural History of Generation* (New York: T. W. Strong, 1850), v.

43. Mary Pierce Poor diary, Mar. 6, 8, 13, 15, 20, 1852, box 6, Poor Family Collection.

44. Elizabeth Dwight Cabot to Ellen Dwight Twistleton, Feb. 24, 1861, sec. 2, box 2, folder 20, Elizabeth Dwight Cabot Letters.

45. "Editor's Table," *Godey's Lady's Book* 48 (May 1854): 462–63.

46. John B. Blake, "Mary Gove Nichols, Prophetess of Health," *Proceedings of the American Philosophical Society* 106 (June 29, 1962): 220–21.

47. Martha H. Verbrugge, "The Social Meaning of Personal Health: The Ladies' Physiological Institute of Boston and Vicinity in the 1850s," in *Health Care in America: Essays in Social History*, ed. Susan Reverby and David Rosner (Philadelphia: Temple University Press, 1979), 48, 51, 56, 62.

48. "Editor's Table," *Godey's Lady's Book* 49 (July 1854): 80. The figure here may be somewhat exaggerated. In this editorial Sarah Josepha Hale was encouraging women to go into medicine. Some educators also recognized the need for women to know something about physiology. In the 1830s Emma

Willard was among the first to teach the subject to young women in her Female Seminary in Troy, N.Y. See Alma Lutz, *Emma Willard: Daughter of Democracy* (Boston: Houghton Mifflin, 1929), 181.

49. Sarah Ripley Stearns diary, Jan. 1, 1815, Stearns Collection, Schlesinger Library.

50. Anna Colton Clayton to John Clayton, July 16, 1847, Anna Colton Clayton Letters.

51. Miriam Whitcher to sisters, father, mother, and brothers, Jan. 2, 1848, Frances Miriam Berry Whitcher Letters.

52. Elizabeth Dwight Cabot to Ellen Dwight Twistleton, July 1, 1861, sec. 2, box 2, folder 20, Elizabeth Dwight Cabot Letters.

53. Some who have offered this view are Charles Strickland, "A Transcendentalist Father: The Child-Rearing Practices of Bronson Alcott," *Perspectives in American History* 3 (1969): 29; Linda Gordon, *Woman's Body, Woman's Right: A Social History of Birth Control in America* (New York: Penguin, 1976), 24; Wertz and Wertz, *Lying-in*, 78–79; Degler, *At Odds*, 59.

54. George Templeton Strong, *The Diary of George Templeton Strong: The Turbulent Fifties, 1850–59*, ed. Allan Nevins and Milton Halsey Thomas (New York: Macmillan, 1952), 62, 70; George Templeton Strong diary, May 17, 23, 1856, vol. 3, pp. 131, 133, George Templeton Strong Papers, New-York Historical Society.

55. Mary Harris Lester diary, Oct. 10, 13, 15, 21, 24, 29, 1848, Nov. 16, 18, 28, 29, 30, 1848, Dec. 17, 1848, Andrew Lester Papers, New-York Historical Society.

56. Harriet Hanson Robinson diary, Feb. 5, 14, 21, 1859, Mar. 11, 21, 28, 1859, Apr. 16, 19, 20, 25, 29, 1859, Robinson-Shattuck Papers, Schlesinger Library. For other examples, see Sedgwick journal, 1827, 49; Sally Logan Fisher diary, Apr. 12, 20, 1794, Historical Society of Pennsylvania; Elizabeth Dwight Cabot to Ellen Dwight Twistleton, Dec. 19, 27, 1858, sec. 2, box 2, folder 17; [Jan. 1859], Jan. 18, 23, 31, 1859, sec. 2, box 2, folder 18; Aug. 26, 1861, sec. 2, box 2, folder 20, Elizabeth Dwight Cabot Letters; Jeannie McCall to Peter McCall, June 18, [1847,] Jeannie McCall Letters, McCall Section, Cadwallader Collection, Historical Society of Pennsylvania; Stearns diary, Aug. 29, 1813, Sept. 5, 9, 11, 1813, Stearns Collection; Poor diary, Oct. 27, 31, 1842, Nov. 1, 2, 4, 5, 8, 10, 1842, May 23, 25, 1844, June 13, 16, 1844, Oct. 7, 12, 16, 18, 19, 20, 21, 1848, Aug. 16, 18, 19, 20, 21, 22, 23, 27, 28, 1853, Poor Family Collection; Mary Brown Askew diary, Dec. 26, 1860, Jan. 23, 1861, Historical Society of Pennsylvania.

57. Frances Elizabeth Appleton Longfellow journal, Feb. 28, 1844,

Frances Elizabeth Appleton Longfellow Papers; Wagenknecht, ed., *Mrs. Longfellow*, 111.

58. Elizabeth Dwight Cabot to Ellen Dwight Twistleton, Dec. 27, 1858, sec. 2, box 2, folder 17, Elizabeth Dwight Cabot Letters.

59. Elizabeth Dwight Cabot to Ellen Dwight Twistleton, Sept. 2, 1861, sec. 2, box 2, folder 20, Elizabeth Dwight Cabot Letters.

60. Bessie Huntting Rudd to Mary Huntting Bush, [spring 1860,] box 3, folder 52, Bessie Huntting Rudd Letters, Huntting-Rudd Family Papers, Schlesinger Library.

61. Sedgwick journal, 1847, 49.

62. Hannah Webster Foster, *The Coquette; or, The History of Eliza Wharton* (Boston: E. Larkin, 1797), 20.

63. Julia Ann Hartness Lay diary, Dec. 27, 1852, Jan. 22, 1853, Rare Books and Manuscripts Division, Astor, Lenox and Tilden Foundations, New York Public Library.

64. Jenny Lawrence, "Miriam Berry Whitcher Speaks Her Mind: Letters Home, 1846–1852," *New-York Historical Society Quarterly* 63 (Jan. 1979): 48–49.

65. Ibid., 49.

66. For a discussion of this issue, see Ann Douglas Wood, "'The Fashionable Diseases': Women's Complaints and Their Treatment in Nineteenth-Century America," *Journal of Interdisciplinary History* 4 (Summer 1973): 25–52.

67. Miriam Whitcher to sister, Feb. 25, 1848, Frances Miriam Berry Whitcher Letters; Lawrence, "Miriam Berry Whitcher," 49.

68. Lawrence, "Miriam Berry Whitcher," 34.

69. Clair Elizabeth Fox, "Pregnancy, Childbirth, and Early Infancy in Anglo-American Culture: 1625–1830" (Ph.D. diss., University of Pennsylvania, 1966), 105.

70. Claudia Kidwell, "Short Gowns," *Dress* 4 (1978): 30, 45, 50.

71. For examples of such garments, see dresses catalogued as CI 45.97.3, CI 51.90.6, CI 44.35, 1975.227.9, CI 49.43.2ab at the Metropolitan Museum of Art, N.Y. For mention of wrappers, see Jeannie McCall to Peter McCall, Oct. 27, [late 1840s,] Jeannie McCall Letters; Lay diary, Oct. 6, 1855.

72. Elizabeth Dwight Cabot to Ellen Dwight Twistleton, Dec. 27, 1858, sec. 2, box 2, folder 17, Elizabeth Dwight Cabot Letters.

73. Anne Buck, *Victorian Costume and Costume Accessories* (New York: Universe, 1961), 27–28.

74. Wagenknecht, ed., *Mrs. Longfellow*, 107.

75. For examples, see dresses held by the Costume and Textiles Depart-

ment, State Historical Society of Wisconsin, and dresses catalogued as CI 52.61.2, CI 51.90.6, and 43.126.29 at the Metropolitan Museum of Art. The earliest example of these garments is dated in the 1840s. It is difficult to tell what sort of clothing pregnant middle- and upper-class women wore before that time.

76. Mary Shaw Ryan, *Clothing: A Study in Human Behavior* (New York: Holt, Rinehart and Winston, 1966), 3; Marilyn J. Horn, *The Second Skin: An Interdisciplinary Study of Clothing* (Boston: Houghton Mifflin, 1968), 4, 10, 12, 57, 90–92, 109.

77. Elizabeth Dwight Cabot to Ellen Dwight Twistleton, Dec. 27, 1858, sec. 2, box 2, folder 17, Elizabeth Dwight Cabot Letters.

78. Bessie Huntting Rudd to Hattie Huntting, Feb. 28, 1862, box 3, folder 61, Bessie Huntting Rudd Letters.

79. Seaman, *Midwives Monitor*, 74–75. This belief had been popular for some time; see Charles White, *A Treatise on the Management of Pregnant and Lying-in Women* (London: Edward and Charles Dilly, 1773), 76–77; Buchan, *Advice to Mothers*, 55–61. Buchan also advised a flowing rather than a tight dress as did British obstetrician Alexander Hamilton. See Alexander Hamilton, *Outline of the Theory and Practice of Midwifery* (North-hampton, Mass.: Thomas and Andrews, 1797), 130–31.

80. "Editor's Table," *Godey's Lady's Book* 16 (Jan. 1838): 47–48. While recognizing the importance of fashion to establishing or maintaining one's place in society, Hale felt that bowing to the demands of fashion was a kind of bondage inappropriate for a citizen of a republic.

81. Matthew Carey, *Philosophy of Common Sense* (Philadelphia: Blanchard, 1838), 68. For a similar comment, see M. Angeline Merritt, *Dress Reform Practically and Physiologically Considered* (Buffalo: Jewett, Thomas, 1852), 77.

82. Frederick Hollick, *The Matron's Manual of Midwifery, and the Diseases of Women during Pregnancy and in Child Bed* (New York: T. W. Strong, 1848), 169–70; Thomas Ewell, *Letters to Ladies, Including Important Information concerning Themselves and Infants* (Philadelphia: W. Brown, 1817), 119–20; Andrew Combe, *Treatise on the Physiological and Moral Management of Infancy* (Boston: Saxton and Kelt, 1846), 78–80; John Eberle, *A Treatise on the Mental and Physical Education of Children* (Cincinnati: Corey and Fairbank, 1833), 10; Hamilton, *Outline*, 130–31.

83. Ryan, *Philosophy of Marriage*, 263; Combe, *Treatise*, 79–80; Pendleton, *Parents' Guide*, 173; Aristotle, *The Works of Aristotle, the Famous Philosopher, in Four Parts* (New England: n.p., 1813), 35.

84. Skinner, *Female's Medical Guide*, 91.

85. Ibid., 90.

86. Thomas Bull, *The Maternal Management of Children, in Health and Disease* (Philadelphia: Lindsay and Blakiston, 1853), 23.

87. Henry C. Wright, *The Unwelcome Child; or, The Crime of an Undesigned and Undesired Maternity* (Boston: Bela Marsh, 1858), 24.

88. Fox diary, Aug. 9, 1849, box 13, folder 30, Logan–Fisher-Fox Papers.

89. Ibid., Aug. 10, 11, 21, 1849.

90. Horace Adams, "A Puritan Wife on the Frontier," *Mississippi Valley Historical Review* 27 (June 1940): 81.

91. Elizabeth Dwight Cabot to Ellen Dwight Twistleton, Jan. 23, 1859, sec. 2, box 2, folder 18, Elizabeth Dwight Cabot Letters.

92. Miriam Whitcher to Alice, [spring 1848,] Frances Miriam Berry Whitcher Letters.

93. Lester diary, Dec. 10, 1848, Andrew Lester Papers.

94. Mary Guion diary, Jan. 23, [1814,] New-York Historical Society.

95. Anna Colton Clayton to John Clayton, July 16, 1847, Anna Colton Clayton Letters.

96. Bessie Huntting Rudd to Edward Rudd, May 27, 1860, box 6, folder 110, Bessie Huntting Rudd Letters. See also Stearns diary, Aug. 29, 1813, Stearns Collection.

97. Mary Pierce Poor to Lucy Pierce, June 9, 1853, box 7, folder 97, Mary Pierce Poor Letters. See also Bessie Huntting Rudd to Edward Rudd, May 27, 1860, box 6, folder 110, Bessie Huntting Rudd Letters.

98. Stearns diary, Aug. 29, 1813, Stearns Collection.

99. Lester diary, Dec. 10, 1848, Andrew Lester Papers.

100. Mrs. Markoe to [Sally] Hughes, May 12, 1837, folder 3, Sally Hughes Letters, Maxcy-Markoe-Hughes Collection, Historical Society of Pennsylvania.

101. Adams, "Puritan Wife," 77.

102. Jeannie McCall to Peter McCall, [1847,] Jeannie McCall Letters.

103. Anna Colton Clayton to John Clayton, July 16, 1847, Anna Colton Clayton Letters.

104. Miriam Whitcher to Alice, [spring 1848,] Frances Miriam Berry Whitcher Letters.

105. Mary Pierce Poor to Lucy Pierce Hodge, July 10, 1853, box 12, folder 126, Mary Pierce Poor Letters.

106. Adams, "Puritan Wife," 75.

107. Black journal, Apr. 8, 1847, in *Victorian Women*, ed. Hellerstein, Hume, and Offen, 218–19.

108. Ann Douglas, "Heaven Our Home: Consolation Literature in the Northern United States, 1830–1880," *American Quarterly* 26 (Dec. 1974):

496–515; Ann Douglas, *The Feminization of American Culture* (New York: Knopf, 1977), 240–72.

109. Elizabeth Dwight Cabot to Ellen Dwight Twistleton, Dec. 27, 1858, sec. 2, box 2, folder 17, Elizabeth Dwight Cabot Letters. One month before the birth of her second child in 1861, Cabot again wrote out instructions for the disposal of her personal property. See Elizabeth Cabot, *Letters of Elizabeth Cabot*, 2 vols. (Boston: privately printed, 1905), 1:295.

110. Bessie Huntting Rudd to Edward Rudd, May 27, 1860, box 6, folder 110, Bessie Huntting Rudd Letters.

111. "A Mother's Trials," *Godey's Lady's Book* 55 (June 1857): 21.

112. Elizabeth Dwight Cabot to Ellen Dwight Twistleton, Dec. 27, 1858, sec. 2, box 2, folder 17, Elizabeth Dwight Cabot Letters.

113. Adams, "Puritan Wife," 78–79.

114. Wagenknecht, ed., *Mrs. Longfellow*, 194.

115. Quoted in Nancy F. Cott, *The Bonds of Womanhood: "Woman's Sphere" in New England, 1780–1835* (New Haven: Yale University Press, 1977), 91. For other examples of depression, see Eleanor Parke Custis Lewis to Elizabeth Bordley Gibson, May 19, 1826, Eleanor Parke Custis Lewis Letters; Sarah Connell Ayer, *Diary of Sarah Connell Ayer* (Portland, Maine: Lefavor-Tower, 1910), 235; Peggy Dow, *Vicissitudes; or, The Journey of Life* (Philadelphia: Joseph Rakestraw, 1816), 604; Katherine Minot Channing, ed., *Minot Family Letters: 1773–1871* (Sherborn, Mass.: privately printed, 1957), 65.

116. Timothy Shay Arthur, "The Wife: A Story for My Young Countrywomen," in *Three Eras of a Woman's Life: The Maiden, Wife and Mother* (Philadelphia: Henry F. Anners, 1848), 157; see also Alice B. Neal, "A Mother's Wages," *Godey's Lady's Book* 55 (July 1857): 39.

117. Mrs. Markoe to [Sally] Hughes, May 12, 1837, folder 3, Sally Hughes Letters.

118. James MacDonald, "Puerperal Insanity," *American Journal of Insanity* 4 (Oct. 1847): 113–14.

119. Hollick, *Matron's Manual*, 88.

120. Ewell, *Letters*, 121; Howard, *Treatise*, 32; "Dr. Huston's Lecture," *Boston Medical and Surgical Journal* 23 (Jan. 27, 1841): 405; Ryan, *Philosophy of Marriage*, 261; Burns, *Principles*, 191; Denman, *Introduction*, 137; Samuel K. Jennings, *The Married Lady's Companion; or, Poor Man's Friend* (New York: Lorenzo Dow, 1808), 91; William A. Alcott, *The Physiology of Marriage* (Boston: John P. Jewett, 1856), 173.

121. Burns, *Principles*, 365.

122. Fleetwood Churchill, "On the Mental Disorders of Pregnancy and Childbed," *American Journal of Insanity* 7 (Jan. 1851): 265.

123. A. F. Wedd, ed., *The Fate of the Fenwicks: Letters to Mary Hays* (London: Methuen, 1927), 143.

124. Elizabeth Parker to Susan Parker, n.d., Elizabeth Parker Letters, Parker-Brinley Papers, Historical Society of Pennsylvania.

125. Worthington Hooker, *Physician and Patient; or, A Practical View of the Mutual Duties, Relations and Interests of the Medical Profession and the Community* (New York: Baker and Scribner, 1849), 323. For a general discussion of this belief, see Norman Dain, *Concepts of Insanity in the United States, 1789-1865* (New Brunswick, N.J.: Rutgers University Press, 1964), 88-90. For a discussion of its continuing relevance in the post–Civil War period, see Donald Meyer, *The Positive Thinkers: A Study of the American Quest for Health, Wealth, and Personal Power from Mary Baker Eddy to Norman Vincent Peale* (Garden City, N.Y.: Doubleday, 1965), 22–26.

126. Benjamin Rush, *Medical Inquiries and Observations upon the Diseases of the Mind* (Philadelphia: Kimber and Richardson, 1812), 59. See also Churchill, "On the Mental Disorders," 259–60. For a discussion of traditional beliefs emphasizing the influence of the reproductive organs on the character of women, see Natalie Zemon Davis, *Society and Culture in Early Modern France: Eight Essays* (Stanford: Stanford University Press, 1975), 124–25. For discussion of the influence of such ideas on the nineteenth-century diagnosis and medical treatment of women, see Wood, "Fashionable Diseases," 3; Carroll Smith-Rosenberg, "Puberty to Menopause: The Cycle of Femininity in Nineteenth-Century America," in *Clio's Consciousness Raised*, ed. Hartman and Banner, 24; Meyer, *Positive Thinkers*, 72.

127. Bright, *Mother's Medical Guide*, 227.

128. MacDonald, "Puerperal Insanity," 115–16.

129. Ibid., 142; J. D. Jeffrey, "Case of Puerperal Mania," *Eclectic Journal of Medicine* 3 (July 1839): 335. Doctors were not the only ones to observe and analyze the emotional stresses that might plague pregnant women. A. Bronson Alcott wrote that the period of gestation destroyed the "harmony of the organic and instinctive functions" and dimmed the imagination by a "cloud of nervous pressure" ("Observations on the Experience of an Infant during the First Year of Its Existence, 1832–3," 5, Houghton Library).

130. Churchill, "On the Mental Disorders," 297.

131. Bright, *Mother's Medical Guide*, 97–98.

132. Burns, *Principles*, 191; William P. Dewees, *Treatise on the Physical and Medical Treatment of Children* (Philadelphia: Carey and Lea, 1825), 36–37; McNair, *Suggestions*, 209; Denman, *Introduction*, 137.

133. Wedd, ed., *Fate of the Fenwicks*, 143.

134. M. Esquirol, "On the Mania of Lying-in Women and Nurses," *Med-*

*ical Repository*, [4th ser.,] 6 (1820): 168; Churchill, "On the Mental Disorders," 301; MacDonald, "Puerperal Insanity," 115; Denman, *Introduction*, 137.

135. Denman suggested bleeding at the beginning of the century (*Introduction*, 137). By mid-century some sort of moral support was considered the best therapy. See Churchill, "On the Mental Disorders," 301; McNair, *Suggestions*, 209.

136. Wagenknecht, ed., *Mrs. Longfellow*, 109. For other comments about making baby clothes, see Lay diary, Oct. 6, 1855; Kate Ross to Edward C. Ross, June 22, 1836, Edward C. Ross Letters; Fox diary, Jan. 8, 1850, box 13, folder 30, Logan–Fisher-Fox Papers; Eleanor Parke Custis Lewis to Elizabeth Bordley Gibson, Nov. 4, 1799, Eleanor Parke Custis Lewis Letters.

137. Charles D. Meigs, *A Lecture Introductory to the Course of Obstetrics in Jefferson Medical College of Philadelphia, Delivered November 5, 1842* (Philadelphia: Merrihew and Thompson, 1842), 19. See also Charles D. Meigs, *Obstetrics: The Science and the Art* (Philadelphia: Blanchard and Lea, 1856), 638.

138. Mary Pierce Poor to Lucy Pierce Hodge, Aug. 17, 1853, box 12, folder 126, Mary Pierce Poor Letters; Poor diary, Mar. 6, 8, 13, 15, 20, 1852, box 6, Poor Family Collection.

139. Elizabeth Parke Custis Lewis to Elizabeth Bordley Gibson, Dec. 1, 1826, Eleanor Parke Custis Lewis Letters.

140. H. Hobart to Benjamin Drake, Feb. 8, 1834, Benjamin Drake Letters, Benjamin Drake Papers, Rare Books and Manuscripts Division, Astor, Lenox and Tilden Foundations, New York Public Library.

141. Mother to Jeannie McCall, n.d., Jeannie McCall Letters.

142. Elizabeth Dwight Cabot to Ellen Dwight Twistleton, Sept. 9, 1861, sec. 2, box 2, folder 20, Elizabeth Dwight Cabot Letters.

143. Arthur, "The Wife," 159.

144. A. D. Mayo, *Selections and Writings of Mrs. Sarah C. Edgarton Mayo: With a Memoir, by Her Husband* (Boston: A. Tomkins, 1849), 109.

145. Alcott, "Observations," 5.

# To "Stand on the Trembling Verge": Attitudes toward Childbirth

LIKE THE PREGNANCY that preceded it, childbirth was an intensely private experience, and the details regarding its conduct were not normally discussed in public. Novelists and other popular writers rarely mentioned, let alone described, the birth of children in the early nineteenth century. Typical of the way that a novelist handled the matter was the technique used by Caroline E. Rush in *The North and the South*, published in 1852. "Years rolled on," she wrote, "and our pretty bride had changed to the blooming matron, the mother of a large, fine family of children."[1] Other authors used similarly vague references to the birth of children when they found it necessary to account for their presence in the family.[2] Such consistent avoidance of all mention of the experience of childbirth prompted twentieth-century novelist E. M. Forster to observe that in sentimental novels babies were often delivered between chapters and came "into the world more like parcels than human beings."[3]

Only when the story line required them to acknowledge the event did authors explicitly discuss childbirth. In *Charlotte, a Tale of Truth*, Susanna Rowson wrote of the birth of Charlotte's child, "A surgeon was sent for; he bled her, she gave signs of returning life, and before dawn, gave birth to a female infant."[4] Similarly, Mrs. P. D. Manvill described childbirth in her novel, *Lucinda; or, The Mountain Mourner*, in the most general of terms: "Alternate hope and fear prevailed for many hours; at length the rising sun, and the birth of a lovely female infant, in a measure dispelled the gloom which pervaded every heart."[5] In each case it was necessary for the authors specifically to mention a child's birth because both infants were illegitimate and both mothers died after delivery.

While it may not have been considered an appropriate topic for literary discussion, the birth experience was discussed by childbearing women and members of their families in their private papers and by doctors in their professional literature. All had reasons to be ambivalent about the process. A woman recorded her responses to childbirth because she viewed it as one of the more important events in her life. She and her friends and family knew that as it was being born, her child could cause her pain and threaten her life before it bestowed upon her the blessings of motherhood. As a result childbearing women were receptive to the claims being made by doctors that the risks of childbirth could be reduced by the application of medical technology.

Physicians knew that there were good reasons to study midwifery and attend women during the birth of their children. "Women seldom forget a practitioner," wrote Dr. Walter Channing of Boston in 1820, "who has conducted them tenderly and safely through parturition. . . . It is principally on this account that the practice of midwifery becomes desirable to physicians. It is this which insures to them the permanency and security of all their other business."[6] Despite their awareness that midwifery could serve as the basis for establishing a more general medical practice,[7] however, doctors had reservations about practicing obstetrics. Midwifery cases did not supply an especially attractive source of income. Doctors in urban areas charged separate fees for obstetrics cases, and those fees did rise during the period.[8] But the value of the fees was offset to some extent by the fact that lying-in cases were time-consuming. They could require constant attendance on short notice for an unpredictable length of time, forcing the physician to postpone or forgo attendance on other fee-paying patients. Valentine Seaman of New York complained in 1800 that "physicians cannot afford to give up so much of their time from their other business, as would be necessarily employed upon such occasions, for the small compensation."[9] Charles Meigs, who taught at Jefferson Medical College in Philadelphia in the 1840s, warned his students about the same problem when he observed that "a practitioner of midwifery . . . is more hampered than any other member of the profession."[10]

Fear of pain, permanent injury, or death, willingness to defer to the demands of fashion, the belief that birth posed special dangers to affluent, well-bred women, and the availability of doctors, private nurses, and new medical technology all contributed to changing attitudes toward the birth process and to willingness of northern middle- and upper-class women to modify the way lying-in was conducted in the early nineteenth century. Fear as well as concern for establishing or maintaining their reputations as genteel and respectable, for example, encouraged women to accept the medical definition of childbirth as an illness and to hire doctors as testimony to their economic and social status. They increasingly sought the services of doctors and private nurses in addition to or rather than those of midwives, female relatives, and friends. This practice combined with a willingness to have their husbands present during labor and birth began to undermine the female support system that had been a traditional part of the lying-in process. The presence of male midwives during labor and delivery increased the tension level in the delivery room as doctors, parturient women, and their attendants struggled to determine the degree to which each would control the conduct of birth. And finally, the ability of doctors to use medical technology in the form of ergot, which could speed up the process of labor, and anesthesia, which could eliminate its pain, to confirm the legitimacy of their presence during normal labor and uncomplicated delivery forced medical practitioners to address questions of medical ethics and to reassess their attitude toward women in general and their female patients in particular, the social responsibilities of mothers, and the function of pain.

Because they feared the pain that might accompany labor and delivery and were concerned that they might die during parturition, childbearing women believed that the thread of life was particularly strained during childbirth. Their relatives shared their concern and frequently wrote to express their relief that loved ones had survived the experience. In the fall of 1848, following the birth of her fourth child, Sarah Watson Dana suffered from a severe hemorrhage. For seven hours two doctors worked to save her life. Shortly thereafter Dana received congratulatory letters typical of those received by others in similar circumstances. "Little did we think as we parted from you," wrote her aunt, "that you were so soon to stand on the trembling verge. Thanks, to our Heavenly Father that brought you safe up again. We feel that we could ill spare one so very dear to us." A few days later Sarah's sister sent her a letter expressing similar sentiments: "I am thankful to hear that you are recovering so well after being brought so low. One's life seems to hang upon a thread at these perilous times. How can we be grateful enough that you were preserved."[11] In the eyes of her relatives, Dana's accomplishment was not merely that she had borne a living child. She had survived the process as well. That survival was cause for special rejoicing.

The tendency to associate childbirth with death was not unique to the nineteenth century. The birth process had always been considered hazardous. Early New England Puritan divines were only more articulate than most when they warned parturient women that their fate, a legacy of Eve's sin, was in the hands of God. They believed that confinement was an opportune time for women to prepare their souls as they prepared to deliver their babies.[12] Cotton Mather was merely being realistic when in the seventeenth century he suggested that while they carefully made arrangements for their lying-in, expectant mothers should never forget that they might soon "need no other linnen . . . but *a Winding Sheet*, and have no other chamber but a *grave*, no neighbors but *worms*."[13]

There was little anyone could do in the seventeenth and early eighteenth centuries to influence the outcome of childbirth. Doctors were usually unavailable. Few physicians immigrated to the colonies,[14] and there was no reason to suppose that doctors who did immigrate or were trained by preceptors in America had skills superior to those of local midwives who along with friends and neighbors attended women by preparing them for delivery and supervising its conduct. Most midwives were not prepared either by inclination or by training to interfere with the progress of natural labor.[15] Those with skill and knowledge could affect the outcome of labor by administering herbs, turning the fetus, or removing an obstruction. But if the labor was prolonged or the baby impacted, they would have to send for a doctor, if one was available, whose attempts to remove the child from the womb with the use of a crotchet inevitably resulted in the death of the child if not the mother.[16] Until the public introduction of the Chamberlen forceps in England in the early eighteenth century, medical science did not provide doctors the technology to reduce the chance of fetal and maternal death.[17] Human agency had little effect on the outcome of labor. Midwives invited doctors to attend women in confinement only under the most unpromising of circumstances.

By 1800 this situation had begun to change for some women. Unlike their seventeenth-century forebears, middle- and upper-class urban women in the nineteenth century had less reason to depend solely on God's agency to determine the outcome of childbirth. Available to those women who sought to guard themselves against the hazards of childbearing were doctors trained in obstetrics abroad or in newly founded American medical schools. Although their training was usually devoid of clinical experience, young physicians had access to the knowledge of anatomy as well as the use of obstet- rical forceps.[18] Concerned about providing the best possible care for childbearing women and desirous of establishing medical practices, they offered their services as male midwives in such metropolitan areas as Boston, New York, and Philadelphia.[19] At first childbear- ing women in urban areas, who could afford to do so, hired these doctors in the hope of ensuring their own safety during complicated deliveries. By the 1820s many of them routinely called doctors rather than midwives to attend normal deliveries as well.[20]

Some doctors and health reformers felt that the desire for safety was not the only reason why such women wanted male midwives to attend them. They believed that the decision to hire physicians who practiced obstetrics was motivated by the desire of the socially mobile to use their choice of attendant as a way of testifying to their affluence and social position by submitting to the demands of fashion.

In 1818, when two prominent Boston physicians decided to give up the obstetric portion of their general practice, they invited a formally trained midwife from Scotland to immigrate to the United States in order to serve the needs of their female patients.[21] In a protest pamphlet published two years later, Walter Channing ob- jected to the reentry of women into the practice of midwifery in Boston on the grounds that, among other things, female midwifery might become fashionable among the rich and influential. The effect of this, he feared, would be to drive physicians from the business of obstetrics as the middle classes followed the lead of their social betters.[22]

Those who opposed the practice of male midwifery were also sensitive to the influence of fashion in determining a woman's choice of attendants. In 1847 A. M. Mauriceau, the author of a popular health manual, complained that only "fashion" and the "credulity" of women sustained the demand that doctors attend deliveries.[23] The next year Samuel Gregory, a Boston health reformer dedicated to training women in medicine and obstetrics, wrote that one of the principal reasons why men had gained ascendancy in obstetrics in the first place had been that their employment had appealed to those concerned with establishing their refinement, respectability, and affluence. Gregory's statement is revealing because he carefully distinguished the factors he believed contributed to the employment of male midwives: "Many husbands employ gentlemen to attend their wives, not because they think it necessary, but because their neighbors will consider them unfashionable, and say they are niggardly, and unwilling their ladies should have the best assistance, and perhaps call their wives countrified and homespun, because they can have children without a scientific operator."[24]

The protests of these critics were clearly self-serving. Nevertheless, they all agreed that an important factor in determining who members of the middle and upper classes chose as their lying-in attendant was the need to distinguish themselves from their economic and social inferiors. Implied in their criticism was the concern that in bowing to fashion in this way, childbearing women and members of their families were being capricious and selfish.

The practice of hiring physicians to attend the birth of middle- and upper-class women during labor and delivery encouraged doctors to abandon the notion that pain and danger in childbirth were a punishment from God, a legacy from Eve. Civilization rather than original sin, they began to argue, was responsible for placing childbearing women at risk. Working on the assumption that "women in general, especially in a state of society, endure more pain, are exposed to greater difficulties, and meet with more accidents from labour, than any other animal,"[25] regular doctors in both England and America began to identify the factors that made it difficult for the patients they were likely to serve to bear children.

Difficulty in childbirth, observed John Burns in 1810, results from removing "women from a state of simplicity to luxury and refinement" so that the powers of the reproductive system are impaired.[26] This attitude reflected a romantic view of the state of nature and was a response to the knowledge of other cultures that had been accumulated during 300 years of European exploration and colonization. Such knowledge allowed doctors to compare their state of civilization with that of more primitive peoples. When they did, it seemed apparent to them that primitive women in places such as Greenland, Morocco, and the American West bore their children with much more ease than did British and American women.[27] "In the actual condition of civilized society, much more suffering and danger await women . . . than in other conditions more simple and natural. . . . The habits of females, in highly civilized countries,—their luxurious living, their modes of dress, their neglect of exercise, and erroneous mental and moral culture" combine against their safety, wrote physician Henry Miller.[28]

But civilization alone was not the cause for pain and danger. Nineteenth-century medical authors also had a clear sense of the class differences that were increasingly visible in the urban society where they lived. Either directly or by implication, doctors, especially British doctors published in the United States, indicated that in a state of civilization lower-class women could be expected to deliver their babies with less difficulty than upper-class women. British obstetrician Thomas Denman wrote that lower-class women not only had "fewer complaints than the affluent, but have also more easy labors."[29] In his *Institutes of Marriage*, Robert Culverwell included a poem that illustrated class differences. A field woman "teeming" with child, wrote the poet,

> Weeds the young corn, or harrows down the earth,
> Patient of toil, with careful hand she twines
> And trains the tendrils of the straggling vines,
> Intent on labor; nor as yet forbears

Till pain o'er takes her, 'mid her rustic cares.
*Her bosom's load so easily she yields,*
*One must suppose she found it in the fields.*[30]

Doctors believed that the most refined women could be expected
to have the greatest difficulty in childbirth. The accumulation of
wealth and the life-style that resulted from the expenditure of that
wealth removed women from the state of nature. It allowed them
to avoid physical work and exercise and indulge in excessive and
debilitating pleasure.[31] High living not only contributed to the
travail of women during labor but also made them incapable of
enduring it. According to James Y. Simpson, a Scot obstetrician,
"Unaccustomed by their mode of life to much pain and fatigue,
patients in the higher ranks of life are not fitted to endure either of
them with the same power or with the same impunity as the uncivilized mother, or even as females in the lower and hardier grades of
civilized society."[32]

As they gradually expanded upon secular explanations for difficulty in childbearing, explanations that deemphasized God's role in
the process, British and American physicians not only attempted to
secure their place in the lying-in chamber, they also confirmed what
childbearing women already knew: childbirth was potentially dangerous. What doctors did was to redefine the danger by labeling it
a medical problem particularly for the middle and upper classes, a
problem that justified placing confidence in the value of human
agency in the form of obstetric medicine to reduce the potential for
parturient suffering and danger.

Middle- and upper-class women deferred to the definition of
childbirth as a pathological, potentially life-threatening condition
not only because it fit their preconceived notions about the process
but also because to do so testified to their delicacy and gentility.
Even the term that they and members of their families began to use
to describe labor and delivery reflected their agreement with doctors
that childbirth among women of their class was a condition fraught
with potential medical problems. In earlier days the process of labor
and delivery was commonly referred to as travail. In 1738, for example, Ebenezer Parkman wrote in his diary that "a little after 4 in
the morning my Wife called Me up by her extreme pain prevailing

upon her and changing into signs of Travail."[33] In the 1780s entries in the diary of Martha Ballard, a midwife in Maine, followed the same pattern. Although she occasionally used the word *unwell* to describe a woman in labor, she more often identified them as being "in travail." In a typical entry she wrote, "Called to Mr[s]. Church's about day. She being in travail; was delivered about 5 o'clock, p.m., of a daughter."[34] The use of the word *travail* carried with it the connotation that the woman being described was painfully toiling to bring a child into the world.

As the accumulation of wealth allowed women in the middle and upper classes to avoid the need to perform physical labor, the word *travail* began to fall into disuse. As early as 1795 Elizabeth Drinker, whose daughters both availed themselves of the specialized services of America's foremost obstetrician, William Shippen, Jr., consistently referred to them as being ill rather than as being in travail. In April 1795 Drinker wrote in her diary, "I came to Jacob Downings after tea," and finding her daughter in the first throes of labor, sent word to Shippen that "she is unwell." She used an identical phrase to describe the labors of her daughters in 1797 and 1799.[35] The Drinkers and by association their daughters were among the social elite of Philadelphia at the turn of the century. They could afford the best medical services available in the city and were willing to do so because the Drinker women typically had difficult and tedious labors.

By the 1830s middle- and upper-class women, in describing their childbirth experiences, tended to use the words *sickness* or *illness* almost exclusively. In 1832 Millicent Hunt wrote that before the birth of her fifth child, she "was taken ill between the hours of nine and ten in the evening."[36] In 1847 Persis Sibley Andrews Black noted, "I was confined . . . after having been sick 20 hours— very sick but a short time."[37] Elizabeth Cady Stanton wrote to a friend in 1851 to announce the birth of her fourth son, "I was sick but a few hours."[38] No longer did such women describe the process of bearing a child in terms of work. The rhetoric they used suggested that it was a process requiring more passive endurance than strenuous activity.

Urban women in the middle and upper classes did hire male midwives and indicated their willingness to view childbirth as a medical problem by changing the rhetoric they used to describe their experience. It does not necessarily follow, however, that they were willing to abdicate their right to control the way they experienced childbirth by completely submitting to male medical authority in the lying-in chamber.

Both doctors and their patients wanted labor and delivery to end as quickly as possible in the birth of a healthy child to a healthy mother. But despite agreement about the ultimate goal, their relationship was complicated by a number of factors, including the irrelevance of a physician's special skills in normal cases, his assumptions about the passive and submissive character of the women in the delivery room, the traditional role of women in the ritual of birth, and a doctor's concern about establishing and maintaining clinical control over his obstetrics cases.

As a professional who wanted to establish the need for medical services in normal as well as abnormal childbirth, a physician who attended normal obstetrics cases automatically faced built-in hazards to professional status. In uncomplicated cases the specialized skills and knowledge claimed by doctors were superfluous. A well-trained physician knew that he was medically justified in limiting his treatment to that which midwives had always provided. His job in such cases was to monitor labor, support the head of the baby as it was delivered, cut the umbilical cord, and deliver the placenta. Normal deliveries did not give the doctor an opportunity to demonstrate (and thereby confirm) the utility and benefit of his access to the special skills and technology that had originally justified his presence in the lying-in chamber.

Such realities made doctors open to charges that the services they offered were not usually needed, and therefore physicians, particularly those with a lack of clinical experience who were unduly impressed by textbook emphasis on procedures for abnormal cases, were faced with the temptation to interfere unnecessarily with the normal process of labor and delivery in order to prove to their patients that they were earning their fees. An alternative response was to claim that the mere presence of a physician was enough to make labor easier. According to one doctor, "The very presence of a medical practitioner will often afford relief, without the performance of any manual operation whatever. The confident assurance to the patient of her safety will inspire that balmy hope, which will hasten delivery much better than any other means."[39]

Further tensions were produced when doctors unexpectedly found that their female patients and those who attended them might refuse to allow a physician to assume complete control over delivery. Doctors believed that their patients could best serve their own interests by being passive participants in the childbirth experience. A number of factors encouraged this belief. First, doctors were the products of a culture that expected women to be dependent on men and to submit to their authority.[40] Second, doctors could justifiably assume that most women did not have enough knowledge about their bodies and the mechanics of childbirth to be able to direct their labor themselves, let alone direct a doctor in his work. A woman, wrote William Potts Dewees of Philadelphia, "cannot fail to know less than her physician, therefore she is not entitled to be her own directoress."[41] Third, some physicians believed that at the moment of birth, women could not be expected to be fully conscious. Rapid dilation of the cervix during labor produced, according to one doctor, "a period of extreme distress and pain" and was frequently accompanied by "incoherence or temporary delirium."[42]

These assumptions about women allowed doctors to maintain that having a baby was something that happened to a woman, not something she did. Even Eve, according to Charles Meigs, did not "have" her first child. In an imaginative description of the first case of obstetrics in history, Meigs pictured Eve as falling into unconsciousness at the moment of birth and being "recalled to her senses" only by the cries of her infant "lying upon the grassy floor of the bower near her."[43]

Given the belief that a parturient woman was not expected to be an active participant in the childbirth process, all a woman had to do, according to one physician, was "to keep up her spirits, and to adhere strictly to the rules of her medical advisor."[44] A patient's best interests would be served, according to another doctor, only if she would "place the fullest confidence" in her doctor, "strictly follow his directions, have no opinion of her own, and pay no attention to any contrary advice that may be proposed by her nurse."[45] Dewees agreed, insisting that his colleagues should "let her not indulge in any opinions that may clash with those of her attendant;—let her yield herself entirely to his directions."[46]

Despite their belief that female passivity was particularly desirable during the delivery process, physicians did not always find women sufficiently submissive. Traditionally women had directed the conduct of childbirth without the advice or interference of men. Thus, while they may have been prepared to defer to male authority in other matters, they were not necessarily willing to do so in matters relating to childbirth. As historian Judith Leavitt has pointed out, doctors found it necessary to practice obstetrics in a context established by women.[47] The result was that physicians sometimes felt it necessary to modify both their behavior and their medical treatment in order to accommodate the wishes of patients or their attendants.

Women influenced the practice of obstetrics by adhering to standards of modesty that not only prescribed their own behavior but in the process defined and determined the behavior of those around them, including their doctor. Standards of modesty reflected in part the social and sexual tensions of the day. Modesty not only placed a limit on the intimacy that was possible between two individuals but also helped them to define their relationship with each other. A personal form of privacy, modesty inadvertently gave parturient women some power to define their position in the patient-doctor relationship. Doctors recognized that power, and as a result they took the demands of modesty seriously, recognizing that, as one regular physician put it, "no woman can be placed in a . . . condition compelling her to appeal to the aid of the accoucheur without some sense of a mortified delicacy."[48] An irregular doctor articulated similar concerns: "It must be recollected that the situation of the female at such times is a very peculiar one, and that the presence of one of the other sex, however necessary, must be more or less objectionable to her."[49]

However much they may have recognized the existence of such sensibilities, many doctors found them inappropriate in the lying-in chamber, where, in their opinion, safety and medical freedom to act and not delicacy should have been the primary consideration.[50] Nevertheless, they modified their behavior and often justified their actions in the lying-in chamber to accommodate female demands. For example, while doctors recognized the need to perform a vaginal examination on women in labor in order to determine the position of the fetus and the degree of dilation of the cervix,[51] they also used it as an opportunity to reassure the patient that her physician could be depended upon to behave himself under such intimate circumstances. The procedure, wrote Thomas Denman, assures the patient "of the skill and humanity of the practitioner, and of the propriety of his conduct."[52]

At the very least such an examination was considered to be indelicate. Thus doctors were urged to perform the examination under rigidly prescribed conditions. First, doctors were supposed to propose the examination indirectly through a female attendant, whose duty it was to explain to the patient that such an examination was necessary to her emotional and physical well-being since it would allow the doctor to determine if she was in labor and if any abnormalities existed that might hinder a speedy and normal delivery.[53] Persuading a patient to submit to the procedure was not necessarily easy. Charles Meigs complained to his students that he had "many times been kept out of [his] house all night" attending a woman supposedly in labor who refused to allow the examination. "It is exceedingly vexatious," he wrote, "thus to be baffled by the unreasonable backwardness of the patient to submit to an operation which she knows to be necessary and inevitable."[54]

Once the patient was induced to give her consent, she was placed on her left side facing away from the doctor, thereby eliminating the possibility of eye contact. Meigs encouraged his students to perform the examination during a contraction in order to avoid embarrassing the patient, "whose mind, fully occupied in perceiving the painful sensation, is at the moment somewhat diverted from the awkwardness of the situation."[55] Concern for propriety even went so far as to encourage doctors to conduct the examination with the shutters closed and to deliver infants under a sheet with as little light as possible.[56]

Doctors were also aware that women could directly challenge the authority of the obstetrician and attempt to interfere with his practice by expressing doubts about his treatment, offering impertinent advice, or suggesting alternative methods of dealing with the discomforts of labor. Patients themselves could put a great deal of pressure on a physician, confessed one doctor, and it required a considerable amount of "mental fortitude, many times, to resist the importunate entreaties of the patient for relief."[57] Other doctors proposed various ways to relieve the pressure that patients might try to place on them to take actions not clinically justified. Samuel Merriman suggested that it might prove "expedient to amuse the patient" by giving her a few drops of medicine even though such medicine was ineffective in relieving the discomforts of labor.[58] Another felt that a physician might at least "pretend to assist" during the first stages of labor for the purpose of composing the mind of the patient and inspiring her with confidence. But he warned that a doctor who was monitoring the progress of labor should not really interfere in the process at that point.[59]

Female attendants, whether they were friends, relatives, or private nurses, might also challenge the authority of the attending physicians. Throughout the early nineteenth century, doctors continued to recognize the usefulness of female attendants in the lying-in chamber. Confining their definition of their professional duties to the clinical aspects of the case, doctors willingly admitted that attendants could give patients moral support and perform practical services that the doctor considered inappropriate for a male physician to handle.[60] At the same time, however, doctors realized that allowing others to assume any responsibility in the case threatened their ability to control it.

Interference from attendants was sometimes indirect. In 1810, for example, John Burns complained that female attendants might "by their conversation, disturb the patient, or by their imprudence, . . . diminish her confidence, in her own powers, and also in her necessary attendants."[61] Doctors also recognized that attendants, like their patients, could directly interfere with the conduct of the case by putting intense pressure on doctors to take some action they might not otherwise take. In an article on the use of ergot as a means of speeding delivery, Samuel Akerly admitted that he had on occasion administered the stimulant "more in deference to the solicitude of an attendant matron, than from a conviction that it was indicated."[62] Attendants were also prone to offer the patient advice that the doctor might consider inappropriate or even dangerous. Charles Meigs commented that he often found it necessary to ask bystanders to refrain from encouraging his patients from bearing down in the early stages of labor, a suggestion, he noted, they never failed to make.[63]

In other cases physicians found themselves in the position of trying to practice medicine by consensus. William Potts Dewees, for instance, while attending a particularly difficult labor, decided that the best treatment was to bleed the patient until she fainted. But he did not apply the lancet until he had conferred with and received the permission of the woman's friends.[64] Concerned about the pressure a patient's friends might place upon a physician, Dewees, on the one hand, cautioned his students that they should take care never to be "betrayed into indiscretion" by the attendants' "overweaning anxiety."[65] On the other hand, John Metcalf warned his colleagues that they should "never be deterred from doing whatever" they believed to be "important for the relief of the patient, by the fears, or indecision, or clamour of the attendants."[66] Doctors were clearly concerned that the tendency of childbearing women and their attendants to interfere in the conduct of their obstetrics cases threatened to undermine their professional autonomy.

By the 1830s some doctors also had to contend with the presence of husbands in the lying-in chamber. Close reading of obstetrics and health care manuals indicates that while doctors did not necessarily encourage the presence of husbands during labor and delivery, they sometimes found it necessary to defer to the wishes of their patients in the matter.[67] Richard Henry Dana, Jr., for example, joined the doctor in the delivery room during the births of each of his children and in his journal described his participation in the birth of his first child in graphic detail. On Sunday morning, June 12, 1842, Dana reported that he went for a doctor to attend his wife, Sarah, who was in the early stages of labor. The doctor arrived, examined his wife, and then left to call on another patient. While the Danas waited for labor to progress, Richard was frequently upstairs walking his wife slowly up and down the room. At three in the afternoon she was put to bed, and he went downstairs but was called back a half hour later to join the doctor, a nurse, and his mother-in-law to be with his wife during the last stages of labor and delivery. "I stood beside her," he reported in his journal,

> & held her hand all the time & whispered in her ear, & in her moments of ease she whispered to me & pressed my hand. It is an hour of harrowing anxiety, beside [the] distress of witnessing so much pain. There is surely no pain like it in the world. Poor S[arah], who has great self command, screamed again & again as the last & heaviest came on. All self control is gone & the woman lies a mere passive instrument in the hands of an irresistible power.

Much to the relief of everyone, their daughter was born at 4:45 that afternoon.[68]

One gathers from his journal entries that Dana considered his presence at the birth of his children to be perfectly natural, his support of his wife to be highly desirable, and his relationship with the doctor to be a mutually supportive one. When American doctors began to use anesthesia in obstetrics cases, husbands were even more likely to be present in the delivery room.[69]

We can only guess how doctors felt about the participation of husbands in the birth process. There were good reasons for doctors to feel ambivalent about it. Some felt that husbands, like female attendants, posed a potential threat to the ability of the physician to control the conduct of labor and delivery. Others recognized that husbands could serve as an important source of moral support for a wife in the throes of labor and as insurance that they would not be accused of improper professional behavior.[70] Indeed, occasionally, the presence of a husband was crucial to the very survival of the wife as the case of George and Ellen Strong of New York illustrates. In April 1849 Ellen Strong's labor began with convulsions. Frightened, George sent the servants for help and did what he could to comfort his semiconscious wife, whose convulsions continued unabated. When two doctors arrived, they bled her, administered chloroform, and sent for a third doctor. Her labor and convulsions continued all day, and that evening she bore a stillborn child. Ten minutes after the delivery the doctors informed her anxious husband that "it was hopeless" and that "she could not live two hours, that her speedy death was inevitable." She appeared unconscious, her convulsions were continuing, her pulse was fading, and she was having difficulty swallowing. Seeing that the doctors did not intend to do anything further to help his wife, George made one last, desperate attempt to save her life by rubbing her lips and the inside of her mouth with ice and applying a rag soaked in water and brandy to her lips. She swallowed, and, as he put it in his diary, "the tide was turned."[71] The doctors in charge had abdicated their control over the case to the husband, and it was his administration of medical therapeutics that saved the life of the patient.

The tension that existed between a doctor's wish to control the way he practiced clinical obstetrics and his patients' desire to directly or indirectly, through their attendants, influence the way that the birth of their children was conducted was also evident in the debates that arose over the use of ergot and anesthesia. In 1807 Dr. John Stearns of Saratoga County, New York, introduced ergot, a fungus that commonly grows on rye, to the medical profession by reporting in the *Medical Repository* that he had used it in cases of "lingering parturition" when the contractions of the uterus began to lose their strength. In his letter he was very careful to note the danger of its use and warned that it was necessary to determine if the fetus presented normally or if there was any obstruction in the way of normal delivery. Once ergot was administered, he cautioned, it caused "violent and almost incessant action" of the uterus, making turning the fetus or removing an obstruction impossible. "The pains induced by it are peculiarly *forcing;* though not accompanied with that distress and agony, of which patients frequently complain when the action is much less." He also mentioned another advantage of using ergot that had a great deal of potential appeal to a busy physician anxious to deliver a baby speedily so that he might attend to his other duties. It saves, he wrote, "a considerable portion of time."[72]

Ergot, which was probably used by midwives in some areas, was readily available. In 1815 Samuel Akerly wrote in the *Medical Repository* that he had earlier attended a woman whose labor was particularly tedious and long. Discussing the patient's condition with her concerned husband, Akerly mentioned the benefits of using ergot under such circumstances. The husband, he reported, immediately went out to his rye field and collected enough ergot to fill half a tea cup.[73]

Because it was so accessible, ergot could easily be abused by doctors interested in expediting the progress of normal labor. Akerly wrote that since ergot began working within six to fifteen minutes after being administered, he had been able to attend three deliveries within ten hours and cover a distance of thirty-four miles.[74] Maria D. Brown remembered being administered ergot when she was in labor with her first child. "First he bled me," she recalled. "Then, after he had taken a pint of my blood, he gave me a cup of ergot to hasten labor. I was young and strong and he was anxious to be off."[75] Brown clearly believed that her physician had administered the substance to her as a convenience to himself rather than as a response to evidence that it was clinically indicated. But at the time she was young and inexperienced and did not feel herself in any position to stop him.

The availability of such a substance allowed the physician to comply with the demands of his patients to limit their suffering by shortening their labors. By using it he could demonstrate the utility of his presence. However, the use of ergot in normal labors for the convenience of patient or doctor verged on abuse. By 1820 doctors were condemning its indiscriminate use as unethical in medical journals and were recommending that it be administered only in difficult labors when normal uterine contractions failed to effect the expulsion of the fetus.[76]

Physicians could use ergot to speed the process of labor, but its application did nothing to reduce the discomfort of uterine contractions. Anesthesia had the potential for reducing or eliminating the pains associated with labor. Parturient women, sensitive to the pain they faced during childbirth, expressed few reservations about using anesthesia. The question of whether to administer ether or chloroform to women in labor was more complicated for physicians, however, because it forced them to confront their attitudes toward their female patients and toward the function of pain in labor.

Childbearing women expected the birth process to be painful and a source of suffering. But they also recognized that the amount of discomfort they felt during labor and delivery could vary in intensity and degree. Some suffered a good deal. Millicent Hunt remembered the "severe pain" she had to endure during the delivery of her fifth child.[77] Mary Harris Lester wrote, "I suffered severely until about ¼ before 9 o clock, when I by the goodness of God was safely delivered of a fine son."[78] Other women expressed surprise at not having suffered more. "I have been highly favoured thro' the whole of this illness—having had as little suffering as is possible for any one to *escape* with," reported Mehetable Goddard in 1821 after the birth of her child.[79] Mary Pierce Poor expressed similar sentiments: "My whole sickness has been a pleasant one. I have been more 'comfortable' than could have been 'expected.'"[80]

Still other women wrote of their pain in relative terms comparing it with that which they had suffered before or that which others may have endured. Elizabeth Cady Stanton wrote to a friend about the birth of her fourth son: "Theodore Stanton bounded upon the stage of life with great ease—comparatively!!"[81] Persis Sibley Andrews Black recalled: "I was confined . . . after having been sick 20 hours. . . . Upon the whole, they called it a pretty *comfortable time*."[82] And a friend of Agnes Lamb Richards wrote: "You heard I suppose all about my sickness when Addie was born, did not you? Nothing like *your* time, *Ag I assure* you! ah no! no! Yet I did not suffer as much as I thought I would."[83]

Childbearing women would have found their belief that childbirth was painful reflected occasionally in the popular literature of the day. Although most authors ignored the act of giving birth, a few made isolated references to it in novels and essays that tended to confirm that women could expect to suffer. In *Fresh Leaves*, for example, Fanny Fern argued for a mother's right to the custody of her children partly on the ground that in bearing them she had gone through a "terrible ordeal" during which she had been "called upon to endure agonies that no man living would have the fortitude to bear more than once, even at their shortest duration."[84] And P. D. Manvill described the main character in the novel *Lucinda* as laboring "through the horrors of an awful night . . . in all the agonies of excruciating distress."[85]

The medical community also subscribed to the belief that childbirth was frequently a painful experience. Although they disagreed over the role that pain played in the birth process and argued over the use of anesthesia during childbirth, James Y. Simpson of Edinburgh and Charles Meigs of Philadelphia were both convinced that some women could and did suffer during the process. Simpson described a woman in the last stages of natural labor as in "anguish" and asserted that "the degree of actual pain usually endured during common labor is as great, if not greater, than that attendant upon most surgical operations."[86] Meigs in turn wrote that for some though not all women, labor was "a great and terrible conflict" during which the intensity of perceived pain was "absolutely indescribable, and comparable to no other pain," an "agony."[87] Yet while they agreed that women often suffered great pain during the birth process, they did not agree on the best way to deal with it.

Modern scholars in search of effective ways of evaluating the feeling of pain have suggested that the intensity of perceived pain is usually directly connected with the degree to which the sufferer associates the pain he or she is feeling with death or "annihilation." The more a person feels her existence threatened by the source of pain, the more pain she is likely to feel.[88] The intense anxiety expressed by pregnant women in the early nineteenth century about the fear of death in childbed must have made it difficult for them to separate their pain from their fear. Even Meigs, who opposed the use of anesthetics during childbirth, wrote that women during labors that progressed slowly and painfully were likely to repeat over and over, "I can never bear all this, I shall surely die."[89] This inability on the part of childbearing women to dissociate the discomforts that accompanied childbirth from the fear of death may well have contributed to their increased sensitivity to the pain of labor and helps to explain their willingness to experiment with the use of anesthesia.

The historian James Turner has pointed to an increasingly humanitarian concern in the nineteenth century for eliminating the sources of pain. While he is unclear about what factors or combination of factors were the most important for encouraging the development of this concern, he writes that "for the first time, men and women developed that dread of pain—that 'instinctive' revulsion from physical suffering even of others—uniquely characteristic of the modern era."[90]

Although Turner notes a dramatic change in attitudes toward pain in general, there was a certain continuity in popular attitudes toward a specific type of pain, labor pain. For centuries midwives and doctors had been trying to find some substance that would effectively relieve the discomforts suffered by women in childbirth. In the seventeenth century, for example, folk remedies were used during childbirth to ease the pain of the contractions. In 1612 James Guillimeau suggested a recipe for "a drinke to make easie the deliverie." An attendant should "take Oile of sweet Almonds, drawen without fire, water of Parietary, two ounces, mingle them together, and let her drinke it."[91] In England Dr. Thomas Raynalde, who believed that women during labor suffered in "great paine and untollerable anguish," devoted a whole chapter in an edition of his midwifery manual, *The Birth of Man-kinde*, published in 1634, to "Remedies and Medicines, by which the labour may be made more tollerable, easie and without great paine." He suggested, among other things, a pill composed of various ingredients including cinnamon, myrrh, and opium to be taken with four ounces of "good old Wine."[92]

In seventeenth-century Salem, Massachusetts, a self-styled doctor, Zerobabel Endicott, prescribed a concoction of powdered virgin's hair and twelve ant's eggs dissolved in the milk of a red cow or some ale to mitigate the pains of labor.[93] Another popular manual, *Aristotle's Masterpiece*, published as early as 1684 and widely read in America well into the nineteenth century, also contained suggestions for relieving the pains of labor. In an American edition published in 1813, the author suggested that powdered "piony seeds" and oil applied to the loins and private parts could be expected to give "deliverance very speedily, and with less pain than can be imagined."[94]

Early nineteenth-century doctors followed the example of their predecessors and continued to devise therapies designed to reduce parturient pain. Benjamin Rush, believing that childbirth pain was "not entailed upon the female sex by an immutable law," encouraged the practice of venesection during labor because he believed that it was the most effective way to relieve the discomfort of uterine contractions.[95] Rush's contemporaries William Potts Dewees and Peter Miller both wrote essays expressing their agreement with Rush that doctors had a responsibility to relieve women of pain in childbirth and prescribing bloodletting as the best way to do it.[96]

Because they were generally satisfied with the therapeutic value of bloodletting for relieving parturient pain, doctors tended to ignore the potential that other substances had for relieving the pain that some women experienced during labor. In 1772 Joseph Priestly discovered the analgesic effects of nitrous oxide, and by 1800 Sir Humphrey Davy had suggested that this gas be used to reduce pain in surgical cases.[97] Shortly thereafter morphine was isolated and its analgesic properties discovered.[98] But most practitioners made no attempt to experiment with these substances. By the 1830s, it is true, some doctors were using laudanum, a derivative of opium, to mitigate the pain of childbirth, but more traditional physicians like Dewees opposed such practices and continued to recommend bleeding.[99] It was not until October 1846 that William T. Morton, assisting Dr. John Collins Warren of Boston, demonstrated the effectiveness of ether in alleviating pain in surgery.[100] Three months later in Edinburgh, James Y. Simpson administered ether to an obstetrics patient in an attempt to alleviate the pains associated with labor. Dissatisfied with its use, he began experimenting with chloroform in November 1847.[101]

The first American woman to be given ether during labor was Fanny Appleton Longfellow. Longfellow's case is significant not only because it was the first in the country, but also because it offers a unique opportunity to view the introduction of a revolutionary medical technology through the eyes of a patient, her family, her friends, and members of the medical community.

Fanny Appleton married Henry Wadsworth Longfellow in 1843. The daughter of a wealthy Boston merchant, she lived with her husband in a spacious house in Cambridge, Massachusetts, facing the Charles River just a short way from Harvard Yard. Both of the Longfellows had shown previous interest in irregular methods of medical treatment. Henry used hydropathy, and Fanny used homeopathy to help ease pain in her legs. Therefore, it was not out of character for them to have taken an interest in the new anesthetic discovery. In the early spring of 1847, Fanny was already the mother of two children. Pregnant again, she had heard of Simpson's experiments.[102]

The Longfellows tried unsuccessfully to persuade various Boston doctors to agree to administer ether to Fanny during her labor. They eventually had to hire a local dentist, Nathan Colley Keep, to administer the vapor while Dr. Bigelow, Sr., of Boston delivered the baby. [103]

On April 7, 1847, Fanny's labor began. After five and one-half hours of regular but mild contractions, her pains became more severe. At that point Keep began to administer the ether. For the next twenty minutes he monitored her condition carefully, noticing the frequency and severity of each contraction and administering just enough ether to alleviate the pain but not enough to allow her to fall into unconsciousness. After her fourth contraction he stopped administering the ether so that he could observe the progress of her labor without anesthetic. The labor appeared to be proceeding normally, but Fanny's discomfort increased perceptibly without the ether. Keep again began to administer the vapor, but Fanny was in the throes of her last contractions, and the ether did not have sufficient time to take effect. The whole process took only thirty minutes. The result, according to Keep, was "highly satisfactory." [104]

Henry Longfellow was less reserved in his assessment of the experiment. His enthusiasm knew no bounds. His wife safely delivered, he dashed off a note to his good friend Charles Sumner, announcing the birth of their new daughter. "My dear Charles," he wrote, "the great experiment has been tried, and with grand success! Fanny has a daughter born this morning, at ten. Both are well. The *Ether* was heroically inhaled." [105] On the same day he wrote in his journal: "Fanny heroically inhaled the vapor of sulphuric ether . . . and all the pains of labor ceased, though the labor itself went on and seemed accelerated. This is the first trial of ether at such a time in the country. It has been completely successful. While under the influence of the vapor there was no loss of consciousness, but no pain. All ended happily." [106] The next day Longfellow wrote to his mother in Portland, Maine: "The trial proves, that the new discovered *Letheon* may be used not only with perfect safety in such cases, but with the most beneficial results afterwards. Fanny has never before seemed so quiet and well after a confinement." [107]

Writing to her sister-in-law shortly after her confinement, Fanny said, ether is "the greatest blessing of this age," and she referred to it as "a gift of God." [108] Members of her family and close friends were apparently less certain. Letters written by both Henry and

Fanny Longfellow were by their tone designed not only to announce the birth of their daughter but also to reassure friends and family that the ether they had made arrangements to use against the advice of various Boston doctors had damaged neither mother nor infant. Family members, including Henry's sister Anne Longfellow Pierce, had obviously shown considerable concern for their safety, since Fanny wrote shortly after her confinement: "Many thanks for your warm sympathy in my new joy and etherial bravery. . . . I never was better or got through a confinement so comfortably. . . . I am very sorry you all thought me so rash and naughty in trying the ether. Henry's faith gave me courage, and I had heard such a thing had succeeded abroad. . . . I feel proud to be the pioneer to less suffering for poor, weak womankind." [109] And later in May Henry wrote to his sister, "Fanny—(that is what you want to know)—is very well—remarkably well—better than ever before, after a confinement; so that *Ether* still reigns triumphant, and wears its laurels untarnished." [110]

Friends also wrote one another discussing the Longfellow experiment. "Fanny has immortalized herself by boldness, Longfellow by daring," wrote Francis Leiber to George Hillard. But in Leiber's opinion the risk they had taken had been very great. "How could he know that the ether would not stop the active energies of nature so indispensable during parturition?" Hillard reported that the use of ether had "excited a 'furore' among all the 'femmes couvertes' of our community. The curse of Eve is felt to have glanced aslope and fallen to the ground." [111] Indeed, Fanny's contemporaries were very interested in the innovation. In the wake of her experiment, a number of her friends in the Boston area demanded and found someone to administer the vapor to them during labor. To her sister-in-law Fanny wrote, "Two other ladies, I know, have since followed my example successfully," and in another letter she wrote, "Mrs. John Bryant has an etherial baby, another girl, which is the latest and best news." [112]

In his correspondence with Hillard regarding the experiment with ether, Leiber had anticipated that a struggle would ensue within the medical community, as well as between physicians hesitant to use the new medical technology and their obstetrical patients who would demand it. "I have no doubt whatever," he

*Figure 4.* Portrait of Fanny Appleton Longfellow (1859) by Samuel Worcester Rowse. Frances Appleton Longfellow was the first American woman to arrange to have anesthesia in the form of ether administered to her during the birth of her third child in 1847. She and her husband, Henry Wadsworth Longfellow, lived in Cambridge, Mass. Courtesy of the Longfellow National Historic Site, National Park Service, Cambridge, Mass.

wrote, "that some *regulars* will seriously object to this removal of Eve's curse, as they preached against vaccination—indeed far more so." [113]

As Leiber had accurately predicted, the response of the medical community was mixed. Some doctors apparently read about the use of obstetric anesthesia in professional publications such as the *Boston Medical and Surgical Journal*, where Keep's description of the Longfellow experiment appeared one week after the delivery of their child. [114] Others learned about its application through an informal social network such as the one used by Henry Longfellow to inform two physicians in Maine about the innovation. In a letter to his mother on the day after the birth of the baby, Longfellow wrote: "Pray tell Dr. [William] Wood and Dr. [John Taylor Gilman] Davies of this. The ether is inhaled from a glass vessel, having two orifices; one to be placed at the mouth or nose, the other to admit air; as it is essential to have atmospheric air inhaled with the vapor." [115] On April 10 Alexander Longfellow, Henry's brother, replied, describing the response of the two Maine doctors to Henry's information: "The doctors were much interested in the medical fact stated in your note, the taking of Letheon which they seemed to regard as a somewhat hazardous experiment. Davies could not refrain from a pun on the occasion. If you had asked your wife which she should prefer, a boy or a girl, she would have replied I will take *ether*." [116]

Other physicians took the innovation a little more seriously. In May Dr. Walter Channing of Harvard Medical School began his campaign as the primary American champion of obstetrical anesthesia. In the *Boston Medical and Surgical Journal*, he described the salutary effects of ether in one of the most distressing kinds of obstetrical cases, the performance of a craniotomy (crushing the head of the infant to extract it from the womb). As the year progressed, Channing continued to write articles for the Boston journal as well as a pamphlet on the use of ether in obstetrics. In 1848 he published a book intended to provide incontrovertible clinical evidence that ether was a safe way to relieve women in the agony of childbirth. [117]

Not surprisingly, not all doctors were as enthusiastic about the use of anesthesia as Channing. Both members of the regular medical community and sectarians opposed its use. Among the most articulate and influential spokesmen for the opposition was Charles Meigs of Philadelphia, who objected to the use of anesthesia in obstetrics on religious, philosophical, social, and medical grounds.

Meigs hesitated to use anesthesia because he believed that to do so would be to interfere with God's desire to punish women with pain in childbirth for Eve's role in tempting Adam in the Garden of Eden.[118] While he was not alone in raising this objection, religious scruples to the use of anesthesia in childbirth appear to have been less strong in the United States than in Scotland. There James Y. Simpson lost no time in answering objections raised by the clergy. Through a philological manipulation of the Hebrew text of the Old Testament, Simpson argued that the Hebrew word for *sorrow* should not be translated as "pain" but as "labor." He added also that in causing a deep sleep to come over Adam in the creation of Eve, Christians had clear evidence that God could not possibly object to the use of anesthesia since he had acted as the world's first anesthetist.[119] Simpson's "Answer to Religious Objections" arrived in Boston by steamer in January 1848, only a month after it had been published in Edinburgh.[120] It apparently met the clergy's most immediate objections so persuasively that the editors of the major American religious periodicals did not consider it worthwhile to debate the issue before the Civil War. By May the *Boston Medical and Surgical Journal* announced that in the opinion of the editor, the religious objections to the use of anesthesia had "been adroitly met,"[121] and in the same year the American Medical Association committee on obstetrics dismissed the religious objections to obstetric anesthesia as "absurd and futile."[122]

Meigs's philosophical objections could not be so easily dismissed because they involved issues concerning the character and function of pain itself. Meigs maintained that the pain suffered in childbirth was functional. It was, he wrote, a "most desirable, salutary, and conservative manifestation of life-force." According to Meigs pain was not only important to the birth process, it continued to be necessary to the life process because it served as a physiological expression of power or force.[123] Anesthesia interfered with part of the life process, and therefore its use was undesirable. Such an opinion placed Meigs squarely within the school of thought, described by his colleague Samuel Dickson, that viewed pain as the awakener

87

of life and intellect, a stimulant necessary to life and whose absence, by implication, produced a condition akin to death.[124] Supporters of anesthesia like Channing and Simpson, however, viewed pain as a negative rather than a positive force. Channing saw pain as dysfunctional.[125] Simpson wrote that pain was not essential to the birth process and that "all pain" was *per se . . . destructive.*"[126]

In addition to religious and philosophical concerns, Meigs objected to the use of obstetric anesthesia because he believed its use had the potential for disrupting family relationships and for undermining a woman's claim to respectability. These objections were based on the assumption that maternal affection provided the glue that held the family together and that mothers helped to establish the base upon which the family's respectability rested. Anything that jeopardized their ability to do either of these things threatened the position of the family and by implication the stability of society.

There were many in both the medical and lay communities who believed that pain in childbirth contributed to the affection mothers felt for their children. Mother love, wrote Eliza Farnham in an essay appearing in the *Ladies Wreath* in 1847, "is kindled into being amid mortal agony and peril."[127] Similarly, Louisa Barwell wrote in her advice book to mothers that the effect of labor pain appeared "to make the infant more dear."[128] According to a University of Pennsylvania medical student who presented his M.D. thesis in 1849, "The associations connected with the pangs of parturition may play an important part in framing the indissoluble link which binds a parent to its offspring."[129] Another physician wrote, "The very suffering which a woman undergoes in labor is one of the strongest elements in the love she bears her offspring."[130] Those who held this position implied that when women self-indulgently chose to use anesthesia to alleviate the pains associated with labor, they did so at the risk of jeopardizing the bond of affection mothers should feel for their children.

Anesthesia was also objectionable because its use altered a woman's consciousness, an alteration that could appear to approximate that of intoxication. Walter Channing had indicated a sensitivity to this issue early on. In his defense of ether in 1848, he had dogmatically insisted that whatever the condition of women under its influence, "the etherized person is not *drunk,*—is not *intoxicated.*"[131] But the issue did not die with authoritative denial. An 1851 article in the *Boston Medical and Surgical Journal* compared the effects of ether to the effects of alcohol,[132] a theme that Meigs more explicitly and completely developed five years later in his obstetrics text. According to Meigs: "To be insensible from whiskey, and gin, and brandy, and wine, and beer, and ether, and chloroform, is to be what in the world is called Dead-drunk. No reasoning—no argumentation is strong enough to point out the ninth part of a hair's difference between them." The only difference he saw between the two was the time it took to become intoxicated and the transitiveness of the influence of ether. Although he eventually admitted that he occasionally used ether in complicated obstetrics cases, he complained that since the woman was intoxicated, he sometimes had to stop administering it so that the "motor powers of the womb" could recover from the "stupefying influence of the intoxication or dead-drunke[n]ness of the woman."[133] Meigs was concerned about protecting the reputation of his genteel female patients from any influence that might destroy their credibility as the guardians of familial morality and respectability.

Meigs's final group of criticisms about the use of obstetrical anesthesia concerned its medical safety. It seems clear that to some degree the battle over the use of anesthesia in childbirth became a struggle over the best way to manipulate the childbirth experience medically in order to avoid death. Both sides argued that their position was the one most effectively designed to sustain the lives of their parturient patients. Meigs allowed pain because he believed it was a physiological expression of life. Simpson and Channing were willing to banish the worst effects of pain to protect those same lives from its destructive influence. Thus, rejecting the evidence from Channing's case studies, which had shown anesthesia to be safe, Meigs wrote that he would not use it in any but the most complicated deliveries. He further testified that he felt obliged to refuse the demands of his patients for anesthesia.[134] When he finally did begin to experiment with it, he remained obstinately unimpressed with the results.[135]

It is impossible to tell precisely how the professional debate over the use of anesthesia in childbirth affected the majority of American physicians. Certainly it must have forced many doctors to evaluate carefully the professional risks and benefits of adapting the new technique to their practice. Humanitarian considerations often held sway over other considerations. Acknowledging the effectiveness of ether and chloroform in reducing the pain of parturition, some doctors decided to administer the substance when their patients demanded it.[136]

And demand it they did. John Metcalf reported to the Massachusetts Medical Society in 1856 that when physicians arrived to deliver a baby, they should be prepared to respond to the question, "Have you brought the chloroform?"[137] There is no evidence to indicate that parturient women or members of their families were in the least concerned with any of the religious, philosophical, or social issues being debated by members of the medical community. Their own experience or what they knew of the experience of others told them that they could expect to suffer during labor. They were quite willing to try something that might relieve them in their anticipated agony. In 1851 George Templeton Strong of New York described the labor of his wife: "At about 7:30, she went to bed in a good deal of suffering, and from that time till the finale, suffered terribly. . . . She bore up bravely, only begging sometimes for chloroform, which Johnston [the attending physician] most stoically and imperturbably declined giving." Strong did not explain why their doctor refused to administer the chloroform that his wife requested. At her next confinement, however, Johnston was replaced with another doctor, who, when called to the Strong residence, began administering chloroform at once. Strong reported that the anesthetic relieved some of her pain without producing "insensibility nor even any apparent confusion of thought or difficulty of speech." The chloroform apparently did not offer much relief during the final stage of labor, however, for Strong described the last "four or five paroxysms" as "piteous and terrible to see."[138] Richard Henry Dana, Jr., was somewhat more impressed with the effect of anesthesia on his wife during delivery and reported in his journal on September 1, 1848, that she felt very little pain "under the blessed effects of Chloroform."[139] Some women found no relief at all from the use of anesthesia. In October 1848 Helen Garrison's midwife attempted to administer ether to her during labor. William Lloyd Garrison reported in a letter that it "seemed to excite rather than allay distress," and they soon discarded it.[140] Thus, while child-bearing women were willing to experiment with anesthesia in order to avoid the pain that they expected to accompany the delivery of a child, they were not universally satisfied with the results.

On the one hand the demand of women that their lying-in attendants provide them with a pain-relieving vapor served as an example of the way in which childbearing women manipulated the practice of medicine in an effort to direct the conduct of their own childbirth experience. Because obstetrics cases were important in building and maintaining a medical practice, physicians could not afford to discount their private patients' desire for anesthetic relief. Simpson had been convinced from the very beginning that women, unwilling to suffer "when suffering is so totally unnecessary," would force the use of anesthesia on the profession.[141] He even found that his obstetrical patients in Scotland were so enthusiastic about its use that they set out as missionaries to convince their friends of its benefits.[142]

On the other hand, however, by demanding that they be administered anesthesia, childbearing women placed themselves in a position that made it easier for their doctors to assume more control over the birth process. It was the doctor, after all, who ultimately decided whether or not anesthesia would be used. Women came to them as suppliants. Moreover, anesthesia was guaranteed to render childbearing women incapable of interfering with the doctor's practice of obstetrics.

Whatever the willingness of doctors to submit to female demands for pain relief during normal childbirth, that willingness was confined to their practice among middle- and upper-class women who delivered their children at home, who paid their physician his required fee, and whose social status was such as to command a doctor's respect. In his study of the use of anesthetics in mid-nineteenth-century America, Martin Steven Pernik pointed out that ether and chloroform were used selectively by American physicians to relieve the pain in labor of those middle- and upper-class women who, they felt, were the most likely to suffer excessively and were believed to be the least likely to be able to bear it.[143] For this reason as well as for economic considerations, the use of obstetrical anesthesia in normal cases did not filter below that class of people who could afford to hire attendants skilled in its application and willing to take the time to administer it. At the turn of the twentieth century, half of the women in America were still being delivered by midwives who generally did not have the training to administer anesthesia to their patients.[144] Even those lower-class women who delivered in charitable lying-in hospitals were not likely to be offered the opportunity to obtain anesthetic relief during normal labors. Added to the fact that doctors believed lower-class women less likely than their private patients to suffer during childbirth, an 1896 report of the Massachusetts General Hospital indicated that the ever-increasing need to provide basic services such as shelter, food, and nursing care for charity cases prohibited the extra cost and time required to administer general anesthesia to obstetrics patients.[145]

However selective doctors were in administering anesthesia to women during childbirth, its use did give physicians an opportunity to confirm the assertion that had been made by medical authorities since the beginning of the century that the services of a doctor could make a difference in the way a woman experienced even a normal delivery. It also allowed doctors effectively to separate the pain of childbirth from a parturient woman's anxiety about fear of death in childbed. Frederick Hollick, an irregular doctor, wrote in 1848 that anesthesia was a blessing not just because it caused a reduction in pain but also because it reduced the fear of such pain, a fear that in his experience had been known to cause death.[146] Simpson of Scotland also noted the effect that the possibility of using anesthesia had on the attitude of his parturient patients. "A number of patients," he wrote, "have spontaneously told me, that the prospect of being enabled to pass through the ordeal of parturition with the assistance of anaesthetic agents . . . has destroyed, in a great measure, that state of anxiety and dread of anticipation, which in former pregnancies, had, for weeks and months previously, silently annoyed and haunted them."[147] In 1848 an American Medical Association obstetrical committee reported the same findings, that anesthesia was as effective in reducing fear and anxiety as it was in reducing pain.[148]

No matter how gripping the fear of childbirth, severe the pain during labor, or dangerous the process of delivery, early nineteenth-century women were typically able to bury whatever ambivalence or resentment they felt once they were out of danger. They responded to the birth of their children as women had done since the time of the early Christian scribe who wrote in John 21:16, "When a woman is in travail she has sorrow, because her hour has come; but when she is delivered of a child, she no longer remembers the anguish, for joy that a child is born into the world." Doctors, authors, and childbearing women themselves wrote of the transition from misery to comfort and joy that accompanied the birth of a child and of the unwillingness of new mothers to dwell on memories of unpleasantness.

"When a child is born," wrote botanic practitioner Thomas Hersey in 1836, "the sudden transition from misery, pain and fear, has a most transporting influence on female feelings." [149] Frederick Hollick agreed, writing in his popular midwifery manual that after a baby is born the "female feels, as most of them express it, *in heaven;* there is an almost instantaneous change, from the most agonizing pain to a state of perfect ease." [150] Even rare literary references to the birth of a child described this change. A poem published in a ladies' magazine in 1808 attempted to describe the mixed emotions felt by women who bore children amid anxiety and pain:

> Welcome thou little dimpled stranger,
> O! welcome to my fond embrace;
> Thou sweet reward of pain and danger,
> Still let me press thy cherub face.
>
> Dear source of many a mingled feeling,
> How did I dread but wish thee here!
> While hope and fear, in turns prevailing
> Serv'd but to render thee more dear.
>
> How glow'd my heart with exultation,
> So late the anxious seat of care,
> When first thy voice of supplication
> Stole sweetly on thy mother's ear. [151]

In 1849 Ann E. Porter wrote in her essay "Cousin Helen's Baby": "Need I tell anyone who has been a mother, of the joy which one experiences at the birth of their first-born. It is like the glorious sunlight of morning after a night of storm and darkness." [152] Early nineteenth-century doctors and authors perpetuated and confirmed the belief that the unpleasant aspects of childbirth were redeemed by the birth of a living child.

Middle- and upper-class urban women commonly acknowledged the pain and anxiety associated with childbirth but did not dwell on memories of unpleasantness. Mary A. Willson's letter to Sarah Watson Dana is typical of this response. Willson and Dana had borne their children at approximately the same time, thus Willson may have assumed that Dana's memories of that experience were fresh and needed no explicit description. The birth of their children, she wrote, "which a few months ago looked so threatening and awful is now over and we have been carried through in safety. I cannot look back on it as a scene of suffering, on the contrary, I can feel nothing but happiness. I hope it may be the same to you." [153] Willson did not deny her suffering; she merely dismissed it. Other women expressed similar sentiments. Three weeks after the birth of a son in 1853, Julia Ann Hartness Lay wrote that when she gazed upon "perfect and faultless form" and "sparkling eyes" of her new baby, she felt "well repaid" for her "hours of suffering." [154] And Abigail Alcott wrote to her brother shortly after the birth of her first child that the joy she felt at the moment of her daughter's birth was more than "sufficient compensation for the anguish of 36 hours." [155]

It is not surprising that when women wrote about their birthing experiences, they did not dwell on their more unpleasant memories. Grateful at having escaped the danger of those few hours and distracted by the presence of their infants and the conduct of their recovery, they tended to look forward to the future rather than back into the recent past. Their next goal was to recover from their "sickness" and assume their maternal responsibilities.

## Notes

1. C[aroline E.] Rush, *The North and the South; or, Slavery and Its Contrasts, a Tale of Real Life* (Philadelphia: Crissy and Markley, 1852), 30.

2. Catharine Read Arnold Williams, *Religion at Home, a Story, Founded on Facts* (Providence: Marshall and Hammond, 1829), 70; C. M. Sedgwick,

*Home* (Boston: James Munroe, 1835), 50; [S. S. B. K. Wood,] *Amelia; or, The Influence of Virtue: An Old Man's Story* (Portsmouth: William Treadwell, 1802?), 240; Timothy Shay Arthur, *The Mother* (Philadelphia: E. Ferrett, 1846), 25; Timothy Shay Arthur, *Our Children: How Shall We Save Them?* (New York: Brognard, 1850), 20; Maria J. McIntosh, *Charms and Counter-charms* (New York: D. Appleton, 1848), 394.

3. E. M. Forster, *Aspects of the Novel* (New York: Harcourt, 1927), 81. For a similar observation, see Herbert Ross Brown, *The Sentimental Novel in America, 1789–1860* (Durham, N.C.: Duke University Press, 1940), 122.

4. Susanna Rowson, *Charlotte, a Tale of Truth*, 2 vols. (Philadelphia: Mathew Carey, 1794), 2:154.

5. P. D. Manvill, *Lucinda; or, The Mountain Mourner* (Johnstown: n.p., 1807), 114.

6. [Walter Channing,] *Remarks on the Employment of Females as Practitioners in Midwifery* (Boston: Cummings and Hilliard, 1820), 19. See also Charles D. Meigs, *Introductory Lecture to a Course on Obstetrics, Delivered in Jefferson Medical College, November 4, 1841* (Philadelphia: Merrihew and Thompson, 1841), 10.

7. Catherine M. Scholten, "'On the Importance of the Obstetrick Art': Changing Customs of Childbirth in America, 1760–1825," *William and Mary Quarterly* 34 (July 1977): 438; Jane B. Donegan, "Man-Midwifery and the Delicacy of the Sexes," in *"Remember the Ladies": New Perspectives on Women in American History*, ed. Carol V. R. George (Syracuse: Syracuse University Press, 1975), 91; Richard W. Wertz and Dorothy C. Wertz, *Lying-in: A History of Childbirth in America* (New York: Free Press, 1977), 67. The same was true of British doctors. See Jean Donnison, *Midwives and Medical Men: A History of Inter-Professional Rivalries and Women's Rights* (London: Heinemann Educational Books, 1977), 37, 92, 177; M. Jeanne Peterson, *The Medical Profession in Mid-Victorian London* (Berkeley: University of California Press, 1978), 87.

8. For a discussion of medical fee schedules, see George Rosen, *Fees and Fee Bills: Some Economic Aspects of Medical Practice in Nineteenth Century America* (Baltimore: Johns Hopkins, 1946), 4, 5, 9, 13, 20, 44.

9. Valentine Seaman, *The Midwives Monitor and Mothers Mirror* (New York: Isaac Collins, 1800), v–vi.

10. Charles D. Meigs, *A Lecture Introductory to the Course of Obstetrics in Jefferson Medical College of Philadelphia, Delivered November 5, 1842* (Philadelphia: Merrihew and Thompson, 1842), 19. For a discussion of similar attitudes on the part of British doctors, see Peterson, *The Medical Profession*, 87, 99-100.

11. Richard Henry Dana, Jr., *The Journal of Richard Henry Dana, Jr.*, ed.

Robert F. Lucid, 3 vols. (Cambridge, Mass.: Belknap Press, 1968), 1:355–56; Aunt Lydia to Sarah Watson Dana, Sept. 25, 1848, box 15, folder 23; Mary Watson Willson to Sarah Watson Dana, Oct. 6, 1848, box 15, folder 17, Sarah Watson Dana Letters, Dana Family Papers, Schlesinger Library, Radcliffe College, Cambridge, Mass.

12. James Axtell, *The School upon a Hill: Education and Society in Colonial New England* (New York: W. W. Norton, 1974), 62–63; Lyle Koehler, *A Search for Power: The "Weaker Sex" in Seventeenth-Century New England* (Urbana: University of Illinois Press, 1980), 34; Gordon E. Geddes, *Welcome Joy: Death in Puritan New England* (Ann Arbor: UMI Research Press, 1981), 49–54.

13. Quoted in Axtell, *School*, 63.

14. Joseph Kett, *The Formation of the American Medical Profession: The Role of Institutions, 1780–1860* (New Haven: Yale University Press, 1968), 5.

15. For a discussion of midwifery training for women in Britain in the late eighteenth century, see Donnison, *Midwives and Medical Men*, 39–41.

16. For discussions of colonial midwifery, see Donegan, "Man-Midwifery," 90; Judy Barrett Litoff, *American Midwives, 1860 to the Present* (Westport, Conn.: Greenwood Press, 1978), 6; Janet Bogdan, "Care or Cure? Childbirth Practices in Nineteenth-Century America," *Feminist Studies* 4 (June 1978): 93; Scholten, "'On the Importance,'" 429–34; Wertz and Wertz, *Lying-in*, 6–18.

17. For discussions of the significance of the Chamberlen forceps, see Wertz and Wertz, *Lying-in*, 34–35, 39; Jane B. Donegan, *Women and Men Midwives: Medicine, Morality, and Mysogyny in Early America* (Westport, Conn.: Greenwood Press, 1978), 26–27, 49–52; Theodore Cianfrani, *A Short History of Obstetrics and Gynecology* (Springfield, Ill.: Charles C. Thomas, 1960), 189–203; Scholten, "'On the Importance,'" 437; W. Smellie, *A Treatise on the Theory and Practice of Midwifery* (London: D. Wilson and T. Durham, 1752), lviii, lxvi, 247–91. Until the beginning of the eighteenth century, the doctors in the Chamberlen family kept knowledge of the instrument a secret.

18. For discussions of early medical education, see Donegan, *Women and Men Midwives*, 115–18, 133; Kett, *Formation*, 9–10; Wertz and Wertz, *Lying-in*, 29, 49–50; Litoff, *American Midwives*, 8; Scholten, "'On the Importance,'" 435–36.

19. The first of these doctors was William Shippen, Jr., of Philadelphia, who advertised both his services as a midwife and a series of lectures on the subject in 1762. Valentine Seaman in New York was equally willing to offer a course of study on midwifery and published a manual for the use of midwives in 1800. *Medical Repository* 2 (1799): 437; ibid. 3 (1800): 302. In 1807 Samuel Bard, also of New York, published a compendium of midwifery practices, *A Compendium of the Theory and Practice of Midwifery* (New York: Collins

and Perkins, 1807). For information on the background and training of such men, see Donegan, *Women and Men Midwives*, 114–30.

20. Donegan, *Women and Men Midwives*, 120; Scholten, "'On the Importance,'" 439. Two of the women in this study hired midwives to attend them during labor and delivery. Doctors attended the lying-in of sixteen others. The rest made no reference to the matter.

21. Edward Warren, *The Life of John Collins Warren, M.D., Compiled from His Autobiography and Journals*, 2 vols. (Boston: Ticknor and Fields, 1860), 2:276.

22. [Channing,] *Remarks*, 12–13, 14–15.

23. A. M. Mauriceau, *The Married Woman's Private Medical Companion* (New York: Joseph Trow, 1847), 195–96.

24. Samuel Gregory, *Man-Midwifery Exposed and Corrected* (Boston: George Gregory, 1848), 39. For more on Samuel Gregory, see Donegan, *Women and Men Midwives*, 198–203; Mary Roth Walsh, *"Doctors Wanted—No Women Need Apply": Sexual Barriers in the Medical Profession, 1835–1975* (New Haven: Yale University Press, 1977), 35–75.

25. Bard, *Compendium*, 94.

26. John Burns, *The Principles of Midwifery, Including the Diseases of Women and Children* (Philadelphia: Hopkins and Earle, 1810), 229.

27. Ibid.; Bard, *Compendium*, 94; William P. Dewees, *An Essay on the Means of Lessening Pain, and Facilitating Certain Cases of Difficult Parturition* (Philadelphia: John H. Oswald, 1806), 7, 39; Seaman, *Midwives Monitor*, ix–x; Charles White, *A Treatise on the Management of Pregnant and Lying-in Women* (London: Edward and Charles Dilly, 1773), 98; James Y. Simpson, "On the Use of Anaesthetics in Midwifery," *Medical Examiner, and Record of Medical Science*, [n.s.,] 5 (May 1849): 275; Hugh L. Hodge, *An Eulogium of William P. Dewees, M.D., Delivered before the Medical Students of the University of Pennsylvania, November 5, 1842* (Philadelphia: Merrihew and Thompson, 1842), 13.

28. Henry Miller, *Report of the Obstetric Committee on Anaesthesia in Midwifery, and the Speculum Uteri* (Louisville: Webb and Levering, 1853), 14.

29. Thomas Denman, *An Introduction to the Practice of Midwifery* (Brattleborough, Vt.: William Fessenden, 1807), 125–26.

30. R. J. Culverwell, *The Institutes of Marriage* (New York: n.p., 1846), 110.

31. John Vaughan, "An Inquiry into the Utility of Occasional Bloodletting in the Pregnant State of Disease," *Medical Repository* 6 (1803): 33.

32. Simpson, "On the Use of Anaesthetics," 276.

33. Quoted in Axtell, *School*, 64.

34. Charles Elventon Nash, *The History of Augusta: First Settlements and Early Days as a Town, Including the Diary of Mrs. Martha Ballard (1785–1812)* (Augusta, Maine: Charles E. Nash, 1904), 240. See also John Pierce to Benjamin Tappan, Mar. 7, 1803, box 1, folder 8; and Oct. 25, 1813, box 1, folder 9, Poor Family Collection, Schlesinger Library.

35. Cecil K. Drinker, *Not So Long Ago: A Chronicle of Medicine and Doctors in Colonial Philadelphia* (New York: Oxford University Press, 1937), 51, 54, 59.

36. Horace Adams, "A Puritan Wife on the Frontier," *Mississippi Valley Historical Review* 27 (June 1940): 82.

37. Persis Sibley Andrews Black journal, May 9, 1847, in *Victorian Women: A Documentary Account of Women's Lives in Nineteenth-Century England, France, and the United States*, ed. Erna Olafson Hellerstein, Leslie Parker Hume, and Karen M. Offen (Stanford: Stanford University Press, 1981), 219.

38. Theodore Stanton and Harriot Stanton Blatch, eds., *Elizabeth Cady Stanton As Revealed in Her Letters, Diary, and Reminiscences*, 2 vols. (New York: Harper, 1922), 2:26. See also Mary Harris Lester diary, Dec. 17, 1848, Andrew Lester Papers, New-York Historical Society, N.Y.

39. Michael Ryan, *The Philosophy of Marriage in Its Social, Moral, and Physical Relations* (London: H. Bailliere, 1839), 279–80.

40. Barbara Welter, "The Cult of True Womanhood, 1820–1860," *American Quarterly* 18 (Summer 1966): 151, passim.

41. William P. Dewees, *Treatise on the Physical and Medical Treatment of Children* (Philadelphia: Carey and Lea, 1825), 38.

42. James MacDonald, "Puerperal Insanity," *American Journal of Insanity* 4 (Oct. 1847): 119. For other references to this phenomenon, see Fleetwood Churchill, "On the Mental Disorders of Pregnancy and Childbed," *American Journal of Insanity* 7 (Apr. 1851): 302; J. H. Worthington, "On Puerperal Insanity," *American Journal of Insanity* 18 (July 1861): 46.

43. Charles D. Meigs, *Obstetrics: The Science and the Art* (Philadelphia: Blanchard and Lea, 1856), 710.

44. Pye Henry Chavasse, *Advice to Wives on the Management of Themselves, during the Periods of Pregnancy, Labour, and Suckling* (New York: D. Appleton, 1844), 57.

45. Ryan, *Philosophy of Marriage*, 269–70.

46. Dewees, *Treatise*, 38.

47. Judith Walzer Leavitt, "'Science' Enters the Birthing Room: Obstetrics in America since the Eighteenth Century," *Journal of American History* 70 (Sept. 1983): 294; see also Judith Walzer Leavitt, *Childbearing in America: 1750 to 1950* (New York: Oxford University Press, 1986), 36–63.

48. Meigs, *Obstetrics*, 286.

49. Frederick Hollick, *The Matron's Manual of Midwifery, and the Diseases of Women during Pregnancy and in Child Bed* (New York: T. W. Strong, 1848), 222.

50. [Channing,] *Remarks*, 4, 16.

51. Burns, *Principles*, 231; Fleetwood Churchill, *On the Theory and Practice of Midwifery* (Philadelphia: Lea and Blanchard, 1843), 204.

52. Denman, *Introduction*, 153.

53. Burns, *Principles*, 231; Robert Lee, *Lectures on the Theory and Practice of Midwifery* (Philadelphia: Ed. Barrington and Geo. D. Haswell, 1844), 216; Ryan, *Philosophy of Marriage*, 284; William P. Dewees, *A Compendious System of Midwifery* (Philadelphia: Carey and Lea, 1826), 189.

54. Charles D. Meigs, *The Philadelphia Practice of Midwifery* (Philadelphia: James Kay, 1838), 156, 157.

55. Meigs, *Obstetrics*, 300–301.

56. Dewees, *Compendious System*, 190; John Throckmorton, "Notebook of Medical School Lectures, 1815–1816," Monmouth County Historical Association, Freehold, N.J.

57. John George Metcalf, "Statistics in Midwifery," *American Journal of the Medical Sciences*, [n.s.,] 6 (Oct. 1843): 328.

58. Samuel Merriman, *A Synopsis of the Various Kinds of Difficult Parturition* (Philadelphia: Thomas Dobson, 1816), 31.

59. Samuel K. Jennings, *The Married Lady's Companion; or, Poor Man's Friend* (New York: Lorenzo Dow, 1808), 113.

60. Seaman, *Midwives Monitor*, 90–91; Daniel H. Whitney, *The Family Physician and Guide to Health* (New York: H. Gilbert, 1833), 151; Thomas Ewell, *Letters to Ladies, Including Important Information concerning Themselves and Infants* (Philadelphia: W. Brown, 1817), 151; H. B. Skinner, *The Female's Medical Guide and Married Woman's Advisor* (Boston: Skinner, 1849), 31.

61. Burns, *Principles*, 241.

62. Samuel Akerly, "Practical Observations on the Medical Qualities and Efficacy of the Ergot, or Spurred Rye: Pulvis ad Parturients," *Medical Repository*, [4th ser.,] 2 (1815): 272.

63. Meigs, *Philadelphia Practice*, 155.

64. William P. Dewees, "A Case of Difficult Parturition, Successfully Terminated by Bleeding," *Medical Repository* 2 (1799): 24–26.

65. Dewees, *Compendious System*, 188.

66. Metcalf, "Statistics," 343.

67. J. Jill Suitor, "Husbands' Participation in Childbirth: A Nineteenth-

Century Phenomenon," *Journal of Family History* 6 (Fall 1981): 283–85. Suitor attributes this development to the emergence of marriages based primarily on affection and companionship, the decline in the birthrate, and an increase in the emphasis placed on children and their relationship with their parents (pp. 287–89).

68. Dana, Jr., *Journal*, ed. Lucid, 1:68–69; see also 1:266–67, 355–56, 2:407. Andrew Lester and William Lloyd Garrison also attended their wives during childbirth. See Lester diary, Dec. 17, 1848, Andrew Lester Papers; William Lloyd Garrison, *The Letters of William Lloyd Garrison: No Union with Slave-Holders, 1841–1849*), ed. Walter Merrill (Cambridge, Mass.: Belknap Press, 1973), 599. In 1806 Lorenzo Dow expected to attend his wife and expressed great disappointment when her other attendants refused to allow it. Their child was born while they were visiting Dublin, where it was apparently considered inappropriate for husbands to attend their wives. See Peggy Dow, *Vicissitudes; or, The Journey of Life* (Philadelphia: Joseph Rakestraw, 1816), 606.

69. A number of husbands commented on the effect of anesthesia on their wives, thereby indicating that they were present when the doctors administered it. See George Templeton Strong, *The Diary of George Templeton Strong: The Turbulent Fifties, 1850–1859*, ed. Allan Nevins and Milton Halsey Thomas (New York: Macmillan, 1952), 274; Henry Wadsworth Longfellow journal, [Apr.] 7, [1847,] Houghton Library, Harvard University, Cambridge, Mass.

70. Suitor, "Husbands' Participation," 284–85.

71. George Templeton Strong, *Diary of George Templeton Strong: Young Man in New York, 1835–1849*, ed. Allan Nevins and Milton Halsey Thomas (New York: Macmillan, 1952), 348–49.

72. John Stearns, "Account of the Pulvis Parturiens, a Remedy for Quickening Child-birth," *Medical Repository*, [2d ser.,] 5 (Nov., Dec., Jan. 1807–8): 308–9.

73. Akerly, "Practical Observations," 271–72.

74. Ibid., 272.

75. Harriet Conner Brown, *Grandmother Brown's Hundred Years, 1827–1927* (Boston: Little, Brown, 1929), 93.

76 Ansel W. Ives, "On the Modus Operandi of Ergot in Parturition," *Medical Repository*, [4th ser.,] 6 (1820): 19–28; Ansel W. Ives, "Further Observations on the Modus Operandi of Ergot," ibid., 403–13; John Johnston Kelso, "On the General Utility of the Ergot of Rye in Obstetric Medicine," *Eclectic Journal of Medicine* 3 (Oct. 1839): 453–56; "Bibliographical Notice," *Medical Examiner, and Record of Medical Science* 4 (May 22, 1841): 325; Meigs, *Obstetrics*, 677–78; Metcalf, "Statistics," 344.

77. Adams, "Puritan Wife," 82.

78. Lester diary, Dec. 17, 1848, Andrew Lester Papers.

79. Mehetable May Dawes Goddard to Ann Goddard, Aug. 12, 1821, box 1, folder 15, Mehetable May Dawes Goddard Letters, May-Goddard Collection, Schlesinger Library.

80. Mary Pierce Poor to Feroline P. Fox, Oct. 9, 1853, box 12, folder 169, Mary Pierce Poor Letters, Poor Family Collection. See also Mary Rodman Fisher Fox diary, Apr. 23, 1850, Sept. 28, 1851, box 13, folder 30, Logan-Fisher-Fox Papers, Historical Society of Pennsylvania, Philadelphia; Frances to Arabella Carter, Jan. 14, 1836, box 1, folder 6, Timothy Carter Papers, Maine Historical Society, Portland, Maine.

81. Stanton and Blatch, eds., *Elizabeth Cady Stanton*, 2:26.

82. Black journal, May 9, 1847, in *Victorian Women*, ed. Hellerstein, Hume, and Offen, 219.

83. Elizabeth to Agnes Lamb Richards, Dec. 9, 1839, Agnes Treat Lamb Letters, Lamb Papers, New-York Historical Society.

84. Fanny Fern, *Fresh Leaves* (New York: Mason and Bros., 1857), 88.

85. Manvill, *Lucinda*, 113.

86. James Y. Simpson, *The Obstetric Memoirs and Contributions of James Y. Simpson, M.D., F.R.S.E.*, ed. W. O. Priestly and Horatio R. Storer, 2 vols. (Philadelphia: Lippincott, 1855–56), 2:530, 529.

87. Charles D. Meigs, *On the Nature, Signs, and Treatment of Childbed Fever in a Series of Letters Addressed to the Students of His Class* (Philadelphia: Blanchard and Lea, 1854), 227; Simpson quoting Meigs, *Obstetric Memoirs*, 2:574; Charles D. Meigs, *Lecture on Some of the Distinctive Characteristics of the Female, Delivered before the Class of the Jefferson Medical College, January 5, 1847* (Philadelphia: T. K. and P. G. Collins, 1847), 18–19.

88. George Pitcher, "The Awfulness of Pain," *Journal of Philosophy* 67 (July 23, 1970): 490; David Bakan, *Disease, Pain, and Sacrifice: Toward a Psychology of Suffering* (Chicago: University of Chicago Press, 1968), 79–90.

89. Meigs, *Lecture Introductory*, 21.

90. James Turner, *Reckoning with the Beast: Animals, Pain, and Humanity in the Victorian Mind* (Baltimore: Johns Hopkins, 1980), 34, 80, xi–xii.

91. James Guillimeau, *Child-birth; or, The Happy Deliverie of Women* (London: A. Hatfield, 1612), 116.

92. Thomas Raynalde, *The Birth of Man-kinde* (London: A. H., 1634), 41, 111–15.

93. Roy Finney, *The Story of Motherhood* (New York: Liveright, 1937), 155; Koehler, *Search for Power*, 58.

94. Aristotle, *The Works of Aristotle, the Famous Philosopher, in Four Parts* (New England: n.p., 1813), 40.

95. Benjamin Rush, "On the Means of Lessening the Pains and Danger of Child-Bearing, and of Preventing Its Consequent Diseases," *Medical Repository* 6 (1803): 26, 28.

96. Dewees, *Essay*, 61–95; Peter Miller, "An Essay on the Means of Lessening the Pains of Parturition," in *Medical Theses, Selected from among the Inaugural Dissertations . . .*, ed. Charles Caldwell (Philadelphia: Thomas and William Bradford, 1805), 350. For a more detailed discussion, see A. Clair Siddall, "Bloodletting in American Obstetric Practice, 1800-1945," *Bulletin of the History of Medicine* 54 (Spring 1980): 101-10. Lack of evidence makes it difficult to determine whether or not women who were bled experienced relief from parturient pain. By distracting them or providing them with the assurance that everything possible was being done to make them more comfortable, bleeding may have served as a psychological boost more than anything else. ·

97. Andrew M. Claye, *The Evolution of Obstetric Analgesia* (London: Oxford University Press, 1939), 54; John Duffy, "Anglo-American Reaction to Obstetrical Anesthesia," *Bulletin of the History of Medicine* 38 (Jan.-Feb. 1964): 32; Turner, *Reckoning*, 166 n.

98. Turner, *Reckoning*, 82.

99. Dewees, *Essay*, 55–56.

100. Duffy, "Anglo-American Reaction," 33.

101. Ibid.; Victor Robinson, *Victory over Pain: A History of Anesthesia* (New York: Henry Schuman, 1946), 201–2.

102. Edward Wagenknecht, ed., *Mrs. Longfellow: Selected Letters and Journals of Fanny Appleton Longfellow (1817–1861)* (New York: Longmans, Green, 1956), ix, 113, 114, 115, 119.

103. Ibid., 130; N. C. Keep, "The Letheon Administered in a Case of Labor," *Boston Medical and Surgical Journal* 36 (Apr. 14, 1847): 226; Augustus K. Gardner, *A History of the Art of Midwifery: A Lecture Delivered at the College of Physicians and Surgeons, November 11, 1851* (New York: Stringer and Townsend, 1852), 26.

104. Keep, "Letheon," 226.

105. Henry Wadsworth Longfellow, *The Letters of Henry Wadsworth Longfellow*, ed. Andrew Hilen, 4 vols. (Cambridge: Harvard University Press, 1972), 3:134.

106. Henry Wadsworth Longfellow journal, [Apr.] 7, [1847].

107. Longfellow, *Letters*, ed. Hilen, 3:134. The vapor of ether that Fanny Longfellow used was called letheon because its effects were said to be similar to those experienced when a mythical river of antiquity washed away memory of "sorrow and crime." See Samuel Henry Dickson, *Essays on Life, Sleep, Pain, Etc.* (Philadelphia: Blanchard and Lea, 1852), 122.

108. Wagenknecht, ed., *Mrs. Longfellow*, 130.

109. Ibid., 129–30.

110. Longfellow, *Letters,*, ed. Hilen, 3:135.

111. Edward Wagenknecht, *Longfellow: A Full-Length Portrait* (New York: Longmans, Green, 1955), 243.

112. Wagenknecht, ed., *Mrs. Longfellow*, 130, 131. John Duffy and Claude Heaton have suggested that when Queen Victoria allowed the use of chloroform during the birth of her eighth child, Prince Leopold, in 1853, the use of obstetric anesthesia gained respectability and became more popular in the United States (Duffy, "Anglo-American Reaction," 35–36; Claude Edwin Heaton, "The History of Anesthesia and Analgesia in Obstetrics," *Journal of the History of Medicine and Allied Sciences* 1 [Oct. 1946]: 568–69). There is no direct evidence to support this suggestion. It is even difficult to determine how the general public became aware of her use of anesthesia. Although the queen's obstetrician informed his colleagues of its use soon after the delivery of the prince, neither the London *Times* nor the *New York Times* mentioned the fact in their announcements of his birth.

113. Wagenknecht, *Longfellow*, 243.

114. Keep, "Letheon," 226.

115. Longfellow, *Letters*, ed. Hilen, 3:134.

116. Ibid., 135 n.

117. Walter Channing, "A Case of Inhalation of Ether in Instrumental Labor," *Boston Medical and Surgical Journal* 36 (May 19, 1847): 313–18; Walter Channing, "Inhalation of Ether in a Case of Laborious Labor," ibid. (May 26, 1847): 335–37; Walter Channing, "Inhalation of Ether," ibid. (June 2, 1847): 366; Walter Channing, "Cases of Inhalation of Ether," ibid. (June 24, 1847): 415–19; Walter Channing, *A Treatise on Etherization in Childbirth Illustrated by Five Hundred and Eighty-one Cases* (Boston: William D. Ticknor, 1848). Claude E. Heaton also makes reference to a pamphlet written by Walter Channing on the subject of anesthesia ("History of Anesthesia," 570).

118. Meigs, *Obstetrics*, 368.

119. Simpson, *Obstetric Memoirs* 2:551, 558.

120. *Boston Medical and Surgical Journal* 37 (Jan. 26, 1848): 524.

121. Ibid. 38 (May 31, 1848): 366. The use of obstetric anesthesia may have become an issue after the Civil War. For a reference to objections expressed in the *Bibliotheca Sacra* in 1888, see Duffy, "Anglo-American Reaction," 41.

122. "Report of the Committee on Obstetrics," *Transactions of the American Medical Association* 1 (1848): 226.

123. Meigs, *Obstetrics*, 372–73. For another discussion of nineteenth-century ideas about the benefits of pain, see Martin Steven Pernik, "A Calculus

of Suffering: Pain and Professionalism in the Practice of American Medicine and Surgery, 1840–1867" (Ph.D. diss., Columbia University, 1978), 69–98.

124. Dickson, *Essays on Life*, 92.

125. Channing, *Treatise on Etherization*, 20.

126. James Y. Simpson, "On the Use of Anaesthetics in Midwifery," *Medical Examiner, and Record of Medical Science*, [n.s.,] 5 (Apr. 1849): 211; Simpson, *Obstetric Memoirs* 2:536. For another discussion of nineteenth-century ideas concerning the danger of pain, see Pernik, "Calculus of Suffering," 13–34.

127. Eliza W. Farnham, "Women's Ministration," *Ladies Wreath* 1 (1847): 142.

128. Louisa Mary Barwell, *Advice to Mothers on the Treatment of Infants* (Philadelphia: Leary and Getz, 1853), 18.

129. Quoted in Pernik, "Calculus of Suffering," 79.

130. Channing, *Treatise on Etherization*, 142.

131. Ibid., 40.

132. E. Sanford, "Analogies between Alcoholic Intoxication and Anaesthesia by Inhalation of Ether," *Boston Medical and Surgical Journal* 45 (Nov. 5, 1851): 274–76.

133. Meigs, *Obstetrics*, 368, 373, 376. For another discussion of anesthesia as an intoxicant, see Pernik, "Calculus of Suffering," 110–13.

134. Simpson, "On the Use of Anaesthetics," 206; Meigs, *Obstetrics*, 372.

135. Meigs, *Obstetrics*, 376. For a discussion of the objections to the use of anesthesia in surgery as well as obstetrics, see Pernik, "Calculus of Suffering," 54–127.

136. *American Journal of the Medical Sciences*, [n.s.,] 37 (Jan. 1859): 282; Channing, *Treatise on Etherization*, 6.

137. Duffy, "Anglo-American Reaction," 36.

138. Strong, *Diary of George Templeton Strong: The Turbulent Fifties*, ed. Nevins and Thomas, 70, 274. Harriet Hanson Robinson also found that anesthesia did little to alleviate pain during the last stage of labor. In 1854 she wrote that despite the drug, she did not "escape the finale. Nature was stronger than ether" (Harriet Hanson Robinson diary, Oct. 6, 1854, Robinson-Shattuck Papers, Schlesinger Library).

139. Dana, Jr., *Journal*, ed. Lucid, 1:355.

140. Garrison, *Letters of William Lloyd Garrison*, ed. Merrill, 599.

141. Meigs, *Obstetrics*, 370; James Y. Simpson, "Discovery of a New Anaesthetic Agent More Efficient Than Sulphuric Ether," *Medical Examiner, and Record of Medical Science*, [n.s.,] 4 (Jan. 1848): 73.

142. Simpson, *Obstetric Memoirs*, 2:538.

143. Pernik, "Calculus of Suffering," 328.

144. Donegan, *Women and Men Midwives*, 3; Leavitt, "'Science' Enters the Birthing Room," 295.

145. Massachusetts General Hospital, *The Semi-Centennial of Anaesthesia, Oct. 16, 1846–Oct. 16, 1896* (Boston: Massachusetts General Hospital, 1897), 54–55.

146. Hollick, *Matron's Manual*, 447.

147. Simpson, *Obstetric Memoirs* 2:575.

148. "Report," 228.

149. Thomas Hersey, *The Midwife's Practical Directory; or, Woman's Confidential Friend* (Baltimore: Hersey, 1836), 158.

150. Hollick, *Matron's Manual*, 238. See also Burns, *Principles*, 247.

151. "The Mother to Her Child," *Lady's Weekly Miscellany* 7 (May 21, 1808): 64.

152. Ann E. Porter, "Cousin Helen's Baby," *Godey's Lady's Book* 39 (Oct. 1849): 236.

153. Mary Willson to Sarah Watson Dana, continuation of a letter from Mary Watson to Sarah Watson Dana, Sept. 8, 1848, box 15, folder 12, Sarah Watson Dana Letters.

154. Julia Ann Hartness Lay diary, Mar.–Apr. 1853, Rare Books and Manuscripts Division, Astor, Lenox and Tilden Foundations, New York Public Library.

155. Abigail Alcott to Samuel May, Mar. 27, 1831, box 1, folder 25, Abigail May Alcott Letters, Alcott Family Papers, Houghton Library; see also Kate Ross to Edward C. Ross, Aug. 9, 1836, Edward C. Ross Letters, Chrystie Family Papers, New-York Historical Society; Elizabeth Ellery Sedgwick journal, 1824, 1, Houghton Library; Dana, Jr., *Journal*, ed. Lucid, 1:69.

# "On a Thread Slender and Weak": Attitudes toward the Recovery Period

IN HER LAST NOVEL, *Ernest Linwood*, Caroline Hentz told the story of the saintly Gabriella St. James, who married Ernest Linwood only to find that his insane jealousy isolated them both from the outside world. Early in the story the orphaned Gabriella learned of her parentage by reading a manuscript written by her mother years before. In the memoir, Rosalie St. James described the birth of her daughter and the danger she faced during her recovery from childbirth. "At length," she wrote, "you were given to my arms, and the deep pure fountain of a mother's love welled in my youthful bosom. But my life was wellnigh sacrificed to yours. For weeks it hung trembling on a thread slender and weak as the gossamer's web." [1] Hentz did not indicate the nature of the problem that threatened the life of Rosalie St. James, but she quite clearly believed that danger in childbirth did not end with the birth of a child.

Few would have challenged Hentz's suggestion that for women who had recently delivered a child, the recovery period was fraught with potential danger. Bearing a child could drain a woman's strength and could lead to emotional or physical complications that might delay recovery or even cause death. Thomas Ewell warned in a popular health manual published in 1817 that women recovering from childbirth made a serious mistake if they disregarded the "hazards of the succeeding month," and he estimated that for every woman who died during delivery, two died during the immediate postpartum period. [2] C. Croserio, a homeopathic physician, was similarly alarmed at the death rate of childbearing women during the period immediately following birth. He felt that the weakness which resulted from suffering in labor, loss of blood, contraction of the uterus, and secretion of milk placed a woman in potential danger and estimated that nine out of ten women who died sometime during the process of parturition did so during the period of recovery.[3]

Pre–Civil War mortality statistics are too unreliable to verify or refute their estimates. Whatever the actual mortality rate, the friends and relatives of childbearing women typically expressed great relief when they were assured that a loved one who had recently delivered a child was well on her road to recovery. Elizabeth Watson Daggett, for example, wrote to her sister: "I remember well the all gone feeling I had and as the cause continued much longer with you wonder how you survived it. But I am happy that anxiety from that source is over and that you are preserved through another time of trouble."[4]

Medical interest in the physical and emotional vulnerability of parturient women during recovery did little to comfort those who were afraid that childbirth might result in death or debility. The concern of medical practitioners combined with the inability of the geographically mobile to depend on help from family and intimate friends during confinement, the search for privacy when surrounded by strangers in an urban environment, and the tendency to use the conduct of confinement as testimony to affluence, delicacy, and gentility encouraged childbearing women in the middle and upper classes to prolong the recovery period for four weeks and to seek the services of a monthly nurse to assist during delivery, care for mother and child after birth, and teach new mothers to care for their newborns. These social practices altered female relationships by weakening the female support system that had traditionally provided practical services and emotional support to women during labor and after delivery.

There were a number of serious physical disorders that could threaten the life of a woman during her recovery. Sarah Watson Dana began hemorrhaging after the birth of her third child in 1848. Walter Channing, the attending doctor, "held his hand firmly to the necessary parts" and "applied every medicine" as he watched her life slipping away. Exhausted, Channing finally sent for another doctor to help him, and for seven hours they took turns applying the pressure necessary to stop the bleeding. Eventually the bleeding stopped, and Dana was weak but out of danger.[5] Bessie Huntting Rudd's recovery was complicated by what she called a "wound," and her doctor ordered her to lie still in bed until it healed.[6] Ellen Ruggles Strong, who delivered a stillborn child in 1849 and almost died in the process, suffered from pain, bleeding, convulsions, and a severe cough for almost three weeks after her ordeal.[7]

Fevers that appeared a few days after delivery were particularly frightening because they could mark the onset of puerperal fever, a disease doctors viewed as both "fearful" and "complicated."[8] Puerperal fever, also known as childbed fever, was first identified by Edward Strother in England in 1716.[9] An infection of the womb, it struck without warning. An apparently healthy woman, still weak but recovering normally from childbirth, might develop chills, headache, nausea, and abdominal pain soon after delivery.[10] The prognosis was bleak even though the disease was not always fatal.

Throughout the first half of the nineteenth century, physicians on both sides of the Atlantic argued over the cause and the cure of the dread disease. Without knowledge of bacteria and the nature of infection, doctors could only speculate about its origin. At one time or another many causes were suggested: the state of pregnancy itself, intemperate behavior, constipation, the presence of an obstruction, the effects of climate, even fear of danger. "There are in fact no diseases about which there exists greater discrepancy of medical opinion, or which are involved in more embarrassing speculations," wrote the French obstetrician A. C. Baudelocque.[11] The choice of treatment was just as vast, although in the United States bloodletting was apparently viewed by many as the most effective remedy.[12] Without antibiotics nineteenth-century physicians could not have cured childbed fever even if they had known what caused it. Prevention had to be the cure, and it was over this issue that American physicians debated.

In 1843 Dr. Oliver Wendell Holmes published an article in the *New England Quarterly Journal of Medicine and Surgery* in which he argued that puerperal fever was contagious and was carried from woman to woman by their attendants. At about the same time, an obscure Hungarian doctor named Ignaz Semmelweiss, having come to the same conclusion, began collecting clinical evidence in a Vienna hospital that would eventually prove Holmes to be correct. The solution to the problem, according to Holmes, was to keep the infecting agent away from the patient by means of an antiseptic or by temporarily removing the doctor who had carried the infection once a case of the disease appeared in his practice. Holmes called doctors who through carelessness transmitted the disease from patient to patient "a private pestilence" and suggested that their conduct verged on the criminal. [13]

Acknowledging the possibility that the physician might be carrying the disease struck at the very roots of the somewhat insecure position of the regular practitioner. Having organized the American Medical Association in 1848 in an effort to improve medical standards and drive irregular doctors from practice, and knowing that they had yet to gain the confidence and respect of the public, regular physicians could see their position further threatened by the charge that they were responsible for causing the deaths of their parturient patients. The Holmes-Semmelweiss theory posed a moral dilemma for all physicians practicing obstetrics. In 1850 the editor of the *Medical Examiner* wrote that every practitioner had to be anxious "for he must either continue his practice at the conscious hazard of destroying those entrusted to his care, or he must impoverish himself by abandoning his professional duties, a hard alternative to a man dependent for his living on such exertions." [14]

The Holmes-Semmelweiss theory posed a particular professional problem for Charles Meigs. In 1842 Meigs edited a book of essays on puerperal fever, in which he expressed his belief that childbed fever was an inflammation rather than a fever. [15] Meigs was deeply disturbed by the Holmes-Semmelweiss theory. Not only had he just authoritatively denied that the disease in question was contagious, but he also found the moral consequences of accepting the theory appalling. "Could I but once bring myself to believe in the contagion of childbed fever, I could never afterwards be induced to practice my Art," he wrote. [16] Believing his art was designed to save lives, not take them, he could never see past his feeling of guilt to appreciate the preventive techniques that might have protected him and his patients. He felt that a man who continued to practice after accepting the theory "must be an unfeeling and wicked wretch, who, believing in the contagion of childbed fever, should yet continue to exercise his ministry at the risk of carrying death and desolation into whatever family he should be called on to act the part of the obstetrician." [17]

Although it is likely that most obstetricians had to deal with occasional cases of childbed fever, and while it is true that they had no effective way to treat it, it is unclear how prevalent the disease was or how many women it killed. One irregular doctor, Frederick Hollick, charged that "two females die out of every three attacked by it," but he provided no statistics to substantiate his claim. [18] Another doctor, writing of an outbreak of puerperal fever in Philadelphia during the winter of 1841–42, testified that seventy cases appeared in his practice alone. Fifteen of these women died. [19]

More comprehensive statistics are available from the mortality records kept by the municipal governments of Philadelphia, Boston, and New York. But most of those figures, published in medical journals and specifically showing reported deaths from puerperal fever, are of limited use. They allow only the comparison of such deaths to all other deaths reported in a given city in the same year. For example, medical journal statistics indicate that in Philadelphia for the period from 1807 through 1826, 190 out of 53,004 recorded deaths (three-tenths of 1 percent) were the result of puerperal fever. During the period between 1827 and 1840 in Philadelphia, the highest annual recorded death rate from the disease occurred in 1833 when 32 women reportedly died. Their deaths constituted seven-tenths of 1 percent of all of the 4,400 deaths recorded. [20]

Records from Boston and New York show a similar pattern. In Boston the number of puerperal fever deaths during the period from 1821 through 1848 was slightly under .09 percent of the total recorded deaths (47 out of 52,728). [21] In New York from 1805 through 1808, such deaths comprised about .1 percent of the total reported deaths (10 out of 8,903). [22] These statistics are meaningless in any attempt to judge the seriousness of the threat that puerperal fever posed to parturient women because it is not possible to compare the number of women who reportedly died with the number of women who in the same year bore children and were therefore at risk.

One medical statistician, however, did collect both birth statistics and puerperal fever statistics for the same years for the city of Philadelphia and published them in the *American Journal of the Medical Sciences*. While there is some reason to question the accuracy of both sets of figures, they indicate that for the years from 1831 through 1840, reported puerperal fever deaths made up one-tenth of 1 percent of all women reported giving birth in each year with three exceptions. In 1831 and 1840 they composed two-tenths of 1 percent, and in 1833 they comprised four-tenths of 1 percent.[23] Thus, even in those years when an exceptionally large number of women reportedly died from childbed fever, the death rate remained under 1 percent of all women who were at risk. This percentage seems low and could hardly have accounted for the alarm that cases of puerperal fever appear to have caused.

Statistics gathered by Hugh L. Hodge at Pennsylvania Hospital indicate that lower-class women who delivered their babies there were probably at greater risk than their middle- or upper-class counterparts who delivered their babies at home. In an article published in 1833, a year in which an unusually high number of childbed-fever deaths occurred in Philadelphia, Hodge reported that since its founding in 1803, the hospital had had forty deaths from the fever out of 733 labors (about 5 percent).[24]

Despite the apparent value of these figures, however, there may be good reason to discount them. Even though city ordinances in New York, Boston, and Philadelphia required municipal officers to collect and publish mortality statistics,[25] it remained for the doctors to determine the cause of death. And there is some evidence that doctors may have intentionally misrepresented puerperal fever deaths to city and hospital officials. Doctors as well as their patients were terrified of the disease. "The very name of childbed fever is a word of fear," wrote Meigs in 1854. In a letter published in 1843 and again in a book published eleven years later, Meigs described the alarm created in the community when word of a fever reached the public. "They know," he admitted, "that any one of our women, seized with childbed fever, is at once placed in a most perilous position." He felt that the public had little confidence in the ability of the medical profession to cure or stop the spread of the pestilence and recognized that a case of childbed fever was all it took to make the public even more dissatisfied with the medical care that regular doctors offered.[26]

An acknowledged case of childbed fever hurt a doctor's reputation and could ruin his practice. Meigs had apparently experienced the effects of admitting the presence of fever among his patients. His humiliation, sense of betrayal, and anger were apparent when he wrote, "I have been unceremoniously set aside, after having been for months engaged, even for some who owed me impayable gratitude for the services I had for years rendered them." He felt his dismissal undeserved, and he was indignant at being looked upon as a "peripatetic pestilence, or poisoner of women for love of gain, or what is worse, stupidity."[27]

For Meigs and others the question of the contagiousness of puerperal fever was an emotionally charged one. Because they felt personally and professionally threatened, they resisted both the implications of the Holmes-Semmelweiss theory and the suggestions made for the prevention of the disease. Only in the late 1870s, after Louis Pasteur had isolated the bacteria that caused the infection and Joseph Lister had developed effective antiseptic techniques, would puerperal fever decline as a cause of postpartum death.[28]

Hemorrhage, fever, and other physical complications represented only one kind of pathological response to childbirth. References to troublesome emotional reactions also appeared in both private writings and the medical literature of the early nineteenth century. Early in the century Sarah Ripley Stearns wrote of a friend who, having delivered a little girl, "died in a state of mental derangement."[29] In 1859 Elizabeth Dwight Cabot told her sister that "nothing can be as bad as that nervous depression—I had a little of it after the baby came & I had infinitely rather go through all the physical torture of the proceeding, than have it over again."[30] Neither Stearns nor Cabot discussed how long the emotional difficulties they referred to lasted, how incapacitating they were, or how they were treated.

Slightly more information can be found in references to depression in the diary of Sarah Connell Ayer for December 1826. "About tea-time," she wrote, "I was surprised to see Mrs. Webster enter the room. She has not been well since the birth of her little son, and has been in a state of great darkness of mind occasioned no doubt by ill health." The distressed Mrs. Webster had left her home and family intending to spend the night with a friend. Not finding the friend at home, she went to look for her doctor, and finding him out as well, she came to the Ayer home and asked to spend the night there. Ayer comforted Webster as best she could and sent for Webster's husband, her own husband, who was a physician, and Webster's physician. The doctors administered medicine to calm Webster's nerves, but her condition remained essentially the same. "My heart was sad," wrote Ayer. "I fear'd that unless she could obtain some refreshing sleep soon, and composed spirits, her reason would take its flight forever." It took over a week for Mrs. Webster to improve, and during that time she remained in the Ayer home. When she left, she went to stay with another friend rather than return home to her husband and family. By the middle of January, Ayer reported that Mrs. Webster appeared to be "quite comfortable."[31]

Although they showed considerable concern for the problem of what today would be called postpartum depression, none of these women showed any degree of surprise that it should have occurred. Their attitude paralleled closely that of the medical profession. According to Fleetwood Churchill it was common for women to suffer from emotional problems after delivery.[32] Concerned about identifying and categorizing pathological emotional responses to childbirth, doctors labeled such responses as puerperal insanity and divided them into two categories. The first they called melancholy, a disorder characterized by depression. The second they called mania, a disorder characterized by overexcited, aggressive, or disruptive behavior.

Depression was probably less likely than mania to have been diagnosed and treated by a doctor. Since it was considered normal for a woman to suffer from a certain amount of depression during the whole cycle of childbearing, there was a fine line between those cases of depression that were considered normal and those that were defined as pathological. In some instances even a fairly severe case of depression may not have created too much of a stir or disrupted middle- or upper-class households. The symptoms usually were not difficult to handle at home; moreover, those in the middle and upper classes had servants available to relieve the mistress of many of her domestic responsibilities.

The tendency to ignore or tolerate the symptoms of postpartum depression unless they became really frightening may explain why one doctor felt that manic cases of puerperal insanity were more common than melancholic ones.[33] Those most likely to write about the disease were doctors in Europe and America who either directed mental hospitals or diagnosed and treated patients in them. They would have come into contact with the most extreme cases, patients whose symptoms were severe enough to have justified institutionalization. Institutionalized patients, therefore, rather than private patients cared for by family and friends within the home, were especially likely to find their way into a doctor's case book and from there into the medical journals, thus providing the basis for professional discussion of puerperal insanity.

Although authorities agreed that the disease could occur at any time during the process of childbearing and lactation, they believed that a woman was more susceptible to mental collapse shortly after birth than during pregnancy. At that time physicians felt that a woman's resistance to disease was reduced by her loss of sleep due to fear and discomfort during the last weeks of pregnancy, by the shock of giving birth, and by the exhaustion induced by nursing the baby.[34]

Descriptions of the symptoms that indicated the manic form of puerperal insanity reflected not only the degree to which doctors believed there to be a connection between a woman's mental state and her reproductive organs but also the degree to which they sentimentalized the maternal role. They saw the manic form of puerperal insanity as fearful because it forced women to reject their most feminine domestic function. It interfered with their ability to fulfill their role as mothers.[35]

Doctors described an aversion to the newborn as well as to husband, nurse, family members, or friends as a common symptom of the manic form of puerperal insanity. By directing hostility toward those whom a mother was supposed to love and appreciate, manic women abdicated their role of holding the family, and by extension the community, together. If that were not enough, manic women also demonstrated a good deal of aggressive behavior clearly inappropriate for anyone who had pretensions to being a lady. Manic cases could be socially embarrassing. Patients might weep or laugh "immoderately compared with the cause" or depress everyone around them by looking "at the dark side of everything," fearing evil in the future, or articulating the belief that they were losing their minds.[36] But the symptom that appeared to be most shocking to the doctors was the propensity of such women to use obscene language in their conversations. "It is true," reported James Mac-Donald, "that in mania, modest women use words, which in health are never permitted to issue from their lips,—but in puerperal insanity, this is so common an occurrence, and is done in so gross a manner, that it early struck me as being characteristic."[37] Alone or in combination with other symptoms such as "destructiveness, sleeplessness, and vociferousness," such behavior was deemed disruptive and dangerous. A woman was expected to be loving, nurturing, cheerful, decorous, and self-controlled. These women clearly were not. Their behavior was deviant, and doctors labeled their malady puerperal insanity.

Once the disease was diagnosed, treatment could begin. Early in the century Benjamin Rush, assuming that insanity was a physical disorder, bled his mental patients in conformity with his belief that madness was seated in the blood vessels of the brain.[38] Most other authorities were not convinced that bleeding was likely to cure their patients.[39] As early as the 1820s doctors recognized that physical suffering, individual conditions of the mind, and environmental factors combined to produce what they called puerperal insanity, and they began to develop alternative treatments for the malady intended to enable women to reestablish their self-control.[40] More important than medicating or depleting the body, these treatments emphasized the need to remove the woman from irritating influences, which might include both her baby and other members of her family. Doctors also advised those responsible for her treatment to humor her whims, provide her with sedatives so that she could rest, watch her carefully, and give her time to recover.[41] What doctors, then, were recommending was that women be relieved of and removed from the very pressures and responsibilities of motherhood against which they were rebelling. This is precisely the kind of treatment that those in charge of caring for Ayer's friend, Mrs. Webster, followed. Medical authors found that the recovery rates of patients treated in this way were impressive.[42]

Some women, of course, convalesced without either emotional or physical complications after childbirth. Until the 1850s, however, only women of advanced thinking seem to have been in a hurry to assume their regular activities after the experience. Rachel Gleason, a practicing water cure doctor in New York State, wrote of her recovery after the birth of her first child in 1850 that on the day of the delivery she sat up, wrote a letter to her mother, and tended her baby. "Three days after," she remembered, "I rode out, and in a week was about the house as usual." Within a week after her second confinement in 1855, she resumed her medical practice. When the baby was two weeks old, she went into town to deliver another woman's baby and shortly thereafter "went to Livonia and Buffalo to see patients."[43]

Some irregular practitioners, particularly those such as Gleason, who advocated water cure, advised activity after the birth of a child. In 1854 Harriet Hanson Robinson hired a "cold water nurse" to attend her and was able to take a walk in the garden on the fifth day following the birth of her child. She used the cold water treatment every day during her recovery and reported that she "was never so well nor so free from sick days and nights as at this time, no long wearisome confinement[,] no fever, no medicine, not even *castor oil*, all to be attributed to the free and faithful use of *cold water*."[44]

Three years earlier Elizabeth Cady Stanton wrote to a friend that the day after the birth of her fourth son, she got up, bathed herself, and wrote several letters. About eighteen months later she announced to Lucretia Mott that she had delivered her latest baby with only the help of a nurse and a female friend after a short and easy labor. "I sat up immediately, changed my own clothes, put on a wet bandage, and, after a few hours' repose, sat up again." However proud she was of her behavior, Stanton was the first to admit that it was, to say the least, unusual. "Am I not almost a savage?" she wrote to Mott, "for what refined, delicate, genteel, civilized woman would get well in so indecently short a time?"[45]

Stanton was not the only one who realized that some people were likely to view rapid recovery from childbirth as coarse and vulgar. In 1848 Frederick Hollick noted in his midwifery manual that he had known "a lady who, by the adoption of a proper course of training and treatment, passed through her confinement so quickly, and with so little exhaustion, that she was up and travelling about in three days." According to Hollick the woman's friends were horrified by her behavior, considering it *vulgar in the extreme.*" Someone even remarked that "she must be a *very common person, and* no Lady!"[46] Peer pressure was and remained a powerful incentive to postpone resumption of normal activities. In 1864 Elizabeth Cabot wrote to a friend three weeks after the birth of her second child that she had recovered very rapidly after delivery but had stayed upstairs "out of deference to the prejudice" of her friends.[47]

By the 1850s social custom demanded that any genteel woman convalesce for about a month. Typically a postpartum woman would remain immobilized for at least the first week. During the second week she might sit up. Sometime around the third week she could venture downstairs. By the end of the month, she might take her first outing. Women recorded these various activities precisely in their diaries and letters as if to document their steady but well-paced progress toward normality.

Some during this period may have felt a subtle and unconscious tension between their desire to regain their health as fast as possible and their attempt to conform to prevailing custom. In 1860 Bessie Huntting Rudd reported to her concerned but absent husband: "I am improving slowly. Yesterday & to-day I have sat up twice—from 10 till 1—& again from 5–7. . . . I hope to go out in the dining room to tea by Friday." Eight days later she wrote: "Today I rode to the Bridge & it seemed delightful to breathe the fresh air. Oh! how happy I shall be, to get my strength again."[48] With Rudd and no doubt with others, each activity was carefully recorded to provide confirmation that they were both strong enough to survive the trauma of childbirth and genteel enough to need to postpone the resumption of their normal activities.

The letters and diaries of women like Mary Pierce Poor of Bangor, Maine, Mary Rodman Fisher Fox of Philadelphia, Sarah Watson Dana of Boston, and Mary Harris Lester of New York demonstrate the precision with which the various steps toward recovery were recorded. Poor's child was born on November 10, 1842, one week before Thanksgiving. Because she felt too weak to go downstairs, her husband had a table set in her room and joined her there for Thanksgiving dinner. He probably did not share her fare, however, for she ate only a bowl of weak chicken broth. A little over a week later she managed her first visit to the parlor and by November 30 was receiving callers. Like Rudd, she considered her escape from the confines of her home an event of some significance, for she wrote to her sister: "Today is quite an era in my history as I have taken my first walk. . . . It seems like escaping from a prison to be able to breathe the fresh outdoor air once more."[49] Fox, like Poor and Rudd, recorded the stages of her progress toward normality with care. Seven days after the birth of her child in late September 1851, she reported in her diary, "I sat up for a little while today." Three days later she ventured into the nursery for the first time. Eleven days after that she appeared downstairs at dinner. In November she felt strong enough to travel and went to Pittsburgh.[50]

Earlier that year Dana had also borne a child. Nine days after the birth she sat up and had tea in her room with her husband and two of her friends. A little less than two weeks later she was able to take her first drive. One month to the day after the birth of her child, she attended a wedding reception.[51] Mary Harris Lester, like the others, also left a record of the conduct of her recovery. Seven days after the delivery of her child on December 17, 1848, she noted that she was receiving friends. Six days later she sat up for an hour. Two weeks after that she went into another room several times. By the end of January she was able to go out for a short ride.[52]

It is unclear if the recovery patterns of these women reflect any substantial change from those in the eighteenth century. It may very well be that these patterns had prevailed earlier. Historian Catherine Scholten has written that during the period from 1760 to 1825, a woman was, ideally, confined to bed from three to four weeks after the delivery of a child while family members and friends carried out her domestic responsibilities.[53] However, diaries that describe recovery at the turn of the century indicate that some women did not remain in bed as long as Scholten suggests. Molly Drinker Rhoads of Philadelphia, who experienced a particularly difficult delivery in 1797, got up after four days to have her bed made and within the first week was walking about with the help of her nurse.[54] In 1798 Sarah Snell Bryant noted briefly in her diary that the day after the birth of her son, she got out of bed. The next day she was busy making a petticoat for the child. Ten days after giving birth, she went out to visit a friend.[55] Of course, these women may have been exceptions to the general rule. The significance of their behavior, however, may be not that they failed to stay in bed for a prolonged period, but that they showed no concern that their behavior in any way threatened their respectability as it would have done in the 1850s.

Whatever the length of time a woman might spend recovering from childbirth, she needed during that period some practical assistance in caring for herself and her infant and in running her household. In earlier times friends, neighbors, and relatives had provided such services. They could be counted on not only to help the midwife during labor and delivery but also to run the household during the recovery period. By the early decades of the nineteenth century, that practice was changing. Slowly and with an unevenness characteristic of changes in social ritual, affluent women, who could afford to do so, began to replace midwives with doctors to deliver their children and to replace friends and relatives with nurses who would direct their recovery. In the beginning old and new practices overlapped as the case of John and Lucy Pierce demonstrates. In March 1803 Lucy Pierce bore their first child. When Lucy's labor began, her husband sent for two neighbors, traditional sources of support and practical assistance at such a time. He also, however, sent for a doctor and a nurse. Writing to his father-in-law, John Pierce remarked, "Our nurse, Miss Murdock, is with us universally allowed to be the most experienced and skilful woman in the business she has undertaken, whom we have in these parts." After the birth of Pierce's child, the two neighbors continued to come whenever they were called to help the nurse carry out her duties. The nurse, however, remained in charge of Lucy Pierce's recovery.[56]

Historians concerned with the changes in childbirth customs in the early nineteenth century have blamed doctors for discouraging the attendance of friends and relatives at birth.[57] While it is true that some doctors did discourage the practice, there is no reason to assume that middle- and upper-class women stopped asking such people to attend them merely because doctors opposed their presence. A number of other factors may have contributed to this change in custom. For some, geographic mobility may have made it difficult to depend on the comforting presence of old friends and family members who, while they may have been willing to help, were too far away to do so conveniently. Mobility also meant that childbearing women might deliver their infants in the midst of relative strangers who may not have been as welcome in the household as longtime associates. The opportunity to acquire wealth engendered by an urban commercial economy and the beginnings of industrial development combined with an increasing pool of servant labor may have made the tradition of women automatically assuming each other's responsibilities during confinement inappropriate and unnecessary in the middle and upper classes. Affluent women, whose status was somewhat dependent upon their freedom from physical labor, could hire someone to perform domestic services for them and were increasingly doing so partly as testimony to their wealth and social standing. Women who did not perform domestic chores in their own homes were not likely to have been eager to perform such chores for their equally affluent friends, who were perfectly able to hire someone to do them.

The change in the number and character of attendants at birth and during recovery does not necessarily mean, however, that women became less supportive of one another. It may simply indicate that the character of the support they expected from and offered to each other came to be increasingly defined in emotional and ceremonial rather than practical terms. Despite hiring a nurse, some childbearing women continued to look to traditional sources for encouragement and moral support. Mothers were particularly welcome guests at this time, and daughters regretted circumstances that kept them away. Mary Rodman Fisher Fox wrote in 1855 that her sister Sarah rather than her mother had been with her at the time of her delivery and for a week afterward. "I have an excellent nurse and wanted no comfort or kindness," she reported, "but nothing is like a Mother's presence." [58] Julia Ann Hartness Lay agreed. On her son's fifth birthday she remembered the joy she had felt when he was born and her pleasure at being able to share it with her mother. "Five years ago George was put in my arms a little chubby baby," she wrote. "Mother was with me. . . . She helped me and rejoiced over me as I did over my new born babe." [59]

Mothers continued to want to be with their daughters when they gave birth because they worried about their safety. In 1826 Eleanor Parke Custis Lewis wrote to a friend: "I am very anxious to go to Cincinnati this winter to stay with my darling Parke. She expects to become a Mother in January or February, & you cannot imagine how anxious I feel for her safety & how much I wish to be with her at that trying time." She may have found comfort in the fact that Parke Lewis Butler's mother-in-law had engaged the best physician and nurse that she could find. [60]

By mid-century some middle- and upper-class urban women may have stopped asking friends and neighbors to attend them during labor, but it appears to have been the custom for such people to pay their respects soon after the birth of a child. For friends to visit a woman recently delivered was no doubt originally a natural result of their willingness to provide practical assistance during convalescence. Once their services were no longer required, these postnatal visits became ritualized. Benjamin Rush wrote in 1805 that in the 1760s Philadelphia women were "obliged" to dress for company and sit up for four or five hours at a time "every afternoon on the second week after their confinement" to greet visitors. Rush considered their exposure to "the impure air of a crowded room" and "long and loud conversations" detrimental to their health. He was gratified to note that by 1805 the custom of "obliging lying-in women to sit up for company" had been abolished. [61]

The rather formal practice of visiting described by Rush may have declined during the first decade of the nineteenth century in Philadelphia, but the custom of casually calling upon a woman following her delivery continued in other places. Persis Sibley Andrews Black of Paris, Maine, for example, wrote in her journal in 1847: "It has been a matter of surprise with me that so much interest has been manifested by the ladies—*every* married lady in the village having called since I was confined—all classes—ten or twelve who never called before. Something owing to [the] custom of the place perhaps, but I wo'd fain believe the longer we live here the more friends we have." [62] Similarly New Yorker Julia Ann Hartness Lay received twenty-four visitors in the eight days following her delivery in 1855.[63] For such women, friends and neighbors continued to play a supportive role in the childbirth process, but that role was more social than it was practical. For practical help many turned to their monthly nurses.

The practice of hiring a nurse to care for mother and infant for the four weeks after delivery began in the late seventeenth century in places like Boston.[64] But the widespread employment of "monthly nurses," as they were called, seems to have directly paralleled the increasing use of male midwives by the middle and upper classes in the late eighteenth century. The origins of these women are obscure. In England the training of monthly nurses was a response to the demands of urban physicians who desired the presence of someone in the lying-in chamber who could monitor the course of labor and send for them just in time to deliver the infant. In an attempt to meet the needs of physicians practicing obstetrics, and as a result of a desire to provide occupational opportunities for indigent women, British Lying-in Hospital in London began courses for monthly nurses in 1826.[65] There was no comparable educational facility for such nurses in the United States, however. Nor is there any reason to assume that formally trained monthly nurses immigrated to the United States to serve the obstetrical needs of American women and their physicians.

One source from which monthly nurses in this country could have been recruited was from the pool of midwives who were being displaced by physicians. Certainly many of them would have had the skills and experience needed to make them valuable assistants. Indeed, there is some evidence to suggest that doctors sought to relegate them to precisely that role. In a eulogy of William Potts Dewees, an early nineteenth-century physician, Hugh L. Hodge described the way in which Dewees sought to reduce the position of the midwives who called him in to consult in difficult obstetrics cases. Hodge recalled that while Dewees was careful not to "run counter to their prejudices, or apparently act in opposition to their interests," he nevertheless "maintained the supremacy of his profession in immediately taking the case exclusively into his own hands, allowing them no further agency than as mere nurses or assistants."[66] Dewees used a delicate balance of tact and professional presence to undermine the authority of midwives and relegate them to a subordinate position.

While midwives may have been qualified to act as nurses, however, there is no evidence that many of them moved from midwifery into nursing. Such a change would have been difficult for some. Those who were married and had domestic responsibilities of their own would have found the commitment to extended care an impossible one to fulfill. Because of economic need or a sense of public service, midwives may have been willing to abdicate their own domestic obligations to spend a few hours or even days practicing their profession. However, like the doctors who were displacing them, they would not have been prepared to provide constant care for as long as a month. Thus those women who became nurses were probably recruited from among women who had experience in infant care but who for some reason were no longer tied to their own homes and became monthly nurses to support themselves.

As a result of these circumstances, the quality of care that monthly nurses were likely to provide ranged from excellent to deplorable depending on their experience and skill. Elizabeth Sedgwick and Abigail Alcott rated the services of their nurses as good.[67] Mary Askew described a nurse hired by a friend as "good for nothing."[68] Persis Sibley Andrews Black was particularly pleased with the nurse whom she had hired. In 1847 she described Miss H. Chesley as "one of the most skilful & experienced in the State— Aged about 43—healthy & smart & has nursed 200 women—is proud of her calling & has a genuine love for infants that amounts to a passion."[69] Like Black, Elizabeth Cady Stanton wrote glowingly of "Mother Monroe," her sister's monthly nurse. "Full of the magnetism of human love," she was "as wise as she was good, and as tender as she was strong, who had nursed two generations of mothers in our village." According to Stanton she was so gentle that it appeared to an observer that an infant "lay as peacefully in her hands as if they were lined with eider down."[70] Chesley and Monroe were perfectly suited to fulfill their role as surrogate mothers.

Not all nurses lived up to those standards, however. Their failings ranged from minor to serious. Stanton's nurse was deficient only in the sense that she did not compare favorably with Mother

Monroe. "She was very pleasant when she had her own way," wrote Stanton. "She was neat and tidy, and ready to serve me at any time, night or day. She did not wear false teeth that rattled when she talked, nor boots that squeaked when she walked. She did not snuff nor chew cloves, nor speak except when spoken to."[71]

Other women were not quite so lucky in their choice of nurses. Harriet Hanson Robinson wrote in her diary on May 4, 1859, that for eight days following the birth of her son, her recovery had progressed satisfactorily. Then, however, she began "to distrust" her nurse. "Soon found her to be lazy, dirty and ignorant." If it hadn't been for the attentions of her mother, she believed that she would have starved to death.[72] William Whitcher had an equally bad experience with the woman who had been hired to attend his wife during her first confinement. The day after the stillborn delivery of their first child, the nurse called him into his wife's room and complained that her patient was "tossin abute" and speaking "quarely." Miriam Whitcher was delirious. William Whitcher reported that "the ignorant old hussy of a nurse had heated the room to 75 degrees, and placed the lamp where it shone directly onto the bed." Furious about what he considered to be the nurse's incompetence, thoughtlessness, and "brutal treatment," he was determined to discharge her.[73]

Finding a good nurse was very important to childbearing women. Besides providing practical services during delivery and for some weeks afterward, a nurse offered her employers both emotional support and educational services, services that childbearing women had once depended on friends and relatives to provide. Women nervously anticipating the onset of labor found the presence of their nurses reassuring. Elizabeth Dwight Cabot, for example, wrote to her sister as she awaited the birth of her first child: "My nurse is in the house & I like her looks and her behavior. I don't feel as if she would be needed quite yet, but it is a relief to Elliot [her husband] to have her here."[74]

By the 1820s nurses had also begun to play an important role in teaching a newly delivered woman how to care for her child. Such knowledge had in earlier times been passed down from one generation to another within the family when older children were expected to accept responsibility for the care of younger ones under the supervision of their mothers. But while some women like Abigail Alcott were so self-confident about their ability to care for their first child that they were anxious for their nurse to leave,[75] other women were not. Maria D. Brown, for example, remembered her anxiety when she was in a similar situation. "I had grown up among babies and cared for them when only a child myself," she recalled, "and yet I was hardly prepared for the ordeal that awaited me."[76]

A number of factors may have reduced the confidence that young mothers had in their abilities to take care of their babies. As the birthrate declined and the age of first marriage rose, more women grew up in households without the recent experience of having taken care of infant brothers and sisters.[77] As geographic mobility began to separate generations of families from one another, traditional sources of advice and information had to be replaced. A woman's mother or her experienced friends might not have been immediately available to give her advice and practical assistance. The demands of the ideology of motherhood encouraged childbearing women to be self-conscious about improving standards of child care. For women affected by these factors, the most immediate source of information became the monthly nurse, whose reputation, experience, and self-confidence placed her in an ideal position to act as teacher. Her presence in the household for at least a month gave her the opportunity to help the young wife adjust to motherhood.[78]

When childbearing women found a nurse who was particularly experienced and attentive, they showed considerable loyalty to her. Sarah Watson Dana wrote to her mother of her disappointment when she attempted to engage a particular nurse but found that she had applied "just one day too late." She comforted herself by hiring another who had the reputation of being "the most patient and faithful of women."[79] Fanny Longfellow was so pleased with the nurse she had hired to care for her during her first confinement that she continued to seek her services in subsequent confinements. Her determination to employ her was so intense that on one occasion, having applied too late for the services of her Mrs. Blake, she hired another nurse to attend her for a few days only until Blake was free.[80]

A nurse's reputation was important. Between the 1830s and the early 1860s, a woman working as a monthly nurse could earn from

$4.00 to $6.00 a week plus room and board in some localities.[81] This was substantially more than the $.80 to $1.48 average weekly pay that a female domestic might expect to earn in Pennsylvania, New York, or Massachusetts in 1850.[82] However, a nurse's ability to earn a steady income at such rates depended on her reputation for being able to provide quality care. It was in recognition of that fact that Miriam Whitcher tried to convince her husband not to dismiss her nurse. "She is a poor woman," she argued, "and you must not dismiss her for it will spoil her reputation to send her away." Her husband relented on those grounds but was determined that the nurse would remain "only as a supernumerary." He considered the life of his wife too valuable "to be hazarded to save the reputation of so shabby a functionary."[83]

The need to protect their reputation also tended to make nurses sensitive to any attempts to interfere with their normal way of carrying out their responsibilities. Thus when Stanton asked her nurse to stop bandaging her baby, the nurse refused for a number of reasons. But clearly her greatest concern was that if the child should die, her reputation as a nurse would be damaged.[84]

A nurse's relationship with doctors differed considerably from her relationship with her employers. Physicians tended to be suspicious of monthly nurses. Recognizing that nurses could pose a threat to their authority during both delivery and convalescence, doctors carefully defined the position and duties of monthly nurses and prescribed the way those duties were supposed to be carried out.[85] The doctors' ability to control the care of their patients during recovery, however, was difficult. Once the birth process was complete and they had assured themselves that both mother and infant were in no immediate danger, physicians were free to attend to other business after having left instructions for patient care with the nurse.[86] They could not assume, however, that their instructions would necessarily be followed. The nurse was under no economic obligation to obey the doctor's orders since she was employed by the patient's family. Therefore she might feel justified in ignoring the doctor's instructions if she felt that carrying them out would not contribute to the welfare of her patient. This did not necessarily mean that the nurse would openly oppose the doctor. It might mean that in his absence she would simply do as she pleased.

William Potts Dewees and Charles Meigs, two of the leading obstetricians in the country, expressed considerable concern about the degree to which doctors could depend on the nurse's willingness to carry out their instructions. Consequently, they advised their students that it was necessary to keep track of her behavior. Dewees, for example, instructed his students to use their ears, nose, eyes, and sense of touch to detect the "backslidings" of the monthly nurse. Should they suspect that she had ignored their instructions, he urged them "at once, without regard to her experience, or respectability, [to] tax her with disobedience." Both doctors felt that a physician should not hesitate to assert his authority and should consider a nurse's interference an intolerable challenge to the physician's "rights."[87]

Concern for the preservation of rights and privileges also dominated the works of popular authors who wrote about the role of the nurse in the household of childbearing couples. In their stories and essays they testified to the nurse's authority and to the social and domestic strains she imposed on the household of young couples who had only recently become parents. They pictured such couples as completely unprepared to deal with either the practical responsibilities of parenthood or the interference of the monthly nurse in their domestic affairs. Such difficulties arose not only because young parents lacked confidence in their ability to care for an infant but also because they failed to define the limits of their nurse's authority in the household.

Fanny Fern described this problem in "Our First Nurse." As young parents she and her husband, Charles Eldredge, recognized that having a baby involved hiring a nurse. "We had," she remembered, "a vague idea that we must have one, and *as* vague an idea of what a nurse was. We thought her a good kind of creature who understood baby-dom, and never interfered with any little family arrangements."[88] Such a vague set of expectations could work to the advantage of a nurse like Mrs. Jiff, a character described by Fern in *Ruth Hall:* "Mrs. Jiff had not nursed five-and-twenty years for nothing. She particularly affected taking care of young mothers, with their first babies; knowing very well that her chain shortened, with every after addition to maternal experience."[89] Jiff realized that the more a woman knew about the conduct of recovery and infant care, the less authority she would allow the nurse to exert. Without a mistress to restrain her, a nurse could assert her control over the household by ordering other servants about, banishing husband or grandmother from the bedchamber, and exerting dictatorial powers over the fate of the newborn. She could do so because young parents understood that if not given her way, the nurse might leave them alone with their new infant to fend for themselves.

Nurses in popular literature demanded that their employers recognize their claim to privileges, rights, and immunities not normally granted to domestic servants. In the presence of a nurse, even a husband could be forced to abdicate his normal position as head of the household. When Edwin Bettyman in "The Housekeeping Husband" attempted to interfere with the nurse's ministrations, "she vowed to leave the house unless allowed her own way with mother and child."[90] Bettyman had to surrender to her authority. Fern's Charles Eldredge was forced out of his wife's room by a nurse who considered it her prerogative to determine who did and did not enter her domain.[91]

By submitting to the domination and power of the nurse, husbands and wives temporarily abandoned their roles as employers and heads of the household. The more passive among them merely submitted to her authority. The title character in *Ruth Hall*, for example, was completely intimidated by the self-assured and dominating Mrs. Jiff. She was afraid to make any demands on her whatever and silently suffered from her inconsiderate thoughtlessness. Only occasionally did she wonder if she could ask Mrs. Jiff to sleep somewhere other than in her bed, if it would be improper to ask Mrs. Jiff "to take the babe and keep it quiet *part* of the night" so that she could sleep, or if she might request that Mrs. Jiff refrain from polishing her false teeth in her presence.[92]

Somewhat more assertive parents resorted to a kind of psychological warfare designed to undermine the position of the nurse rather than directly challenge her authority. Reduced to a sense of powerlessness by their feelings of parental inadequacy, Sarah and Charles Eldredge were too afraid of losing the services of their nurse to express their resentment of her directly. Instead, they conspired like two schoolchildren against her. Sarah spied on the nurse and reported all of her misdeeds to her sympathetic husband. Tired of her restricted diet of gruel, Sarah had Charles sneak into her bedroom a piece of cake concealed in his coat pocket. When the constant click of the nurse's knitting needles began to wear on Sarah's nerves, her husband stole the offending articles. Eventually Sarah got up enough courage to challenge the authority of the nurse directly and refused to wear a nightcap. Having succeeded in asserting herself at that level, she went further. When the nurse insisted that she put "a sticky pitch-plaster" on her neck to soothe her cough, Sarah "clapped it round the bed-post" in a fit of pique.[93]

Elizabeth Cady Stanton responded to the authority of her nurse in much the same way as did the Eldredges. Her nurse rejected untraditional methods of infant care and refused a direct order from Stanton to desist from wrapping the Stanton infant tightly. "She bandaged the child every morning," wrote Stanton, "and I as regularly took it off. . . . She had several cups with various concoctions of herbs standing on the chimney-corner, ready for insomnia, colic, indigestion, etc., etc., all of which were spirited away when she was at her dinner." Stanton resorted to such tactics, she said, because she felt she needed the help of a nurse and could find no other.[94]

Not only did the nurse feel it was her prerogative to interfere with normal household routine and dictate what sort of care the mother and infant would receive, she was also in a position to disrupt both casual and intimate communication between husband and wife by intruding on their privacy. "The very first thing" the nurse did, wrote Fern in "Our First Nurse," "was to make preparation to sleep in my room, and send Charley off into a desolate spare chamber."[95] In *Ruth Hall* she wrote, "Ruth innocently wondered if it was necessary for the nurse to occupy the same bed with 'her lady.'" Ruth Hall also wondered why, "when Mrs. Jiff paid such endless visits to the kitchen, she was always as fixed as the North Star, whenever dear Harry came in to her chamber to have a conjugal chat with her."[96] In both stories the nurse made it as difficult as possible for husband and wife to carry on even the most casual conversations in private. She was an interloper in their private world.

Nurses were also acknowledged to have the reputation for exposing that private world to other outsiders through their gossip. "It is fearful the amount of gossip these nurses pick up knowing by heart every family in town," wrote Fanny Longfellow in 1845.[97] Fictional nurses displayed the same lack of discretion. Fanny Fern described Mrs. Jiff as spending some of her time "pouring into" the "ready ears" of another servant "whole histories of 'gen'lemen as was n't gen'lemen, whose ladies she nursed,' and how 'nobody but herself knew how late they *did* come home when their wives were sick, though, to be sure, she'd scorn to tell of it.'"[98]

The domestic world of a young couple who had just witnessed the birth of their first child was in a state of flux while husband and wife adjusted to their new roles as parents. Into that world came the monthly nurse uniformly depicted by contemporary authors as annoying, presumptuous, and demanding. That she should have been portrayed in such a way is not surprising. At a superficial level she, like the stereotypical interfering mother-in-law, provided authors with a convenient source of conflict. There may have been, however, a more subtle reason why she was portrayed in this way. She also served as the object against which irritation could be legitimately directed. The insecurity of new parents in the face of unfamiliar responsibilities created a social climate that allowed the nurse to step out of her prescribed role as a domestic servant and establish herself as a dominating influence in a young couple's home. By demanding that employers recognize and submit to her claim to special status, a nurse not only made claims for herself but also made them for the child for whom she was temporarily responsible. Thus, while she may in a real sense have been perceived as a threat to the normal distribution of power within the family and social structure, her presence also served as a metaphor for the role that a couple's first child would play in their lives. After the departure of the nurse, that infant might also make demands on their patience, cause a dramatic readjustment in their household routine, and interfere with their privacy. In a society that made much of the selflessness of the ideal mother, resentment expressed toward an infant would have been considered inappropriate. For that reason authors like Fern transferred whatever resentment the parents might have felt toward their newborn to the nurse, whose presence, like that of the child she cared for, they may have both resented and valued.

As the month of the nurse's tenure slowly passed, a woman who had borne her first child had to learn whatever her nurse could teach her about caring for her infant. The presence of someone who had the reputation for understanding the needs of newborn babies was no doubt very reassuring to insecure and anxious mothers not yet familiar with the intricacies of infant care, and the thought of her imminent departure must have left some women with a special sense of desperation.

Doctors and women alike recognized how dependent an inexperienced mother might be on her nurse. The young mother, wrote William Potts Dewees in the first American pediatrics manual, feels a natural and painful solicitude "when for the first time she is left to her own guidance in the management of herself and child, by the departure of her nurse."[99] The diaries and letters of women who had just borne their first child confirm Dewees's observation. A little over a month after the birth in 1842 of her first child, Mary Pierce Poor wrote: "Friday morning the nurse left me & I felt quite melancholy all day, she was a very pleasant person to have in the house & I felt no care or anxiety about the baby while she stayed. Lucy [a friend] came in Saturday morning & washed and dressed her & this morning I performed the operation myself for the first time, rather awkwardly I fancy."[100] Elizabeth Dwight Cabot expressed similar concerns when she reported to her sister her feelings of "horror and despair" at the thought of her nurse leaving. "I have done everything to the baby," she wrote, "except wash and dress him & he still lives. . . . I have behaved better so far than I expected but shall probably break down when Guin [the nurse] has departed." In 1861 after the birth of her second child, she remembered her anxiety at the departure of the nurse two years before, but she reassured her sister that she did not feel quite so helpless as she had the first time: "I do not expect to kill this little creature, within twenty-four hours of the nurse's departure, which was my only expectation before."[101]

While a young woman's sense of inadequacy after the birth of a second child was probably less than when the first was born, the prospect of caring for an infant and a toddler at the same time might be very disconcerting. Concern about juggling the demands of two small children appeared in popular literature as well as in personal letters. In "A Mother's Wages" by Alice B. Neal, which appeared in *Godey's Lady's Book* in 1857, the fictional Mrs. Cooper convalesced slowly from the birth of her second child. Because her baby had been born earlier than she had expected, a guest, Mrs. Henderson, carried out the services normally performed by the nurse. During her recovery Cooper asked Mrs. Henderson if she were well enough to see her son Johnny, a toddler not yet two years old. Immediately Cooper began to worry about her ability to deal with both children at once, thinking to herself, "How *am* I to manage with *two* children?" She clearly needed the reassurance offered by Henderson, who reminded her that sleeping newborns were not easily disturbed by the presence of noisy brothers and sisters and that by the time they became more conscious of their surroundings, older children could be taught to play quietly.[102]

Elizabeth Dwight Cabot was also worried about her ability to manage two young children, a feat she labeled a "double shuffle." In 1861 after the departure of her monthly nurse, she wrote: "The first few days, I thought would end fatally for me, & [that] I should be found prostrated on the floor, having tumbled on top of the baby, knocking Frank into the fire on the way, in some unsuccessful effort to do something to satisfy both at the same moment. This tragic scene however is still deferred, & I begin to hope may be permanently so, as I find I am becoming hardened to a great many small coincidences." Time and experience made her less anxious and more philosophical, and she stopped feeling that her problems were caused "because I am an idiot & don't know how to manage either of them."[103]

The presence of a nurse in the case of Cabot or guest-turned-nurse in the case of the fictional Mrs. Cooper served to postpone for the experienced mother as well as the novice the assumption of maternal cares. The help and advice that she offered allowed a woman to prepare herself physically and emotionally to assume the responsibility for maneuvering her child safely through the frightening hazards of infancy. The nurse's departure was a sign that both immediate danger and apprenticeship were over. The thread of life of both mother and child no longer trembled. Young wives, now mothers, were on their own.

## Notes

1. Caroline Lee Hentz, *Ernest Linwood: A Novel* (Boston: John P. Jewett, 1856), 180.

2. Thomas Ewell, *Letters to Ladies, Including Important Information concerning Themselves and Infants* (Philadelphia: W. Brown, 1817), 209.

3. C. Croserio, *Homoeopathic Manual of Obstetrics; or, A Treatise on the Aid the Art of Midwifery May Derive from Homoeopathy*, trans. H. Cote (Cincinnati: More, Anderson, Wilstack and Keys, 1853), 79–80.

4. Elizabeth Watson Daggett to Sarah Watson Dana, Sept. 8, 1848, addition to Mary Watson letter, box 15, folder 12, Sarah Watson Dana Letters, Dana Family Papers, Schlesinger Library, Radcliffe College, Cambridge, Mass.

5. Richard Henry Dana, Jr., *The Journal of Richard Henry Dana, Jr.*, ed. Robert F. Lucid, 3 vols. (Cambridge, Mass.: Belknap Press, 1968), 1:355–56.

6. Bessie Huntting Rudd to Edward Rudd, Aug. 1, 1860, box 6, folder 111, Bessie Huntting Rudd Letters, Huntting-Rudd Family Papers, Schlesinger Library.

7. George Templeton Strong, *The Diary of George Templeton Strong: Young Man in New York, 1835–1849*, ed. Allan Nevins and Milton Halsey Thomas (New York: Macmillan, 1952), 348–49; George Templeton Strong diary, Apr. 26, 28, 30, 1849, May 5, 9, 1849, George Templeton Strong Papers, New-York Historical Society, N.Y.

8. While both Kate Ross and Sarah Hill Fletcher developed fever after delivery, they apparently did not suffer from puerperal fever. They both recovered without further complications. Mother Berie to Edward C. Ross, July 31, 1836, Edward C. Ross Letters, Chrystie Family Papers, New-York Historical Society; Calvin Fletcher, *The Diary of Calvin Fletcher, 1817–1838, Including Letters of Calvin Fletcher and Diaries and Letters of His Wife Sarah Hill Fletcher*, ed. Gayle Thornbrough (Indianapolis: Indiana Historical Society, 1972), 260; Samuel Kneeland, "On the Contagiousness of Puerperal Fever," *American Journal of the Medical Sciences*, [n.s.,] 11 (Jan. 1846): 45. There is no evidence to indicate that any of the women in this study suffered from puerperal fever, nor did any specifically mention that they were afraid of contracting the disease.

9. Charles D. Meigs, ed., *The History, Pathology, and Treatment of Puerperal Fever and Crural Phlebitis* (Philadelphia: Ed. Barrington and Geo. D. Haswell, 1842), 2.

10. For descriptions of the symptoms, see William Buchan, *Domestic Medicine; or, A Valuable Treatise on the Prevention and Cure of Diseases* (Leominster:

Adams and Wilder, 1804), 329; Samuel K. Jennings, *The Married Lady's Companion; or, Poor Man's Friend* (New York: Lorenzo Dow, 1808), 158–59.

11. A. C. Baudelocque, "Treatise on Puerperal Peritonitis," *American Journal of the Medical Sciences* 10 (Aug. 1832): 425–30; A. Curtis, *Lectures on Midwifery and the Forms of Disease Peculiar to Women and Children* (Cincinnati: C. Nagle, 1846), 255–56; quotation from Baudelocque, "Treatise," 425.

12. Charles D. Meigs, *On the Nature, Signs, and Treatment of Childbed Fever in a Series of Letters Addressed to the Students of His Class* (Philadelphia: Blanchard and Lea, 1854), 237–75; Meigs, ed., *History, Pathology, and Treatment*, 25–26, 28; Charles D. Meigs and Dr. Rutter to the *Medical Examiner, and Record of Medical Science* 6 (Jan. 21, 1843): 3.

13. Herbert Thoms, *Chapters in American Obstetrics* (Springfield, Ill.: Charles C. Thomas, 1933), 61–62; Theodore Cianfrani, *A Short History of Obstetrics and Gynecology* (Springfield, Ill.: Charles C. Thomas, 1960), 307, 319; Irving S. Cutter and Henry R. Viets, *A Short History of Midwifery* (Philadelphia: W. B. Saunders, 1964), 129–36; Oliver Wendell Holmes, *Puerperal Fever, as a Private Pestilence* (Boston: Ticknor and Fields, 1855), 27, 56–57. This last work is a reprint of the original essay.

14. *Medical Examiner, and Record of Medical Science*, [n.s.,] 6 (Aug. 1850): 481.

15. Meigs, ed., *History, Pathology, and Treatment*.

16. Ibid., 17; Meigs, *On the Nature*, 87, 121, quotation on 112.

17. Charles D. Meigs, *Obstetrics: The Science and the Art* (Philadelphia: Blanchard and Lea, 1856), 636.

18. Frederick Hollick, *The Matron's Manual of Midwifery, and the Diseases of Women during Pregnancy and in Child Bed* (New York: T. W. Strong, 1848), 430. The French obstetrician A. C. Baudelocque estimated that puerperal fever killed four out of five women who died in childbed ("Treatise," 435).

19. Meigs and Rutter to the *Medical Examiner*, 3. Due to lack of statistics, it is unclear how many incidents of puerperal fever appeared in cases handled by midwives during this period.

20. Gouverneur Emerson, "Medical Statistics: Being a Series of Tables, Showing the Mortality in Philadelphia, and Its Immediate Causes, during a Period of Twenty Years," *American Journal of the Medical Sciences* 1 (Nov. [1827]): 145, 149; Gouverneur Emerson, "Medical Statistics; Consisting of Estimates Relating to the Population of Philadelphia, and Its Changes As Influenced by the Deaths and Births, during a Period of Ten Years, Viz. from 1821 to 1830 Inclusive," *American Journal of the Medical Sciences* 9 (Nov. 1831): 26, 43; Gouverneur Emerson, "Vital Statistics of Philadelphia, for the Decennial Period from 1830 to 1840," *American Journal of the Medical Sciences*,

[n.s.,] 16 (July 1848): 22; Gouverneur Emerson, "Bill of Mortality of Philadelphia for the Year 1833," *American Journal of the Medical Sciences* 15 (Nov. 1834): 267–74.

21. J. Curtis, "Public Hygiene of Massachusetts; but More Particularly of the Cities of Boston and Lowell," *Transactions of the American Medical Association* 2 (1849): 541–42.

22. Samuel L. Mitchell, "Summary View of the Modes by Which Human Life Terminates in the City of New-York; Digested from the Bills of Mortality, Kept by Order of the Common Council, for 1804, 1805, and 1806," *Medical Repository*, [2d ser.,] 5 (May, June, July 1807): 36, 38; Samuel L. Mitchell, "Abstracts from the Bills of Mortality Kept in the City of New-York, during 1807 and 1808," *Medical Repository*, [3d ser.,] 1 (Feb., Mar., Apr. 1810): 337, 338, 342.

23. Emerson, "Vital Statistics," 18, 22.

24. Hugh L. Hodge, "Cases and Observations regarding Puerperal Fever, As It Prevailed in the Pennsylvania Hospital in February and March, 1833," *American Journal of the Medical Sciences* 12 (Aug. 1833): 327.

25. Emerson, "Medical Statistics" (1827), 117; Mitchell, "Summary," 32; Curtis, "Public Hygiene," 493.

26. Meigs, *On the Nature*, 35. An identical observation was made in Britain in 1870. Noting the panic created when a woman in childbed died of puerperal fever, J. Matthews Duncan wrote that the doctor and nurse were blamed. "Hence for their own reputation's sake, as well as with the charitable motive of not alarming all the pregnant women in the community, the death is imputed to any other possible cause than to the dreaded puerperal" (*On the Mortality of Childbed and Maternity Hospitals* [Edinburgh: Adam and Charles Black, 1870], 7–8).

27. Meigs, *On the Nature*, 103.

28. Roy Finney, *The Story of Motherhood* (New York: Liveright, 1937), 212, 248; Richard W. Wertz and Dorothy C. Wertz, *Lying-in: A History of Childbirth in America* (New York: Free Press, 1977), 125, 126; Cianfrani, *Short History*, 311, 313.

29. Sarah Ripley Stearns diary, Mar. 8, 1818, Stearns Collection, Schlesinger Library.

30. Elizabeth Dwight Cabot to Ellen Dwight Twistleton, June 19, 1859, sec. 2, box 2, folder 18, Elizabeth Dwight Cabot Letters, Hugh Cabot Family Collection, Schlesinger Library.

31. Sarah Connell Ayer, *Diary of Sarah Connell Ayer* (Portland, Maine: Lefavor-Tower, 1910), 269–70.

32. Fleetwood Churchill, *On the Theory and Practice of Midwifery* (Philadel-

phia: Lea and Blanchard, 1843), 511; Fleetwood Churchill, "On the Mental Disorders of Pregnancy and Childbed," *American Journal of Insanity* 7 (Apr. 1851): 303–4.

33. Richard Gundry, "Observations upon Puerperal Insanity," *American Journal of Insanity* 16 (Jan. 1860): 305.

34. James MacDonald, "Puerperal Insanity," *American Journal of Insanity* 4 (Oct. 1847): 143; Gundry, "Observations," 302.

35. Gundry, "Observations," 294–95.

36. Ibid., 303; Theodore Helm, "On Puerperal Diseases," *Eclectic Journal of Medicine* 2 (Aug. 1838): 367; Robert Lee, *Lectures on the Theory and Practice of Midwifery* (Philadelphia: Ed. Barrington and Geo. D. Haswell, 1844), 528–29.

37. MacDonald, "Puerperal Insanity," 147. See also Gundry, "Observations," 308; Dr. Bell, "Insanity Connected with the Puerperal State," *Boston Medical and Surgical Journal* 30 (Apr. 17, 1844): 228; John Burns, *The Principles of Midwifery, Including the Diseases of Women and Children* (Philadelphia: Hopkins and Earle, 1810), 366.

38. Benjamin Rush, *Medical Inquiries and Observations upon the Diseases of the Mind* (Philadelphia: Kimber and Richardson, 1812), 18–19, 185–87.

39. MacDonald, "Puerperal Insanity," 152; Samuel B. Woodward, "Observations on the Medical Treatment of Insanity," *American Journal of Insanity* 7 (July 1850): 26–27; Churchill, "On the Mental," 315; Pliny Earle, "Bloodletting in Mental Disorders," *American Journal of Insanity* 10 (Apr. 1854): 330, 339; Lee, *Lectures*, 529; M. Esquirol, "On the Mania of Lying-in Women and Nurses," *Medical Repository*, [4th ser.,] 6 (1820): 174; Burns, *Principles,* 366; Churchill, *On the Theory,* 512.

40. Esquirol, "On the Mania," 169–70; MacDonald, "Puerperal Insanity," 117; J. H. Worthington, "On Puerperal Insanity," *American Journal of Insanity* 18 (July 1861): 43; J. R. Cormach, "Tendency to Insanity at Childbirth," *Medical Examiner, and Record of Medical Science* 7 (Mar. 23, 1844): 70–71; R. G. Hill, "Moral Treatment of Insanity," *Eclectic Journal of Medicine* 4 (Dec. 1839): 54.

41. Lee, *Lectures*, 530; Burns, *Principles*, 367; MacDonald, "Puerperal Insanity," 162; Churchill, *On the Theory*, 513; Dr. Winn, "Puerperal Mania," *American Journal of the Medical Sciences*, [n.s.,] 29 (Apr. 1855): 541–43; Worthington, "On Puerperal Insanity," 59; Ewell, *Letters*, 237.

42. MacDonald, "Puerperal Insanity," 152; Gundry, "Observations," 314–17; Worthington, "On Puerperal Insanity," 53; A. T. H. Waters, "On the Use of Chloroform in the Treatment of Puerperal Insanity," *American Journal of Insanity* 13 (Apr. 1857): 342; Churchill, "On the Mental," 309; Thomas

Denman, *An Introduction to the Practice of Midwifery* (Brattleborough, Vt.: William Fessenden, 1807), 431.

43. Rachel Brooks Gleason, "Reminiscences of Early Life," 63, 71, privately held by Barbara Bush Wells.

44. Harriet Hanson Robinson diary, Oct. 6, [1854,] Robinson–Shattuck Papers, Schlesinger Library.

45. Theodore Stanton and Harriot Stanton Blatch, eds., *Elizabeth Cady Stanton As Revealed in Her Letters, Diary, and Reminiscences*, 2 vols. (New York: Harper, 1922), 2:26, 44–45.

46. Hollick, *Matron's Manual*, v.

47. Elizabeth Cabot, *Letters of Elizabeth Cabot*, 2 vols. (Boston: privately printed, 1905), 2:20.

48. Bessie Huntting Rudd to Edward Rudd, July 11, 19, 1860, box 6, folder 111, Bessie Huntting Rudd Letters.

49. Mary Pierce Poor diary, Nov. 10, 17, 28, 30, 1842, Dec. 7, 1842, box 6; Mary Pierce Poor to John and Lucy Pierce, Nov. 26, 1842, box 6, folder 89; Mary Pierce Poor to Feroline Pierce Fox, Dec. 10, 1842, addition to Dec. 4 letter, box 12, folder 167, Mary Pierce Poor Letters, Poor Family Collection, Schlesinger Library.

50. Mary Rodman Fisher Fox diary, Sept. 28, 1851, Oct. 5, 8, 19, 25, 1851, Nov. 1851, box 13, folder 30, Logan-Fisher-Fox Papers, Historical Society of Pennsylvania, Philadelphia.

51. Sarah Watson Dana diary, Jan. 3, 12, 25, 1851, Feb. 3, 1851, Dana Family Papers.

52. Mary Harris Lester diary, Dec. 17, 24, 30, 1848, Jan. 14, 30, 1849, Andrew Lester Papers, New-York Historical Society. See also Strong, *Diary*, ed. Nevins and Thomas, 353–54.

53. Catherine M. Scholten, "'On the Importance of the Obstetrick Art': Changing Customs of Childbirth in America, 1760–1825," *William and Mary Quarterly* 34 (July 1977): 434.

54. Cecil K. Drinker, *Not So Long Ago: A Chronicle of Medicine and Doctors in Colonial Philadelphia* (New York: Oxford University Press, 1937), 56–57.

55. Sarah Snell Bryant diary, July 12, 13, 14, 22, 1798, Houghton Library, Harvard University, Cambridge, Mass.

56. John Pierce to Benjamin Tappan, Mar. 7, 1803, box 1, folder 8, Poor Family Collection.

57. Carl N. Degler, *At Odds: Women and the Family in America from the Revolution to the Present* (New York: Oxford University Press, 1980), 58; Scholten, "'On the Importance,'" 443.

58. Fox diary, Mar. 27, 1855, Logan-Fisher-Fox Papers.

59. Julia Ann Hartness Lay diary, June 10, 1855, Rare Books and Manuscripts Division, Astor, Lenox and Tilden Foundations, New York Public Library. For other mention of the presence of mothers, see Harriet Conner Brown, *Grandmother Brown's Hundred Years, 1827–1927* (Boston: Little, Brown, 1929), 93, 94; A. F. Wedd, ed., *The Fate of the Fenwicks: Letters to Mary Hays* (London: Methuen, 1927), 143.

60. Eleanor Parke Custis Lewis to Elizabeth Bordley Gibson, Oct. 28, 1826, Dec. 1, 1826, Eleanor Parke Custis Lewis Letters, Historical Society of Pennsylvania.

61. Benjamin Rush, "The Comparative State of Medicine in the Revolutionary Era," in *The Rising Glory of America, 1760–1820*, ed. Gordon S. Wood (New York: George Braziller, 1971), 221, 226.

62. Persis Sibley Andrews Black journal, Apr. 8, 1847, in *Victorian Women: A Documentary Account of Women's Lives in Nineteenth-Century England, France, and the United States*, ed. Erna Olafson Hellerstein, Leslie Parker Hume, and Karen M. Offen (Stanford: Stanford University Press, 1981), 219.

63. Lay diary, Nov. 23, 1855. See also Lester diary, Dec. 17, 24, 1848, Andrew Lester Papers; Ann E. Porter, "Cousin Helen's Baby," *Godey's Lady's Book* 39 (Oct. 1849): 236.

64. Lyle Koehler, *A Search for Power: The "Weaker Sex" in Seventeenth-Century New England* (Urbana: University of Illinois Press, 1980), 117; Mary Beth Norton, *Liberty's Daughters: The Revolutionary Experience of American Women, 1750–1800* (Boston: Little, Brown, 1980), 139.

65. Jean Donnison, *Midwives and Medical Men: A History of Inter-Professional Rivalries and Women's Rights* (London: Heinemann Educational Books, 1977), 51–53.

66. Hugh L. Hodge, *An Eulogium of William P. Dewees, M.D., Delivered before the Medical Students of the University of Pennsylvania, November 5, 1842* (Philadelphia: Merrihew and Thompson, 1842), 16.

67. Elizabeth Ellery Sedgwick journal, 1826, 33, Houghton Library; Abigail Alcott to Samuel May, Mar. 27, 1831, box 1, folder 25, Abigail May Alcott Letters, Alcott Family Papers, Houghton Library.

68. Mary Brown Askew diary, Jan. 26, 1861, Historical Society of Pennsylvania.

69. Black journal, May 9, 1847, in *Victorian Women*, ed. Hellerstein, Hume, and Offen, 219.

70. Elizabeth Cady Stanton, excerpt from *Eighty Years and More*, in *Victorian Women*, ed. Hellerstein, Hume, and Offen, 226–27.

71. Ibid., 227.

72. Robinson diary, May 4, 1859, box 4, Robinson-Shattuck Papers.

73. William Whitcher to Alice, Apr. 2, 1848, Frances Miriam Berry Whitcher Letters, Whitcher Collection, New-York Historical Society.

74. Elizabeth Dwight Cabot to Ellen Dwight Twistleton, Aug. 20, 1861, sec. 2, box 2, folder 20, Elizabeth Dwight Cabot Letters. See also Edward Wagenknecht, ed., Mrs. *Longfellow: Selected Letters and Journals of Fanny Appleton Longfellow (1817–1861)* (New York: Longmans, Green, 1956), 112; Mary Pierce Poor to Lucy Pierce Hodge, Aug. 17, 1853, box 12, folder 126, Mary Pierce Poor Letters.

75. Abigail May Alcott to Samuel May, Mar. 27, 1831, box 1, folder 25, Abigail May Alcott Letters. Anticipating the "interesting" and "delightful" prospect of taking care of her first child, Alcott wrote to her brother during her confinement, "I am at times most impatient to dismiss my nurse that not even she should participate with me in this pleasure."

76. Brown, *Grandmother Brown's Hundred Years*, 93.

77. Yasukichi Yasuba, *Birth Rates of the White Population in the United States, 1800–1860: An Economic Study* (Baltimore: Johns Hopkins, 1962), 135, 137; Degler, *At Odds*, 184.

78. The nurse in early nineteenth-century America performed a function similar to that of the "doula" described by anthropologist Dana Raphael. The role of the doula was to introduce the mother to her new role, to assist her in accepting and acquiring her position as a mother (Dana Raphael, "Matrescence, Becoming a Mother, a 'New/Old' *Rite de passage*," in *Being Female: Reproduction, Power, and Change*, ed. Dana Raphael [The Hague: Mouton, 1975], 68).

79. Sarah Watson Dana to Mary Marsh Watson, Dec. 16, 1845, box 15, folder 7, Sara Watson Dana Letters.

80. Wagenknecht, ed., Mrs. *Longfellow*, 112, 174; Fanny Appleton Longfellow to Mary Appleton Mackintosh, Dec. 31, 1845, Frances Elizabeth Appleton Longfellow Papers, Longfellow National Historic Site, National Park Service, Cambridge, Mass.

81. Kate Ross of Ft. Hamilton, Long Island, paid her nurse $4.00 per week in 1836. Kate Ross to Edward C. Ross, Aug. 9, 1836, Edward C. Ross Letters. In the Boston area Elizabeth Dwight Cabot paid her nurse $6.00 per week in 1861. Elizabeth Dwight Cabot to Ellen Dwight Twistleton, Sept. 9, 1861, sec. 2, box 2, folder 20, Elizabeth Dwight Cabot Letters.

82. J. D. B. DeBow, *Statistical View of the United States* (Washington, D.C.: Beverley Tucker, 1854), 164.

83. William Whitcher to Alice, Apr. 2, 1848, Frances Miriam Berry Whitcher Letters.

84. Stanton, excerpt from *Eighty Years*, 226.

85. Burns, *Principles*, 241; Michael Ryan, *The Philosophy of Marriage in Its Social, Moral, and Physical Relations* (London: H. Bailliere, 1839), 289–90; William P. Dewees, *A Compendious System of Midwifery* (Philadelphia: Carey and Lea, 1826), 191.

86. The presence of a physician was probably very sporadic at best after the birth of a child, particularly if there were no complications or reasons to be concerned. Michael Ryan advised his colleagues to return twelve hours after delivery (*Philosophy of Marriage*, 305). John Burns agreed (*Principles*, 328). James Hamilton advised the doctor to return to any patient "in the better ranks" within a few hours and then daily until the patient recovered. He also advised that among the "lower ranks" the number of visits should be adapted to the "circumstances" of the patient. It should be noted, however, that he believed that a conscientious doctor should feel obliged to pay more than one postpartum visit (*Practical Observations on Various Subjects Relating to Midwifery*, 2 vols. [Philadelphia: A. Waldie, 1837–38], 2:6). All of the doctors offering specific advice on this matter were British. American authors did not address this issue in their texts and manuals. There is no reason to suppose that the attitudes of American doctors differed substantially from their British counterparts in this matter. Only one letter used in this study mentioned the doctor visiting frequently during the recovery period. See John Pierce to Benjamin Tappan, Mar. 7, 1803, box 1, folder 8, Poor Family Collection.

87. Dewees, *Compendious System*, 204; Meigs, *Obstetrics*, 364. Doctors were not the only ones concerned about the willingness of nurses to prescribe and treat without a doctor's authorization. See Drinker, *Not So Long Ago*, 56.

88. Fanny Fern, "Our First Nurse," in *Fresh Leaves* (New York: Mason and Bros., 1857), 47–48.

89. Fanny Fern, *Ruth Hall: A Domestic Tale of the Present Time* (New York: Mason and Bros., 1855), 42.

90. Py Angele De V. Hull, "The Housekeeping Husband," *Graham's Magazine* 36 (Apr. 1850): 276.

91. Fern, "Our First Nurse," 48.

92. Fern, *Ruth Hall*, 42–43.

93. Fern, "Our First Nurse," 49–50.

94. Stanton, excerpt from *Eighty Years*, 226.

95. Fern, "Our First Nurse," 48.

96. Fern, *Ruth Hall*, 42–43.

97. Fanny Appleton Longfellow to Mary Appleton Mackintosh, Dec. 31, 1845, Frances Elizabeth Appleton Longfellow Papers.

98. Fern, *Ruth Hall*, 42.

99. William P. Dewees, *Treatise on the Physical and Medical Treatment of Children* (Philadelphia: Carey and Lea, 1825), 88–89.

100. Mary Pierce Poor to Lucy and John Pierce, Dec. 18, 1842, continued from Dec. 15 letter, box 6, folder 89, Mary Pierce Poor Letters.

101. Elizabeth Dwight Cabot to Ellen Dwight Twistleton, Mar. 22, 1859, sec. 2, box 2, folder 18; and Oct. 20, 1861, continued from Oct. 14 letter, sec. 2, box 2, folder 20, Elizabeth Dwight Cabot Letters.

102. Alice B. Neal, "A Mother's Wages," *Godey's Lady's Book* 55 (July 1857): 37–38.

103. Elizabeth Dwight Cabot to Ellen Dwight Twistleton, Nov. 9, 1861, sec. 2, box 20, folder 20, Elizabeth Dwight Cabot Letters.

## 4

# "What to Do with a Baby": Attitudes toward Infant Nurture

IN 1842 ELIZABETH CADY STANTON observed that when some of her acquaintances were for the first time faced with the problem of "what to do with a baby," they made the mistake of taking "it for granted that the laws governing" an infant's "life, health, and happiness are intuitively understood, that there is nothing new to be learned in regard to it." Stanton was convinced that the ability to care for an infant had little to do with instinct and that a little common sense combined with judicious use of the advice offered by self-appointed child care authorities could help parents guide their children safely through the hazards of infancy.[1]

As people became convinced that the welfare of children depended as much on careful management as on intuition or divine providence, some parents began to feel overwhelmed with a sense of inadequacy. Beset by self-doubt, Abigail Alcott, for example, wrote to her brother in 1833: "It seems to me at times as if the weight of responsibility connected with these little mortal beings would prove too much for me—Am I doing what is right? Am I doing enough? Am I not doing too much? is my earnest inquiry."[2] Alcott's anxiety about her ability to carry out her maternal role may have been unduly exaggerated, but it was not unusual.

Concerned about the difficulty of ensuring the physical, emotional, and spiritual well-being of children, Alcott's contemporaries frequently used the term "awful" to describe parental responsibilities. In 1812 Henry Lee wrote to his wife that "in the management and education of children, there is an awful responsibility upon parents."[3] Twenty-eight years later Calvin Fletcher described his duties to his children in precisely those same terms.[4] Child care experts used the term in their efforts to impress upon women the importance of their role as mothers. Every woman should early in life "convince herself, that an awful responsibility is attached to the title of 'mother,'" warned William Potts Dewees in his pediatrics manual.[5] Their words did not fall on deaf ears. Even before her first child was born, Fanny Longfellow admitted she found the "awful responsibility" of motherhood intimidating.[6]

There were good reasons for women like Alcott and Longfellow to have felt that their efforts to fulfill their maternal obligations might prove inadequate. Biology and tradition placed the burden of the physical care of infants on women. But in the early nineteenth century, the ideology of motherhood bestowed on childbearing women increasing responsibilities for the moral and political nurture of children as well as for the stability of the family and the happiness of its members. The result was that the private decisions that women made regarding the care of their babies took on increased significance.

Mothers were not without resources in their attempts to fulfill their obligations. When instinct or experience failed them, they could depend on advice from friends, relatives, and child care experts. More empirical than it was scientific, that advice was designed to control the decisions they made by establishing ideal standards for judging maternal behavior. Much of it did not allow for the fact that their success in caring for their children was dependent upon many things over which they had little control. They were expected to provide their babies with a healthy prenatal environment. After birth they had to ensure an adequate food supply, nurture their babies through the discomforts and dangers they believed were likely to accompany the teething process, protect their children against and nurse them through various childhood illnesses, and then wean them without damaging their emotional and physical health. They had to do all this in an age in which, according to contemporary estimates, it was likely that one baby in four would die in places like New York before it reached the age of one.[7] Given public expectations and the infant mortality rate, the joys of motherhood were tempered by a good deal of anxiety, guilt, frustration, and fear.

143

Contemporary child care experts were quick to point out that the responsibilities of motherhood began during gestation. Thomas Bull wrote that a woman "must consider herself a mother . . . from the first moment of its [a child's] conception, and that from that moment her duties commence."[8] John Eberle assured women that both maternal instinct and moral obligation required that they do everything necessary "to protect the nascent being" while it was in the womb.[9] The womb was, in Michael Ryan's opinion, much like a laboratory where mothers carried out their maternal responsibilities by providing the proper prenatal environment for fetal development.[10]

While authors of advice literature and medical texts all agreed that the conduct of a mother during gestation had a profound influence on both the physical and emotional development of her unborn child, they knew very little about fetal development and did not always agree about which things were most likely to pose the greatest threat to the well-being of a fetus. Particularly controversial was the question of whether maternal impressions such as unrelieved desires or emotional shocks during pregnancy could affect the proper physical development of a child. Medical journals were filled with articles like the one that appeared in the *Medical Examiner* describing the case of a woman who, frightened by a bear during pregnancy, bore a child with clawlike hands and an excessive amount of bodily hair.[11]

As early as 1800 some regularly trained physicians began to regard as dysfunctional the idea that deformed children resulted when pregnant women were exposed to sudden shocks or were refused some indulgence. For one thing they felt that the persistence of this idea made it difficult for regular doctors to establish the scientific respectability of their branch of medicine. John Goulding wrote in the *Boston Medical and Surgical Journal* that the idea was "as contrary to reason and to all scientific principles, as that a horse-shoe nailed over the door will secure the occupants of the house from witchery."[12] Doctors also opposed the idea because they felt it contributed to the anxiety experienced by a woman during pregnancy. As early as 1800 Valentine Seaman maintained that it did not matter if the idea was true or false. He believed that doctors had a "duty to discourage the idea" in order to "save women from many an anxious thought, and many an hour of distress." [13]

Despite their efforts, however, doctors found this ancient folk belief hard to dispel. While they claimed the idea was unscientific, they could provide no other convincing explanation for the physical deformities of some newborn children. [14] Moreover, while medical writers sought to suppress the belief, nonmedical writers short-circuited their efforts by continuing to present the idea as fact. In 1841 Frederick A. Rauch, an intellectual interested in the study of psychology, stated categorically that a person's physical makeup could be determined by "a fright of the mother during pregnancy, or the sight of any disagreeable or deformed person." [15] Fourteen years later Henry C. Wright, the author of advice manuals, wrote that "society abounds with facts to show that the psychological, no less than the physiological conditions of the mother during Gestation, may and do affect the child, often producing deformities, in the shape of marks on the skin, the absence of a hand, or arm, or foot, or an incomplete or unnatural development of some part of the body." While he recognized that physicians rejected this idea, his conversations with mothers had convinced him that since there were so many unexplained examples of the phenomenon, the idea must be valid. [16]

While the specific issue of the influence of maternal impressions was not of immediate concern to middle- and upper-class women, they did worry a great deal about the prenatal physical development of their children and were afraid of bearing deformed or dead babies. Miriam Whitcher, for example, wrote to her sister that she hardly dared hope that she might become the mother of a "*living* and *perfect* child." [17] Similarly, mothers who had just given birth expressed great relief that their babies were not deformed in some way. Julia Ann Hartness Lay was not the only one to feel herself "well repaid" for hours of suffering when she gazed at the "perfect and faultless form" of her baby. [18]

Not all women were as fortunate as Lay. In 1836 a friend of Arabella Carter reported that the baby she had been expecting was born dead. The child had apparently been strangled in the womb by the umbilical cord three or four days before birth. The stillbirth of her child was particularly regrettable to her because it left her with the sense that she had somehow failed. "If it could only have been brought into the world alive and then been taken away I think [I] could have parted with it with pleasure in comparison to my present feelings," she wrote. [19]

When Mary Pierce Poor bore a son with a harelip, she felt equally distressed. Concerned about his appearance, she and her husband quickly made arrangements to send him under the care of his nurse into Boston to have his deformity repaired by Dr. J. Mason Warren, a surgeon. In the letters she wrote after his birth, she described her response to what she considered to be a great trial. Worried about the danger of the operation and the need to send her child to Boston during the coldest part of the year, she wrote to her parents in November that she missed her baby so much that she almost wished he had died when he was born so that she would not have become so attached to him. Angry and afraid, she tried to comfort herself with the thought that having a physically deformed child was better than having a morally deformed one. "Still," she wrote, "I cannot help wishing my children to be beautiful, for it seems to me that it is likely to have a bad effect upon the character of a child to feel a sense of inferiority to others in outward attractions." Ultimately, she comforted herself with the belief that, despite feeling "most dreadfully about him" at first, "such things are beyond our control." She found it consoling to blame Providence rather than herself for her child's condition. When the infant returned from Boston, Poor found his appearance so improved that she believed the defect was only barely noticeable to the casual observer. [20]

Once her child was born, a mother had to guarantee her baby a suitable and adequate source of food. There were three possible ways of feeding a baby: maternal breast-feeding, wet-nursing, or hand-feeding. [21] Doctors and child care experts did everything they could to convince mothers that both nature and society demanded that they breast-feed their infants. By stressing the physical, psychological, and social benefits to be derived from nursing, they sought to persuade mothers who were affluent enough to hire a wet nurse or to feed their babies by bottle or cup to obey "natural law" and carry out what doctors considered to be one of motherhood's most important obligations.

Nursing, they pointed out, had physical implications for both mother and child. Emphasizing the benefits of providing an infant with its natural source of food, doctors warned that a child, deprived of its mother's milk, would suffer "inconvenience" and deteriorating health, a situation that was more than likely to result in its death.[22] They also charged that mothers who refused to nurse their babies were guilty of stifling their own maternal yearnings and the dictates of nature and in doing so increased their own susceptibility to disease, their likelihood of bearing unhealthy children, or their chances of finding themselves barren.[23]

Doctors and popular writers also argued that nursing was important for establishing the basis for familial affection. It helped to preserve a mother's love for her baby, to develop in a baby love for its mother, and to solidify love between husband and wife. "It is well known," wrote Michael Ryan in his manual on marriage, "that when children are committed to the care of mercenary nurses, maternal love and tenderness diminish, or almost cease."[24] Similarly Thomas Bull claimed that suckling was "plainly intended to cherish and increase the love of the parent herself, and to establish in the dependent and helpless infant from the first hours of its existence those associations on which its affection and confidence afterwards will be most securely founded."[25] Another author described nursing as "a natural way of cementing the matrimonial tie."[26]

Doctors were especially critical of self-indulgent mothers who abdicated their nursing responsibilities because they considered breast-feeding troublesome or because they resented the confinement that nursing entailed, a confinement that prevented them from enjoying themselves and fulfilling their social obligations outside the home. According to John Bright, "She, who, for the pleasure derived from a party, can deprive her child of the food which nature had ordained for its use, is unworthy of the enduring title of mother."[27] William Buchan charged that any woman who refused to nurse her child lacked "conjugal love, fidelity, modesty, chastity, or any other virtue."[28] Male physicians were deeply suspicious of any interest that had the potential for distracting women from their maternal obligations. They viewed any abdication of those responsibilities as morally delinquent, selfish, and socially disruptive.

Yet they did recognize that there were legitimate reasons for a mother to choose alternative methods of feeding her baby. If she was ill, if she was unable to provide the child with sufficient milk of high quality, or if she suffered from the symptoms of "nervousness," doctors advised a mother to refrain from nursing.[29] Doing so under such circumstances served in their opinion the best interests of both the mother and child.

If a mother decided that she could not breast-feed her baby or did not want to do so, she had at least two alternatives. One was to feed her child sweetened, diluted milk from a cup or bottle.[30] As the nineteenth century progressed, technology made it easier for mothers to use this method. Nursing bottles were widely available in urban pharmacies by 1820. In 1845 Elijah Platt of New York patented a rubber nipple that eventually replaced the ones made of pewter, ivory, or silver. And by the 1860s a commercial baby formula was available.[31] Despite such technological advances, however, authorities like Charles Meigs of Philadelphia continued to consider bottle-feeding risky.[32]

The other alternative was to hire a wet nurse. Wet-nursing does not appear to have gained the same popularity in America that it did in Europe. In the colonial period wet-nursing was most likely to have been used immediately following birth while the mother recuperated from delivery or among women who believed there was something in a mother's milk that had toxic effects on a newborn.[33] The evidence concerning the use of wet nurses by middle- and upper-class urban women in early nineteenth-century America is inconclusive. While the writers of advice literature discouraged it, newspapers published advertisements for wet-nursing services, and the directors of maternity hospitals such as New York's Asylum for Lying-in Women sent ex-patients as wet nurses into middle- and upper-class homes.[34]

There was a variety of ways to go about employing someone to nurse a child. When called on short notice to find a wet nurse for a friend, Elizabeth Dwight Cabot simply went into a working-class neighborhood and invaded *"four* Irish mansions" to raise "a nurse and a woman to take her baby."[35] In 1850 Harriet Beecher Stowe, in poor health and unable to provide milk for her new son, hired a young Irish girl who appeared one day at her door. The woman had recently lost her baby and needed employment.[36] Another method of hiring a wet nurse was to make arrangements with the matrons of a lying-in hospital to hire one of the patients who promised to provide wet-nursing services after her delivery. Jeannie McCall wrote to her husband in the late 1840s that she intended "to go out to the lying-in Hospital to find a nurse."[37] Those who wished to engage a wet nurse no doubt preferred this method since hospitals like New York's Asylum for Lying-in Women screened their patients before they recommended them for positions as wet nurses. In 1852 the managers of the asylum noted in their annual report that "the usefulness of the Society in supplying the demand for nurses is greatly on the increase. Indeed such has been the preference for nurses from the Asylum, from the confidence in the community that none will be recommended who are not virtuous and healthy, that they are frequently engaged previous to their confinement."[38] Proud that they were able to serve the interests of the middle-class community by ensuring that respectable but indigent women would receive medical attention during confinement and an opportunity to find employment afterward, the hospital managers continued to note in their annual reports the number of their patients who served as wet nurses following delivery.[39]

Even though a mother might provide her infant with an adequate food supply, the child could be expected to suffer from any number of physical ailments during its first year or so. The teething process was particularly worrisome. Elizabeth Ellery Sedgwick wrote in her journal in 1825 that the period of teething was "filled with terror to a mother's imagination" and that she "had looked forward to it with unceasing anxiety."[40] Doctors contributed to the concern about teething by defining it as a disease, or as a condition that predisposed an infant to disease, or as a condition that aggravated disease already present. At the very least teething was looked upon as a period of considerable suffering and potential danger.[41] In the 1820s and 1830s medical statisticians frequently listed teething as a cause of death.[42] And Fanny Longfellow wrote in 1847 of a friend who had lost a baby as a result of what she described as "rapid teething."[43] Some doctors even estimated that as many as one in six babies who died did so as a result of the complications that accompanied teething.[44]

Concerned about the discomfort that a child often had to endure during dentition and the changes in temperament that might accompany that discomfort, parents were anxious to find ways of making their children more comfortable. The most commonly employed treatment for such problems was to lance the gums and give the child something hard to chew on. Small articles made of wood, bone, coral, ivory, or hard rubber were among the recommended items.[45] Maria D. Brown's treatment conformed to generally accepted standards. "All of my children cut their teeth on one of the Mexican dollars Dan'l brought back from New Orleans," she remembered long after her children were grown. But one of her children had had a particularly difficult time cutting his teeth. "I just took my penknife," she recalled, "wound it with thread all but the point (so that, if my hand slipped, I couldn't cut him), and then, while he slept one day, took him on my knee and lanced his gums."[46] Less self-sufficient women called in a physician to perform this procedure. Having taken the precaution of removing her baby from Philadelphia to the country, where it would have the benefit of being exposed to the "pure air," Anna Colton Clayton became concerned about the effect of teething on her daughter's health during the summer of 1848. After trying a number of unspecified home remedies, she finally sent for a local doctor, who lanced the baby's gums and prescribed a cooling medicine.[47]

Some mothers, dissatisfied with the treatment normally prescribed and worried about their children's continuing discomfort during teething, were tempted to use patent medicines advertised in local newspapers. A friend of Agnes Treat Lamb Richards wrote in 1839 to inquire whether Richards had rubbed her baby's gums with anything, adding that her own nurse had "just read something highly recommended in the newspaper" that she thought might help. She hesitated to use it, however, because she did not know anyone who had tried the remedy and feared to do so until she was able to get more information about the product.[48] Other mothers were not so cautious. Three days after recording in her diary that her infant son was "quite sick with his teeth," Julia Ann Hartness Lay marched out and purchased a bottle of "Mister Carlson's wild cherry" to assuage his discomfort.[49]

While infants under the age of one could certainly be expected to suffer from teething and were believed to be particularly susceptible to the ravages of such diseases as whooping cough, croup, scarlet fever, and measles during their first year, the one illness that appears to have caused the greatest anxiety to parents and doctors alike was cholera infantum or summer complaint. Often fatal, this disease was most likely to attack infant children during the hot summer months. Fatalities from the disease were so high that one doctor called it "this grand exterminator of our infantile population."[50]

The medical community did not know what caused this illness, which began with diarrhea and vomiting and often ended with the death of a dehydrated and emaciated infant. Empirical observation encouraged physicians to believe it was caused by a combination of factors, including improprieties in food and clothing as well as the effects of teething and hot weather.[51]

Doctors also had no effective way to treat the disease. Their sense of helplessness when confronted with a case of cholera infantum was dramatically demonstrated in the early career of J. Marion Sims. Having just returned to his home in Lancaster, South Carolina, after graduating from Jefferson Medical College in Philadelphia in 1835, Sims was called to attend an eighteen-month-old child suffering from the discomforts of teething and chronic diarrhea. After examining his patient, Sims lanced its gums but admitted years later in his memoirs that at the time he had no idea "what ailed the child, or what to do for it." He hurried back to his office and immediately consulted his copy of John Eberle's textbook on the diseases of children. Turning to the section on cholera infantum, he read it over and over again and concocted various prescriptions to stay the course of the disease. Unfortunately, his treatment failed and the child died. When he attended the funeral, he felt himself to be the "chief mourner." "Certainly its father and mother did not feel so badly over the loss of their child as I did at the loss of my first patient," he wrote.[52]

Since doctors could do nothing to minimize the effects of summer temperatures and could only superficially relieve the discomfort that accompanied the teething process, they tended to advise that parents protect their children from the possibility of contracting summer complaint by removing them from the city for the duration of the summer.[53] Just as affluent parents in the 1940s and 1950s fled to rented cottages in the summer to protect their children from the ravages of polio, so did well-to-do early nineteenth-century parents flock to the countryside between July and September to protect their children from the life-threatening influences of the urban environment.

While there was little that mothers could do to safeguard their babies from infectious disease, they had somewhat more control over the timing and method of weaning their children. Making the decision to wean their babies was very difficult for some women. Harriet Hanson Robinson was particularly candid when she described her feelings about this matter. "Dear little Hattie," she wrote on January 6, 1852, "I have begun to wean her. I have never [hand] fed her any before. She is most fourteen months old." Seven days later she wrote, "Baby weans nicely. She dont seem to mind it much." On January 20 she considered the job accomplished. "The baby has been weaned," she wrote in her diary. "Two days and nights now. She does not seem to mind it much. She did not wake but once last night. Willie [her husband] laughed when I told him. He said weaning was nothing but a *bug bear* after all. Truely it has been for me for I have dreaded it ever since she was born."[54] Other women indirectly testified to their feelings of anxiety at the prospect of weaning by expressing surprise at the ease with which their children accepted being denied access to the breast.[55]

That many women worried about weaning their children, that they felt at the very least ambivalent about it, or even, as in the case of Robinson, dreaded the prospect can be attributed to a number of physical, psychological, and social factors. First, some people believed that weaning could place the health of a child in jeopardy. William Lloyd Garrison, for example, was convinced that the premature weaning of his daughter had weakened her resistance to disease and was therefore a contributing cause to her death from a lung ailment.[56]

Secondly, some women hesitated to wean their babies because they believed that as long as they continued to nurse, they were less likely to become pregnant. "Many women," wrote Michael Ryan in 1839, "suckle for fourteen or twenty months to prevent pregnancy." Some women he had known continued to nurse for up to three years to control their fertility.[57]

Other women postponed weaning because nursing was a source of physical pleasure for them. Niles Newton and Michael Newton have noted in their study of nursing that the response of a female's body to lactation is physiologically similar to its response to coitus. In both cases the uterus contracts, the nipples become erect, and skin changes occur. The contraction of the uterus is particularly significant since this involuntary movement can produce orgasm.[58]

While it is unlikely that the male doctors who wrote about breast-feeding in their texts and popular health manuals were aware of this particular physiological response to lactation, they clearly recognized that nursing mothers could derive real joy from feeding their children. In 1804 William Buchan promised mothers that they would experience "a sweet, thrilling, and delightful sensation" and an "exquisite sense of wedded joy" when they carried out their natural function of nursing their children.[59] In 1825 William Potts Dewees assured mothers that the self-gratification they would experience when their babies suckled was equal to no other "earthly pleasure." This pleasure, he went on to say, was not just social in nature but a "positive pleasure derived from the act itself."[60] Doctors also recognized that weaning could bring an end to such pleasure. In his *Mother's Medical Guide* published in 1844, John Bright acknowledged, perhaps without fully understanding what he was saying, that a woman might feel a sense of loss when she weaned her baby. Weaning, he wrote, could be "a period of much anxiety to the mother, and shows, plainly, the pleasure she has had in suckling the child."[61]

Another reason why nursing mothers did not look forward to weaning their babies was that the process could be very uncomfortable. One source of discomfort was the unrelieved pressure that the milk placed on the breasts. Gertrude Meredith wrote that she was weaning her son gradually because such a method had the advantage of causing her less pain than the abrupt method.[62] A friend of Agnes Treat Lamb Richards wrote that she hoped to postpone her child's weaning because she had so much milk that she did not look forward to the discomfort that weaning would cause her.[63] A second source of physical discomfort, particularly when a woman abruptly weaned a small infant, was what modern authorities call milk fever. Women suffering from this ailment experienced flulike symptoms such as fever, chills, and loss of energy. While this illness lasted for only three to four days and normally indicated only that the body was absorbing the milk products back into the system, it was nevertheless uncomfortable.[64]

Some nursing women may have been ambivalent about weaning their children because nursing was important to them psychologically. The ability to nurse a baby was a source of power. Many middle- and upper-class women lived in a social environment that clearly made them dependent on men for social, economic, and legal status. Only in the domestic sphere were they granted power and some degree of autonomy. Nursing a baby gave them the opportunity to enhance their self-esteem by allowing them to do something men could not do, sustain the life of their child. For those who appreciated nursing as a source of power, weaning would have brought with it a feeling of loss.

Weaning also had profound social significance for mothers. When a woman weaned her child, and particularly if she did so within the first year, she assumed in a rather dramatic way responsibility for the moral training of her baby. From the birth of her infant to the time of weaning, a mother's influence on her child tended to be benign and indulgent. She expected and was expected to meet her infant's demands and provide the child with whatever was necessary for its physical comfort. The weaning process represented a mother's first explicit attempt to force her child to submit to her authority and to acknowledge its own social responsibilities. During the weaning process the mother intentionally frustrated her child's desires. Weaning served as a first step in teaching a child that self-denial was a way that human beings had developed to enable them to live in a group, that social order was based on the sacrifice of the individual for the benefit of others.

While they did not describe the social function of weaning in precisely these terms, some women did recognize weaning as a form of deprivation for which they were responsible. Gertrude Meredith explained her preference for gradual weaning by referring to the "comfort" that she was taking away from her son.[65] Julia Ann Hartness Lay wrote that she had been successful in weaning her son but was "sorry" to have deprived him of "so much comfort."[66] And

Elizabeth Ellery Sedgwick feared that in weaning her child she had denied it totally of its pleasure.[67]

The desire to remain indulgent, to postpone the assumption of a disciplinary role that put a mother's will in direct conflict with that of her child, might have been enough to encourage a mother to postpone weaning as long as possible. Such concerns appear to have motivated Martha Coffin Wright to prolong breast-feeding her son. In a letter to Lucretia Mott, she wrote that as she lay in bed listening to the rain falling against the windows and waiting for her two-year-old to wake and make his usual demands on her, she wondered why she did not wean him—because it seemed "cruel" to her she decided, and because it was so much easier to nurse him and "poke him back into his crib" than to fight with him or "'sit up on ends,'" as she called it, and run the risk of waking her other son upstairs. After bearing six children, she still dreaded "weaning the poor little botherations" because they took "so much comfort in nursing."[68] For women who felt as Wright did, weaning represented an unwelcome change in their relationship with their children.

Because of their concern about weaning their children, nursing women deliberated carefully about the timing of the event and the method they would use. When they were ready, various sources of advice were available to them. Although the field of pediatrics was not yet well established, both regular and irregular physicians were prepared to instruct mothers about the timing and preferred method of weaning children. They were unanimous in their belief that weaning should take place after a child reached the age of nine months and certainly by the time it was a year old. They also tended to agree that gradual weaning was the best method. Nevertheless, they recognized the need to be flexible in the matter in order to accommodate the needs of both mother and child. They recommended, for example, that mothers anticipating the need to wean their children should consider its impact on their own health as well as that of their children. Doctors also advised that mothers should take into consideration the quality as well as the quantity of the breast milk available to their children before they decided that the weaning process should begin. Because teething was believed to place considerable strain on the health of the child, they recommended that weaning not take place during the first process of teething. Finally, doctors sought to discourage weaning during the summer months when young children were particularly susceptible to cholera infantum.[69]

Prescription and practice were similar. Mothers adhered to no hard-and-fast rules regarding weaning and took various factors into consideration before they began the process. Mary Rodman Fisher Fox, for example, decided it was time to wean her child when she found the need to wake during the night to nurse increasingly "troublesome."[70] Others weaned their children because of pressure from family and friends, because they believed their milk supply was inadequate, because they were in poor health, or because they believed that for some reason their breast milk was injurious to their baby's health.[71] Still others decided to wean their infants because they simply felt it was time to do so.[72] Some began the process for a combination of reasons. In 1826, for example, Elizabeth Ellery Sedgwick resolved to wean her baby shortly after birth because he was in good health, because she did not have what she considered an adequate supply of milk, because her friends encouraged her to do so, and because her monthly nurse had agreed to return to help care for the child.[73]

Having decided to begin the weaning process, mothers then had to select the best method for doing so. In the early colonial period, mothers typically separated themselves from their children abruptly. By the eighteenth century, however, the method used by American mothers varied. Some separated themselves from their babies while others adopted a more gradual approach.[74] Both patterns continued into the first half of the nineteenth century, but for some women abrupt weaning was beginning to fall into disfavor because they believed it caused unnecessary trauma to their children. In letters and diaries women expressed concern about the effect that abrupt weaning had on their children's physical and emotional health. When Gertrude Meredith wrote to tell her husband that she had indeed begun to wean their son, she assured him that she was doing it "by degrees." One reason for doing so was that she believed the abrupt weaning may have damaged the health of her older daughter. "It is certainly much better to wean the dear little creatures by degrees than to take so great a comfort from them all at once, as I did from my dear little Gertrude—who is playful and seems well, but does not look so," she wrote.[75]

Lucy Buffum Lovell also expressed dissatisfaction with the abrupt method. When her daughter was about fourteen months old, she left her upstairs with her aunt while she spent the day downstairs. "Towards night I went up and took her," she wrote. "She asked to nurse but did not cry much and soon got down on the floor and began to play. She was easily weaned, seeming to understand that she could not nurse again." Lovell was glad that the process was accomplished with so little difficulty but continued to worry about the effects of such deprivation on her daughter's emotional development. She wrote that for more than a month afterward the little girl cried every time her mother moved away from her. Lovell attributed such disturbing behavior to "my leaving her all day when I weaned her" and was determined never to advise any mother to wean her child in that way.[76]

The problems that mothers in the early nineteenth century faced in keeping their babies alive through infancy differed very little from those that had been faced by other women since the beginning of time. Throughout history an infant's hold on life was tenuous. Estimates of infant mortality in the early nineteenth century suggesting that almost one quarter of all children born every year died before they were one only confirmed what most parents already knew. The probability was great that at least one, if not several, of their children would die in infancy.

Parents were fairly realistic about their chances of losing a child and tended to describe their babies' hold on life as tentative. Anna Colton Clayton, for example, wrote to her husband of the pleasure she felt in her new role as a mother, but she felt compelled to assure him, "I don't forget—she is not wholly ours."[77] Mary Pierce Poor likewise wrote to her parents in 1842, "I do wish you could all see the darling, & if she lives & all is well, I intend you shall see her next spring."[78] John Pierce wrote to his father-in-law, "Often I think when doting upon her, how uncertain is her continuance."[79] While none of their children were in any immediate danger, these parents did not feel comfortable assuming that their infants would be spared when so many others were dying. They were willing to contemplate the deaths of their children because they were afraid not to. To some extent fear had always conditioned the way parents felt about their children. Before the eighteenth century, according to Philippe Aries and others, parents attempted to protect themselves from the reality of infant death by maintaining a detached attitude that bordered on indifference. Efforts to maintain emotional distance from infant children continued well into the nineteenth century.[80] But while there is evidence to suggest that some parents tried in this way to protect themselves from the pain that the loss of a baby might bring, it is not at all clear that their efforts were very successful. In his study of attitudes in New England toward children, Peter Slater found that many seventeenth-century Puritan parents were unable to remain indifferent to the deaths of their infants, and Mary Beth Norton found that parents in the late eighteenth century were as likely as not to mourn deeply the loss of a young child.[81]

Parents in the first half of the nineteenth century were not any more successful than their predecessors in maintaining distance from their infant children. Their fear of losing their babies did not effectively diminish the degree of affection they felt for them. Elizabeth Graeter's emotional commitment to her young son could not have been more complete. "At times, my heart would sink without him," she wrote.[82] Mary Rodman Fisher Fox felt essentially the same way about her child: "In my baby I possess a source of pleasure unallayed even by the anxiety which ever attends any thing so much beloved."[83] Mary Pierce Poor acknowledged that at any time her baby might be removed and expressed serious reservations about the extent to which she thought it safe to commit herself to it. She wrote to her sister, "Do you think I can love her *too* much?" Her concerns were not strong enough to prevent her from making a strong commitment, however. "I do not believe in loving *too* much," she said in answer to her own question.[84]

Loving their children yet fearing they might die placed tremendous emotional strain on mothers. One of the ways they dealt with that strain was to try to prepare themselves for the eventuality that their babies were likely to die. Mary Ann Palfrey wrote of her eight-month-old daughter, "My affections are but too much fixed on her and for my own comfort . . . I daily strive to repress the engrossing fondness I feel for her."[85] Even Mary Pierce Poor, who was willing to commit herself totally to her newborn child, recognized the need to prepare herself for the possibility that God might remove "these objects of our affection from us."[86] Like Poor, Mary Irwin admitted attachment to her baby and at the same time acknowledged her emotional defenselessness. "You judge rightly," she wrote to Eliza Pitkin, "that he is very dear to me. I cannot steadily contemplate the idea of losing him, but my Dear sister do you think this inconsistent with a Christian spirit. . . . I have never expected strength to be resigned to the death of a dear child."[87]

Those with deeply held religious convictions responded somewhat differently to the possibility of losing their infants. Suspicious of the love they felt for their children, they feared that maternal affection was a temptation that placed the life of their child as well as their own spiritual and emotional well-being at risk. Their God was a jealous God unprepared to share with an infant the love that was his due. In 1826, for example, Millicent Hunt grew concerned about what she called her "astonishing impiety." The love she felt for her child made her "forget the Giver," she wrote. "I feel that child possesses *all* my love, that child has weaned my heart from God." Some months later she returned to the same subject: "Too dearly do I love him. Alas I tremble lest my God who will not accept a divided heart should snatch from me this little object of my love."[88] Peggy Dow, the wife of an evangelical Methodist minister, had similar fears: "I found my heart was too much set upon it [her infant daughter], so that I often feared I should love her too well; but strove to give myself and all that I had to my God." After the death of this child in infancy, she wrote that she realized that her separation from the babe was for her own good. "I often felt my heart too much attached to it, so much that I feared it would draw my heart from my duty to God! O the danger of loving any creature in preference to our Savior!"[89] Susan Huntington felt so strongly that deep love for a child could place both its earthly fate and a mother's soul in jeopardy that when she wrote to congratulate a friend on the birth of a son, she felt compelled to issue the following warning: "Beware, my dear friend, of making him your idol. Possibly you might have done this with your first babe. If you did, and God loves you, as I trust he does, you can easily see the 'need be' there was for its removal."[90] The belief that maternal love could jeopardize one's soul was also suggested in popular literature. In an article appearing in a popular religious magazine, a grieving parent admitted that she found comfort in the belief that one of the missions of an infant in this world was to lead its parents to recognize their "worldliness" as represented by the love they felt for their children.[91]

Both of these responses to the possibility of infant death were a form of anticipatory grief, which served as a defense mechanism by preparing parents for an event as painful as it was probable. Both were predictable in a transitional age that on the one hand held that God was ultimately responsible for the fate of humans and on the other was beginning to believe that the application of knowledge and technology could affect the human condition. These two responses met the needs of people who believed that a mother's job was to keep her baby alive and well and at the same time knew that there was little she could do to prevent its death. To blame excessive love for threatening the life of a child was a way of letting a mother off the hook while catching her in a double bind. On the one hand it acknowledged the degree of her attentiveness and the adequacy of her care and thus testified to her competency and her commitment to the ideology of motherhood. On the other hand it held that the degree to which a mother was willing to invest time, energy, and affection in a child placed its very life in jeopardy. It allowed her to preserve her self-esteem while it testified to her vulnerability.

## Notes

1. Elizabeth Cady Stanton, excerpt from *Eighty Years and More*, in *Victorian Women: A Documentary Account of Women's Lives in Nineteenth-Century England, France, and the United States*, ed. Erna Olafson Hellerstein, Leslie Parker Hume, and Karen M. Offen (Stanford: Stanford University Press, 1981), 224.

2. Abigail May Alcott to Samuel May, June 22, 1833, box 1, folder 25, Abigail May Alcott Letters, Alcott Family Papers, Houghton Library, Harvard University, Cambridge, Mass. See also Eleanor Parke Custis Lewis to Elizabeth Bordley, Mar. 23, 1806, Eleanor Parke Custis Lewis Letters, Historical Society of Pennsylvania, Philadelphia.

3. Frances Rollins Morse, ed., *Henry and Mary Lee: Letters and Journals with Other Family Letters, 1802–1860* (Boston: T. Todd, 1926), 116.

4. "I sometimes fear that I do not appreciate the awful importance of the relation of parent and child" (*The Diary of Calvin Fletcher, Including Letters to and from Calvin Fletcher*, ed. Gayle Thornbrough [Indianapolis: Indiana Historical Society, 1973], 188).

5. William P. Dewees, *Treatise on the Physical and Medical Treatment of Children* (Philadelphia: Carey and Lea, 1825), xi.

6. Edward Wagenknecht, ed., *Mrs. Longfellow: Selected Letters and Journals of Fanny Appleton Longfellow (1817–1861)* (New York: Longmans, Green, 1956), 107.

7. Samuel L. Mitchell, "Abstracts from the Bills of Mortality Kept in the City of New-York, during 1807 and 1808," *Medical Repository*, [3d ser.,] 1 (Feb., Mar., Apr. 1810): 336. It is difficult to determine the mortality rate for children under the age of two in the early nineteenth century. Contemporary estimates, for example, usually compared the death of children under the age of one to all those who were dying in the same year rather than comparing them to all those who were born in the same year. See Ansel W. Ives, "Review of Ticknor's Philosophy of Living," *Literary and Theological Review* 3 (June 1836): 285 n.; Charles A. Lee, "Medical Statistics; Comprising a Series of Calculations and Tables, Showing Mortality in New York, and Its Immediate Causes, during a Period of Sixteen Years," *American Journal of the Medical Sciences* 19 (Nov. 1836): 46; Andrew Combe, *Treatise on the Physiological and Moral Management of Infancy* (Boston: Saxton and Kelt, 1846), 24. The most that can be said about this matter is that doctors were concerned about what they viewed as a high infant mortality rate. Modern studies are not much more helpful. They usually provide information on the mortality of children aged five and under. See Maris A. Vinovskis, "Mortality Rates and Trends in Massachusetts before 1830," *Journal of Economic History* 32 (Mar. 1972): 195–201; Richard Alan Meckel, "The Awful Responsibility of Motherhood: American Health Reform and the Prevention of Infant and Child Mortality before 1913" (Ph.D. diss., Brandeis University, 1982), 238–39.

8. Thomas Bull, *The Maternal Management of Children, in Health and Disease* (Philadelphia: Lindsay and Blakiston, 1853), 16–17. Popular nonmedical authors concurred with these sentiments. See Lydia H. Sigourney, *Letters to Mothers* (New York: Harper and Bros., 1840), 27; M. U. L., "The Sphere of Woman," *Monthly Religious Magazine* 8 (Feb. 1851): 64; Henry C. Wright, *The Unwelcome Child; or, The Crime of an Undesigned and Undesired Maternity* (Boston: Bela Marsh, 1858), 20–21.

9. John Eberle, *A Treatise on the Mental and Physical Education of Children* (Cincinnati: Corey and Fairbank, 1833), 1.

10. Michael Ryan, *The Philosophy of Marriage in Its Social, Moral, and Physical Relations* (London: H. Bailliere, 1839), 54.

11. L. Slusser, "Influence of the Imagination of the Mother upon the Foetus," *Medical Examiner, and Record of Medical Science*, [n.s.,] 8 (June 1852): 344–46. For other examples, see Benjamin Taylor, "Remarkable Effect of a Pregnant Mother's Imagination," *Medical Respository*, [2d ser.,] 3 (May, June, July 1805): 89; L. P. S., "Influence of Maternal Feelings—Acephalous Child, etc.," *Boston Medical and Surgical Journal* 24 (Mar. 10, 1841): 72–73; S. L. Kerr, "Mental Influence of Mother on Foetus in Utero Exerted through Two Successive Pregnancies," *American Journal of the Medical Sciences*, [n.s.,] 34 (July 1857): 285–86.

12. John Goulding, "Embryotic Influences," *Boston Medical and Surgical Journal* 16 (July 5, 1837): 347–48. Goulding's opinions were echoed by A. Parker in "Maternal Influences of the Mind on the Foetus," *Boston Medical and Surgical Journal* 18 (Mar. 14, 1838): 92–95.

13. Valentine Seaman, *The Midwives Monitor and Mothers Mirror* (New York: Isaac Collins, 1800), 76. See also Dewees, *Treatise*, 26.

14. *Medical Repository* 4 (1801): 305–6; Dewees, *Treatise*, 31–32.

15. Frederick A. Rauch, *Psychology; or, A View of the Human Soul, Including Anthropology* (New York: M. W. Dodd, 1841), 160.

16. Henry C. Wright, *Marriage and Parentage* (Boston: Bela Marsh, 1855), 88–89. See also Mrs. Hester Pendleton, *Parent's Guide for the Transmission of Desired Qualities to Offspring, and Childbirth Made Easy* (New York: Fowler and Wells, 1856), 128–29.

17. Miriam Whitcher to Alice, [Mar. 1848,] Frances Miriam Berry Whitcher Letters, Whitcher Collection, New-York Historical Society, N.Y.

18. Julia Ann Hartness Lay diary, late Mar. or early Apr. 1853, Rare Books and Manuscripts Division, Astor, Lenox and Tilden Foundations, New York Public Library. See also Mary Rodman Fisher Fox diary, Mar. 27, 1855, box 13, folder 30, Logan-Fisher-Fox Papers, Historical Society of Pennsylvania; and Abigail May Alcott to Samuel May, Mar. 27, 1831, box 1, folder 25, Abigail May Alcott Letters.

19. Frances to Arabella Carter, Jan. 14, 1836, box 1, folder 6, Timothy Carter Papers, Maine Historical Society, Portland, Maine.

20. Mary Pierce Poor to Lucy and John Pierce, Nov. 19, 28, 1848, box 7, folder 95; Mary Pierce Poor to Laura Stone Poor, Feb. 24, 1849, box 12, folder 182; Mary Pierce Poor to Lucy and John Pierce, Jan. 13, 1849, box 7, folder 96, Mary Pierce Poor Letters, Poor Family Collection, Schlesinger Library, Radcliffe College, Cambridge, Mass.

21. Charles D. Meigs, *Obstetrics: The Science and the Art* (Philadelphia: Blanchard and Lea, 1856), 708–9.

22. Ryan, *Philosophy of Marriage*, 46.

23. Ibid.; William Buchan, *Advice to Mothers on the Subject of Their Own Health* (Philadelphia: John Bioren, 1804), 76; Dewees, *Treatise*, 49.

24. Ryan, *Philosophy of Marriage*, 46.

25. Bull, *Maternal Management*, 25. See also A. Curtis, *Lectures on Midwifery and the Forms of Disease Peculiar to Women and Children* (Cincinnati: C. Nagle, 1846), 291.

26. "Maternal Affection," *Lady's Monitor* 1 (Mar. 13, 1802): 238.

27. John W. Bright, *The Mother's Medical Guide* (Louisville: A. S. Tilden, 1844), 242–43. See also Bull, *Maternal Management*, 27.

28. Buchan, *Advice*, 169–70. See also Eberle, *Treatise*, 30; and Dewees, *Treatise*, 49.

29. Eberle, *Treatise*, 33; H. B. Skinner, *The Female's Medical Guide and Married Woman's Advisor* (Boston: Skinner, 1849), 37–38; Combe, *Treatise*, 156.

30. Combe, *Treatise*, 150; Skinner, *Female's Medical Guide*, 39; Ryan, *Philosophy of Marriage*, 273.

31. Robert Sunley, "Early Nineteenth-Century American Literature on Child Rearing," in *Childhood in Contemporary Cultures*, ed. Margaret Mead and Martha Wolfenstein (Chicago: University of Chicago Press, 1955), 154; Carl N. Degler, *At Odds: Women and the Family in America from the Revolution to the Present* (New York: Oxford University Press, 1980), 79; Ernest Caulfield, "Infant Feeding in Colonial America," *Journal of Pediatrics* 41 (Dec. 1952): 684; T. G. H. Drake, "American Infant Feeding Bottles, 1840–1946, As Disclosed by United States Patent Specifications," *Journal of the History of Medicine and Allied Sciences* 3 (Autumn 1948): 510.

32. Meigs, *Obstetrics*, 695.

33. Caulfield, "Infant Feeding," 675; Lyle Koehler, *A Search for Power: The "Weaker Sex" in Seventeenth-Century New England* (Urbana: University of Illinois Press, 1980), 114; Ruth H. Bloch, "American Feminine Ideals in Transition: The Rise of the Moral Mother, 1785–1815," *Feminist Studies* 4 (June 1978): 104.

34. Sunley, "Early Nineteenth-Century American Literature," 154. Mary Beth Norton's research indicates that most American women did not hire wet nurses in the late eighteenth century (*Liberty's Daughters: The Revolutionary Experience of American Women, 1750–1800* [Boston: Little, Brown, 1980], 90); *Twenty-sixth Annual Report of the Managers of the New York Asylum for Lying-in Women*, Mar. 29, 1849, 5, New York Hospital–Cornell Medical Center Archives, N.Y. Northern women may have been more likely than their southern counterparts to use wet nurses as a convenience. Evidence from southern sources indicates that middle- and upper-class women in the South

were self-consciously committed to breast-feeding their own children and turned to wet nurses only when it was absolutely necessary. See Sally Mc-Millen, "Mothers' Sacred Duty: Breast-Feeding Patterns among Middle- and Upper-Class Women in the Antebellum South," *Journal of Southern History* 51 (Aug. 1985): 333–56.

35. Elizabeth Dwight Cabot to Ellen Dwight Twistleton, Apr. 8, 1861, sec. 2, box 2, folder 20, Elizabeth Dwight Cabot Letters, Hugh Cabot Family Collection, Schlesinger Library.

36. Harriet Beecher Stowe to Sarah Beecher, Dec. 17, [1850,] box 3, folder 94, Harriet Beecher Stowe Letters, Beecher-Stowe Collection, Schlesinger Library.

37. Jeannie McCall to Peter McCall, Oct. 27, [late 1840s,] Jeannie McCall Letters, McCall Section, Cadwallader Collection, Historical Society of Pennsylvania.

38. *Twenty-ninth Annual Report of the Managers of the New York Asylum for Lying-in Women*, Apr. 15, 1852, 5.

39. *Thirtieth Annual Report of the Managers of the New York Asylum for Lying-in Women*, Apr. 14, 1853, 5; *Thirty–second Annual Report of the Managers of the New York Asylum for Lying-in Women*, Apr. 12, 1855, 5–6; *Thirty-fourth Annual Report of the Managers of the New York Asylum for Lying-in Women*, Apr. 16, 1857, 3.

40. Elizabeth Ellery Sedgwick journal, 1825, Houghton Library.

41. Dewees, *Treatise*, 283, 304; Thomas Ewell, *Letters to Ladies, Including Important Information concerning Themselves and Infants* (Philadelphia: W. Brown, 1817), 256. Dewees described the symptoms of teething as increased salivation, irritation of the gums, running nose, slight fever, diarrhea, and fretfulness (*Treatise*, 179–81).

42. Teething is listed as a cause of death in the mortality statistics published in the *American Journal of the Medical Sciences* 5 (Nov. 1829): 256–61; 10 (May 1832): 265–66; 12 (May 1833): 265–72; 15 (Nov. 1834): 267–74. See also Gouverneur Emerson, "Medical Statistics: Being a Series of Tables, Showing the Mortality in Philadelphia, and Its Immediate Causes, during a Period of Twenty Years," *American Journal of the Medical Sciences* 1 (Nov. [1827]): 149.

43. Wagenknecht, ed., *Mrs. Longfellow*, 126.

44. Dewees, *Treatise*, 304.

45. Ibid., 308; Samuel K. Jennings, *Married Lady's Companion; or, Poor Man's Friend* (New York: Lorenzo Dow, 1808), 209; Skinner, *Female's Medical Guide*, 46; Curtis, *Lectures on Midwifery*, 323–24.

46. Harriet Conner Brown, *Grandmother Brown's Hundred Years, 1827–1927* (Boston: Little, Brown, 1929), 96–97.

47. Anna Colton Clayton to John Clayton, July 7, [1848,] Anna Colton Clayton Letters, John Clayton Papers, Historical Society of Pennsylvania.

48. Elizabeth to Agnes Treat Lamb Richards, Dec. 9, 1839, case 40, Agnes Treat Lamb Letters, Lamb Papers, New-York Historical Society.

49. Lay diary, Dec. 11, 14, 1851.

50. D. Francis Condie, *A Practical Treatise on the Diseases of Children* (Philadelphia: Lea and Blanchard, 1847), 83; quotation from A. J. Fuller, "Report on Treatment of Cholera Infantum," *Transactions of the American Medical Association* 9 (1856): 485.

51. Dewees, *Treatise*, 396–97; Eberle, *Treatise*, 287, 289; Fuller, "Report," 487; "Popular Medical Observations," *Family Magazine* 5 (1838): 67. In the early twentieth century this disease was called summer diarrhea and was thought to be caused by contaminated food or poor hygiene, which acted to lower the resistance of young children to both bacteria and viruses. The high death rate was due to the inability to prevent dehydration. In the 1940s a technique of administering fluids into the body of an infant through needles inserted either into the veins or under the skin was perfected. The ability to regulate the body fluids of young children enabled doctors to prevent serious dehydration, and the death rate from this disease declined. Raymond L. LaDriere, M.D., St. Louis, interview, July 1983. See also Thomas E. Cone, Jr., *History of American Pediatrics* (Boston: Little, Brown, 1979), 74.

52. J. Marion Sims, *The Story of My Life* (New York: D. Appleton, 1884), 140–45. The text to which Sims referred was probably Eberle, *Treatise*.

53. Edward Miller, "Remarks on the Cholera, or Bilious Diarrhoea of Infants," *Medical Repository* 1 (1800): 65; Dewees, *Treatise*, 407; Eberle, *Treatise*, 298.

54. Harriet Hanson Robinson diary, Jan. 6, 13, 20, 1852, box 4, Robinson-Shattuck Papers, Schlesinger Library.

55. Ann Jefferis Sheppard to Martha Jefferis, July 5, 1843, Ann Jefferis Sheppard Letters, Jefferis Family Letters, Chester County Historical Society, West Chester, Pa.; Gertrude Meredith to William Meredith, Aug. 30, 1800, Sept. 4, 1800, Gertrude Meredith Letters, Meredith Papers, Historical Society of Pennsylvania; Malcolm R. Lovell, ed., *Two Quaker Sisters: From the Original Diaries of Elizabeth Buffum Chace and Lucy Buffum Lovell* (New York: Liveright, 1937), 56; Lucy Tappan Pierce to John Pierce, Sept. 17, 1805, box 1, folder 4, Lucy Tappan Pierce Letters; Sedgwick journal, 1824.

56. William Lloyd Garrison, *The Letters of William Lloyd Garrison: No Union with Slave-Holders, 1841–1849*, ed. Walter Merrill (Cambridge, Mass.: Belknap Press, 1973), 555.

57. Ryan, *Philosophy of Marriage*, 277. Recent medical research has shown

that lactation does seem to inhibit the return of fertility by postponing menstruation for about three months. At any time after the return of menstruation, a nursing mother who resumes normal sexual activity is as likely as not to conceive. Ruth A. Lawrence, *Breast-Feeding: A Guide for the Medical Profession* (St. Louis: C. V. Mosby, 1980), 266–67.

58. Niles Newton and Michael Newton, "Psychologic Aspects of Lactation," *New England Journal of Medicine* 277 (Nov. 30, 1967): 1180.

59. Buchan, *Advice to Mothers*, 79, 164.

60. Dewees, *Treatise*, 50–51.

61. Bright, *Mother's Medical Guide*, 262.

62. Gertrude Meredith to William Meredith, Aug. 30, 1800, Gertrude Meredith Letters.

63. Elizabeth to Agnes Treat Lamb Richards, Dec. 9, 1839, case 40, Agnes Treat Lamb Letters.

64. Lawrence, *Breast-Feeding*, 153.

65. Gertrude Meredith to William Meredith, Sept. 4, 1800, Gertrude Meredith Letters.

66. Lay diary, Dec. 1851.

67. Sedgwick journal, 1824.

68. Gerda Lerner, ed., *The Female Experience: An American Documentary* (Indianapolis: Bobbs-Merrill, 1977), 81.

69. Skinner, *Female's Medical Guide*, 38; Ryan, *Philosophy of Marriage*, 311; Bull, *Maternal Management*, 59; Ewell, *Letters*, 255; Meigs, *Obstetrics*, 712; Combe, *Treatise*, 186–87; Eberle, *Treatise*, 62; M. Trousseau, "The Effects of Dentition on Nursing Children," *Boston Medical and Surgical Journal* 55 (Aug. 7, 1856): 15–19; John Burns, *The Principles of Midwifery, Including the Diseases of Women and Children* (Philadelphia: Hopkins and Earle, 1810), 382; Pye Henry Chavasse, *Advice to Wives on the Management of Themselves during the Periods of Pregnancy, Labour, and Suckling* (New York: D. Appleton, 1844), 88–89; Thomas Hersey, *The Midwife's Practical Directory; or, Woman's Confidential Friend* (Baltimore: Hersey, 1836), 288.

70. Fox diary, Sept. 24, 1855, box 13, folder 30, Logan-Fisher–Fox Papers; see also Mary Pierce Poor to Lucy Pierce, Dec. 27, 1856, box 7, folder 97, Mary Pierce Poor Letters.

71. Lucy Tappan Pierce to John Pierce, Sept. 17, 1805, box 1, folder 4, Lucy Tappan Pierce Letters; Sedgwick journal, 1825 and 1826; Harriet Beecher Stowe to Calvin Stowe, Aug.-Sept. [1849,] box 2, folder 73, Harriet Beecher Stowe Letters; A. F. Wedd, ed., *The Fate of the Fenwicks: Letters to Mary Hays* (London: Methuen, 1927), 189; Cornelia Hand to Noah Hand, July 11, [1823,] folder 4, Cornelia Hand Letters, Hand Family Correspondence, Historical Society of Pennsylvania.

72. Robinson diary, Jan. 6, 13, 20, 1852, box 4, Robinson–Shattuck Papers.

73. Sedgwick journal, 1826.

74. Caulfield, "Infant Feeding," 682. See also Laurel Thatcher Ulrich, *Good Wives: Image and Reality in the Lives of Women in Northern New England, 1650–1750* (New York: Knopf, 1982), 141–44; Norton, *Liberty's Daughters*, 91–92.

75. Gertrude Meredith to William Meredith, Sept. 4, 1800, Gertrude Meredith Letters.

76. Lovell, ed., *Two Quaker Sisters*, 56.

77. Anna Colton Clayton to John Clayton, July 5, 1848, Anna Colton Clayton Letters.

78. Mary Pierce Poor to John and Lucy Pierce, Nov. 26, 1842, box 6, folder 89, Mary Pierce Poor Letters.

79. John Pierce to Benjamin Tappan, Aug. 14, 1803, box 1, folder 8, Poor Family Collection. See Abigail May Alcott to Samuel May, Mar. 27, 1831, box 1, folder 25, Abigail May Alcott Letters.

80. In his study of childhood, Philippe Aries wrote that as long as the death rate for children remained high, "people could not allow themselves to become too attached to something that was regarded as a probable loss" (*Centuries of Childhood: A Social History of Family Life*, trans. Robert Baldick [New York: Vintage, 1962], 38–39). Edward Shorter found that indifference to infant death lasted well into the eighteenth century among ordinary people (*The Making of the Modern Family* [New York: Basic, 1975], 169–75). According to David E. Stannard the Puritans in New England attempted to distance themselves from their young children because they were afraid that they would die (*The Puritan Way of Death: A Study in Religion, Culture, and Social Change* [New York: Oxford University Press, 1977], 58–59). Both Stannard and Philip Greven have suggested that another reason why Puritan parents in America resisted developing a close relationship with their children was that they were repelled by their depravity and concerned for their souls (Stannard, *Puritan Way of Death*, 58–60; Philip Greven, *The Protestant Temperament: Patterns of Child-Rearing, Religious Experience, and the Self in Early America* [New York: New American Library, 1977], 29–31). For references to the nineteenth century, see David Grylls, *Guardians and Angels: Parents and Children in Nineteenth-Century Literature* (London: Faber and Faber, 1978), 22; Lewis O. Saum, "Death in the Popular Mind of Pre-Civil War America," *American Quarterly* 26 (Dec. 1974): 484–86.

81. Peter Gregg Slater, *Children in the New England Mind: In Death and in Life* (Hamden, Conn.: Archon, 1977), 18–19; Norton, *Liberty's Daughters*, 88–90.

82. Elizabeth Graeter to Francis Graeter, Aug. 5–14, 1836, folder 59, Hooker Collection, Schlesinger Library.

83. Fox diary, June 28, 1850, box 13, folder 30, Logan–Fisher-Fox Papers.

84. Mary Pierce Poor to Feroline Pierce Fox, Dec. 10, addition to letter of Dec. 4, 1842, box 12, folder 167, Mary Pierce Poor Letters.

85. Hannah Palfrey Ayer, ed., *A Legacy of New England: Letters of the Palfrey Family*, 2 vols. (Portland, Maine: Anthoensen, 1950) 1:82.

86. Mary Pierce Poor to Feroline Pierce Fox, Dec. 10, addition to letter of Dec. 4, 1842, box 12, folder 167, Mary Pierce Poor Letters.

87. Mary Irwin to Eliza Pitkin, Mar. 11, 1835, folder 58, Hooker Collection.

88. Horace Adams, "A Puritan Wife on the Frontier," *Mississippi Valley Historical Review* 27 (June 1940): 70.

89. Peggy Dow, *Vicissitudes; or, The Journey of Life* (Philadelphia: Joseph Rakestraw, 1816), 607, 611–12.

90. Benjamin B. Wisner, ed., *Memoirs of the Late Mrs. Susan Huntington, of Boston, Mass.* (Boston: Crocker and Brewster, 1826), 254.

91. "The Infant's Mission," *Christian Parlor Magazine* 1 (Oct. 1844): 179.

# "A Very Peculiar Sorrow": Attitudes toward Infant Death

No MATTER how realistic parents were about the possibility that their babies might die, they were seldom able to defend themselves adequately against the emotional pain that inevitably accompanied the loss of an infant. Parents mourned deeply when their babies died. "Days have passed since my sweet babe has lain in the silent ground," wrote Christiana Cowell. "I go about my domestic duties in moaning, sighing over the melancholy void that death has made." Everything around her reminded her of her lost child. "There sits her empty cradle," she continued, "no more to lull the weary pain of my darling babe. I shall never see her sleeping there again. Her clothes, the little chair, the toys *all* bring to my heart a pang of yearning sorrow."[1] Fathers were no less sensitive to the loss of an infant. Two months after the death of his daughter, Henry Wadsworth Longfellow noted in his journal: "I feel very sad today. I miss very much my dear little Fanny. An inappeasable longing to see her comes over me at times, which I can hardly control."[2] Nehemiah Adams summed up their feelings when he asked, "Do you not think that the death of a dear little child is a very peculiar sorrow? It seems to me that I have seen people in more anguish under the loss of little children than in any other affliction."[3]

The number of children that couples were likely to bear was beginning to decline in the early nineteenth century. This factor combined with the cult of motherhood, which demanded that women invest considerable time, effort, and affection in their children and measured their contribution to society by their success in fulfilling their maternal obligations, made the death of an infant a particularly tragic occurrence. In their attempts to cope both emotionally and intellectually with this "affliction," parents in the first half of the nineteenth century began working through the grieving process by performing funereal rituals and making an effort to preserve memories of their dead children. The symptoms of grief they described in their diaries and letters were similar to those exhibited by their twentieth-century counterparts, the most significant differences being that they were much less likely to express directly feelings of guilt or to demand an explanation for their loss. Although they placed great value on their babies' lives and did what they could to protect them, they were well aware that children commonly died in infancy and that there was little they could really do to ensure the survival of infants. They used the loss of infants as an occasion for demonstrating their willingness to submit to the will of God and found comfort in the belief that their children had gone to join him in heaven. For them the death of an infant was a private, family matter.

For authors and editors, however, infant death was a matter of public concern. Literary discussion of infant death in stories and poems published during the 1840s and 1850s was designed to offer solace to bereaved parents by confirming their belief that their children preceded them to heaven.[4] But it was also characterized by an effort to explain God's reasons for calling babies back to their heavenly home. In the process of providing such an explanation, popular authors offered to those who mourned the death of a young child a new strategy, one that suggested that the presence of infants in the household and their subsequent demise helped to redeem other members of the family and ensure their permanent reunion in paradise. They also conveyed the idea that infant death was an instrument through which traditional values vital to the American republic could be perpetuated, implying that the demands of the cult of motherhood could be fulfilled as much by the death of an infant as by the birth of one. By picturing infants as redeemers, these authors helped to establish a basis for redefining the role of young children in the family.

By giving them the opportunity to do one last thing for their child, the rituals involved in preparing and burying the bodies of their babies provided a good deal of satisfaction to parents who were beginning the first stages of the grieving process. Mary Wilder White would allow no one else to perform this service after the death of her six-month-old daughter in 1808.[5] Sometimes husband and wife performed this ritual together. When their infant died in 1832, Lavius Hyde brought his wife water to bathe their "little lump of cherished clay." Despite her sadness and the trembling of her hands, she found comfort in preparing the body to be wrapped in its shroud as it lay in her arms.[6]

Bereaved parents also did what they could to preserve the memories of their children. William Lloyd Garrison had daguerreotypes taken of the corpse of his baby daughter before she was buried.[7] Some commissioned artists to make life-size, lifelike portraits from their children's corpses.[8] Fanny Longfellow lovingly cut off some of her daughter's hair.[9]

Others were concerned that siblings have the chance to say good-bye to the infant either shortly before or shortly after death. The Hydes woke their children up when it was certain their infant son was dying so that they might "witness the dying moments of their little brother."[10] But Elizabeth Ellery Sedgwick waited until the body of her baby was properly prepared before she allowed her other children to see it. She was particularly concerned that they not be exposed to the more unpleasant aspects of death and did not want the sight of their deceased brother to leave a "disagreeable impression" on them. Before she brought her children to see the body, she placed the infant in his cradle and made sure that it was in its usual place in the room so that it would appear as if the baby was only sleeping. She wished to avoid "in this way the images of loneliness and darkness so painful and revolting to young minds." She reported that although her little daughter Lizzie kept running up to the cradle and exclaiming, "How beautiful he is! How still! How sweet he sleeps!" she felt sure that the child realized her brother was dead. She encouraged Lizzie to speak of her brother as if he was still alive, she said, in order to preserve his memory.[11]

Having memories of a dead child was important because it forced those in mourning to accept death and allowed them to focus their grief.[12] Without memories death could never seem quite real to the one who had suffered the loss as the case of Frances Miriam Berry Whitcher demonstrates. In 1848 Whitcher almost died after the stillbirth of a daughter. Her labor was so difficult and the state of her health so precarious after delivery that she had no real memories of having borne a child. The body of the infant was buried well before she was fully aware of what had happened. A year later the Whitchers moved from Elmira to Whitesboro, New York. Once they were settled, they had their baby's body exhumed in order to move it. During the process the coffin was placed on the porch of their house and opened. Miriam Whitcher was hesitant to look at the corpse but felt compelled to do so. After she had seen the body of her dead baby, she sent her husband, who was away at the time, a detailed description of its appearance and her reaction to having seen it. She found it lying "exactly as it was placed at first, with a cotton pillow under the head & the little hands crossed, & the gown smoothed down & drawn over the feet. It did not appear to have fallen away at all. We thought at first there was a cloth laid over the face, but John took hold of it softly to raise it up & found that it was a thin coat of white mould. We could see all the little features distinctly through it." She was "surprised that it was so well pre-served" and "had expected only to see a little heap of corruption with no form to it. The dress and the cotton under the head looked as white as they did when it was first buried. There was no change excepting the mould on the face." It was difficult for her to believe that the body was really that of her child because her "impressions of its birth" were "so dreamlike and strange." Seeing the corpse, however, made the death of her baby real to her, and she felt satisfied. [13]

However important memories were to bereaved parents, they did not shield them from having to work through the grieving process. Each in his or her own way had to deal with sleeplessness, yearning, depression, preoccupation with images of the child, dreams about the baby, changes in attitudes toward other children in the family, shame, and feelings of vulnerability, normal symptoms of grief that were identified in 1944 by Erich Lindemann. [14] Many parents suffered in relative silence, mentioning their feelings only when they felt overwhelmed by them or when they felt it necessary to inform friends and relatives of their loss. Isolated comments written in diaries and letters during the year or so following the death of a child testified to the depth and persistence of their feelings of loss

*Figure 5.* "Death Scene" (1841–42) by Jarvis Hanks. This family portrait is an example of posthumous mourning portraiture. It is unusual in that it incorporates in the same painting both the living and the dead. The mother in the center of the painting is Elizabeth Spencer Stone, who died in 1840. Her infant twins died at the age of five months and six months in the same year. The other figures, Elizabeth's husband, mother, and son, were all living when the painting was done. Note that Elizabeth Stone's posture is that which might have been assumed during childbirth and that the twins are lodged deep between her thighs near the womb. Courtesy of the Ohio Historical Society, Campus Martius Museum, Marietta, Ohio.

*Figure 6.* "Memorial to Nicholas M. S. Catlin" (1852) by Susane Walters. During the period before the Civil War, contemplating a portrait of the dead was a part of the mourning process. This portrait painted after the death of Nicholas Catlin uses such common death symbols as a rose pulled from a growing plant, a boat sailing away, a tomb, and a funeral willow, all intended to remind the bereaved that a loved one has died. Courtesy of the National Gallery of Art, Washington, D.C. Gift of Edgar William and Bernice Chrysler Garbisch.

and desolation. Over a year after the death of two of her children, one of whom was an infant, Lucy Lovell wrote: "A year has passed away since our dear little ones were taken from us. Our hearts still bleed. . . . As time rolls away, we feel our loss more instead of less." [15]

Occasionally, however, parents took the time to describe their mourning in explicit detail. The journals and letters of Fanny and Henry Wadsworth Longfellow, for example, provide a graphic description of the way they experienced the grief that followed the death of their seventeen-month-old daughter in September 1848. Complete despair almost overwhelmed Fanny on the day of the funeral: "Struggled almost in vain with the terrible hunger of the heart to hold her once more. Every room, every object recalls her, and the house is desolation." Henry was somewhat more in control on that day. "Our little child was buried to-day," he wrote. "From her nursery, down the front stairs, through my study and into the library, she was borne in the arms of her old nurse. And thence, after the prayer, through the long halls to her coffin and her grave." For a long time that day, Henry sat alone with his daughter in the library, finding comfort in sight of her body surrounded by unopened roses.

On the day after the funeral, as Henry tried to escape his grief by burying himself in his work, Fanny could think only of her remaining children: "Cannot keep despairing now of the other children, and thinking how they will look when dead. Their gleeful voices agonize me. Charles told Nurse Blake 'Sissy was up in the sky,' and when I told him yesterday, he said, 'Oh, I want to go too.' When Death first enters a house, he throws so long a shadow—it seems to touch every one." Henry was also concerned about his feelings toward his remaining children. "It sometimes seems to me," he wrote four days after the funeral, "as if this blow had paralyzed my affection for my other children. Can this be so? No, it is but benumbed for a moment." Fanny was utterly distracted by visions of her daughter during the next few weeks: "In the garden I see only her merry steps and little hands grasping the flowers with glee and shouting 'Pretty,' and then I see her with them in her cold hands." She imagined her baby's "little white bonnet" at her side day and night and frequently believed that she heard "a cry in the nursery" and would listen intently thinking that the child was still there. Although by November she was beginning to resign herself to her loss, periodically she recognized how vulnerable she was and would "devour my children's faces as if looking my last upon them, and shrink with cowardly terror from the possible future." Months later she reported in her journal, "Dreamed my darling Fanny was restored to me; sitting quietly by my side, she said she had been in heaven." The grief that Fanny Longfellow suffered as a result of the loss of her namesake was modified but not removed by the birth of another daughter in November 1850. She felt that the birth of a girl was an answer to her prayers but tempered her joy with the realization that she could easily lose this baby too.[16]

Fanny and Henry Longfellow were able to carry on with their lives after the death of little Fanny. Occasionally, however, the stress associated with grief was perceived to pose a real threat to a mourner's physical or mental health. Jane Harris remembered that after the death of her baby, she was so overcome with grief that she could not carry out her domestic responsibilities and began to fear that she was losing her mind.[17] Susan Huntington worried about the ability of a friend to survive the death of five children within four or five weeks.[18] Fanny Longfellow was similarly concerned even before she suffered the loss of her own daughter. Referring to a bereaved friend, she wrote, "Such a blow must soon sever, I should think, the mother's slender hold upon life."[19]

The depth of the grief suffered by mothers like Longfellow and Harris testified to the degree to which they were both socially and psychologically dependent upon their babies. For many urban middle- and upper-class women in the early nineteenth century whose lives were increasingly prescribed by their domestic function, nurturing children provided a major focus for their lives. Babies provided these women with a social identity, a time-consuming vocation, and a depository for their love and were therefore the recipients of considerable emotional investment. Mary Lee had reason to write that after the death of her baby, her "occupation was gone."[20] Nehemiah Adams's wife felt much the same way. As she sat with her husband discussing her feelings about the death of their baby, she said, "I hardly know what to do with myself; it seems as though I had nothing to do."[21] The death of their babies deprived middle-

and upper-class mothers, already stripped of any significant role as economic producers, of one of their most demanding and respected domestic functions, especially if there were no other children in the house. When a baby died, its mother suffered a double loss.

Even though parents in the early nineteenth century were willing to invest considerable time, energy, and affection in their children, they did not express anger over the deaths of infants. They asked for no explanation, tended to accept the death of their children as the result of some incomprehensible plan devised by an inscrutable God, and found comfort in the conviction that their children had gone to heaven and were probably better off there. In 1807 Peggy Dow noted sadly in her diary that she had lost her baby daughter but reassured herself that the child's "happy spirit" had "landed on the peaceful shore of *blest eternity*."[22] She took comfort in the thought that her daughter had escaped some of the more unpleasant aspects of life on earth: "I often felt a pleasure of the sweetest kind in contemplating that my child had escaped all the vanities and dangers of this treacherous and uncertain world, for the never-fading glories of paradise."[23] Similarly, Mehetable Goddard convinced herself after the death of her four-month-old son that she would not "wish to recall him" for "it remains for us to be thankful that his spirit is removed *pure* from a world of sin and sorrow."[24]

The belief that infants automatically went to heaven when they died was a rather dramatic departure from the clearly less optimistic view held by those in earlier times who believed, at least in theory, that infants were depraved at birth and were as likely as not to be destined for hell as for heaven. There is some reason to wonder, however, whether even those who were ideologically committed to the doctrine of infant depravity in the abstract were in fact able to apply it to children in their own families.[25] Of a grandchild, dead at eighteen months, Anne Bradstreet wrote in 1665, "Blest babe why should I once bewail thy fate, / Or sigh thy dayes so soon were terminate; / Sith thou art setled in an Everlasting state." Mourning the death of two grandchildren four years later, Bradstreet wrote of one that her heart was cheered at the thought that the child was with its "Savior . . . in endless bliss" and of the other that he would remain "among the blest in endless joyes."[26] Cotton Mather, like Bradstreet theologically committed to the concept of infant depravity, was also unwilling to accept the possibility that his own child, who had died soon after birth in 1693 without benefit of baptism, would go any place but heaven.[27] Even among the most prominent of seventeenth-century Puritans, there appears to have been a difference between intellectual assertion and emotional acceptance. What a latter-day Calvinist despairingly said of parents in the early nineteenth century could just as easily have been applied to those who lived 150 years before. "The truth is," he wrote, "the parent cannot, or will not, believe that *his* child, *his* offspring, *his* darling, is naturally dead in trespasses and sins; that *his* nature is corrupt."[28]

There was a difference, however. Because of their Calvinist heritage, seventeenth-century parents in New England could not escape nagging doubt about the eternal fate of infants. By the nineteenth century many parents did not have to resolve any conflict between religious belief and personal desire for assurance that their children would spend eternity in God's kingdom.

The demise of the doctrine of infant depravity was slow and tortuous. Notions about the condition of the infant soul were influenced by the ideas of the Enlightenment and a softening of Calvinist doctrine. In 1690 in his *Essay on Human Understanding*, John Locke suggested that children were not born with innate characteristics. And as early as 1740 John Taylor, who was among the first theologians to challenge seriously the notion that infants might be damned, denied that guilt could be transferred from generation to generation and concluded that babies were born in a state of moral neutrality. During the last half of the eighteenth century, Charles Chauncy of Boston began suggesting that a child's morally neutral state would only give way to redemption or damnation when the child gained the maturity to act as a moral agent. For the next thirty years liberal theologians quibbled over the relative moral state of children and attempted to determine the point at which they could be held accountable for their actions.[29]

It is not surprising then to find that in the early nineteenth century even those ministers with a conservative bent, who tried to resist change and continued to hold firmly to the belief that infants were born in sin and in need of redemption, were less and less willing to deny parents the comforting thought that babies went to heaven when they died. An entry in the diary of Sarah Ripley

Stearns gives us a clue to how at least one such minister handled this problem from the pulpit. Stearns was a devout woman and attended church regularly. Four months pregnant in April 1813, she sat listening intently to her minister deliver a sermon on infant depravity based on the text "behold I was shapen in iniquity." Mr. P., as Stearns called him in her diary, rejected the idea that children were born innocent on the grounds that only the doctrine of infant depravity had any basis in Scripture. Mr. P was unwilling, however, to insist that unregenerate infants were damned. On that issue, wrote Stearns, "he pretended not to be decided." Nevertheless, he offered those in his congregation reason to hope that their children might go to heaven. "The sovereign arm of mercy," he assured them, "can reach them with infinite ease by means unknown to us—we may charitably hope they are received into glory and dwell with the Father."[30] Caught between his desire to maintain the doctrinal integrity of traditional ideas about infant depravity and the need to defer to the sensibilities of the parents in his congregation, Mr. P. felt compelled to hedge.

The Second Great Awakening, which began in the 1790s and continued into the 1830s, provided yet another opportunity to continue the debate over the spiritual condition of infants. Certainly among the early evangelicals, the sinfulness of even very young children was taken for granted. But as the century progressed and the evangelical movement fragmented, its adherents were unable to maintain a coherent position on major theological issues such as the innate depravity of infants, thus leaving the door open for clergymen like Horace Bushnell to argue that if properly nurtured by Christian parents, an evangelical child could "grow up a Christian, and never know himself as being otherwise."[31]

The long debate over the moral state of infants laid the groundwork for the idea that babies could provide the means for achieving grace and guaranteeing a place in heaven for every member of the family. Symptomatic of the willingness of literate Americans to accept this concept is the degree to which they adopted romantic ideas about children. In the first decade of the nineteenth century, William Wordsworth wrote with real conviction, "Heaven lies about us in our infancy." In his ode on "Intimations of Immortality," the British poet suggested, among other things, that when babies were born, they brought with them a kind of pristine purity that distinguished them from other mortals.[32] Americans were so receptive to Wordsworth's rhetoric that by the 1840s his phrase had become something of a cliché. Testifying to her conviction that belief in the innate innocence of infants was universally held to be true, Sarah Josepha Hale quoted the phrase in her January 1844 editorial in *Godey's*.[33] Following the birth of her second child, Mary Pierce Poor wrote that she wished she could have kept her first child "as perfect as she was at fifteen months." Nevertheless, she wrote, to watch a child change in behavior, to watch her become "capricious and fretful and less obedient" must be viewed as inevitable. "She must, like all the rest of us," Poor continued, "pass through 'trial and self-discipline' before she can return to the Heaven that was around her in her infancy."[34] Like Hale and Poor, S. F. Clapp freely used Wordsworth's phrase in a poem called "Infancy," published in the *Christian Examiner and Theological Review* in 1854. Describing infants as having been born in the "fair season of sweet innocence" with "souls of spotless white," she wrote, "Heaven itself *doth* seem to lie / About blest infancy."[35]

Between 1800 and 1860 many people, having come to the conclusion that babies were born innocent and remained so for an undetermined period of time, were no longer deeply troubled by the idea that infants might be denied a place in heaven.[36] Historians like Mary P. Ryan and Philip Greven have argued that belief in infant purity was closely associated with a change in child-rearing tactics that gave greater responsibilities to mothers for the socialization of children and emphasized bending rather than breaking a child's will.[37] From their point of view, infant children were passive recipients of new socialization techniques. But belief in infant innocence also provided the basis for allowing a young child to take an active role in family life. It prepared parents emotionally and intellectually to accept the idea that babies performed a useful function within the family and that God's purpose for removing infants to heaven was not arbitrary but a part of a divine plan that could serve as the basis for preserving the unity of the family.

Between the late 1830s and the Civil War, novelists and authors whose stories and poems appeared in ladies' magazines and liberal religious periodicals intended for popular consumption exploited the belief in infant innocence to confirm parents' hopes that their children did indeed go to heaven when they died and that they were undoubtedly better off there. Fictional parents reiterated the rhetoric of real parents. In T. S. Arthur's *The Mother*, Anna Hartley grieved for her dead child but admitted to her husband that she found consolation in the belief that the baby was "now safe in her heavenly home."[38] The fictional Amy in E. L. Follen's *Sketches of Married Life* was sustained by the thought that her child had been received into heaven.[39] An article in *Godey's* entitled "The Empty Cradle" described the feelings of a grief-stricken mother: "She feels that heaven was the only atmosphere where her precious flower could unfold without spot or blemish, and she would not recall the lost."[40]

To drive the point home, some authors exaggerated the idea that babies were better off dying before their souls were contaminated by earthly influences. One poet warned, "Whilst on thy infant innocence I gaze / . . . 'Twere wise to wish thee—pure and faultless—dead."[41] Another described a mother who, as she sat watching her infant sleep, began to worry about his inevitable loss of innocence: "She breathed a mental prayer, / that rather now—e'en though so dear, / That now, while undefiled / Pure as when heaven bestowed the gift, / It would recall her child." Her prayer was heard. A few days later the child died, "secure from future ill," and went to heaven.[42]

In a short story depicting infant death, a mother, obsessed with preserving her child's innocence and purity, prayed that God might protect him. She sensed a voice saying to her, "Daughter, go in peace, thy petition is heard, and thy request granted." The mother, dissatisfied with Divine assurance, again petitioned God to save her baby from pain and disappointment. In response to her prayer, a spirit appeared to her saying, "I alone can save your son from the evils you fear will fall upon him. In this world it is *impossible* but that he should be exposed to sorrow, and all the evils incident to human life." He offered to transport the child to "a brighter country, where sorrow never enters; where naught but peace, harmony, and happiness dwell." The mother agreed that her child should be taken there, and the infant died.[43] In another story a mother prayed that her child would not die. But falling asleep she dreamed that the infant spoke to her, saying: "Dearest mother, why would you keep me here? The world is full of sin and trouble; would you keep me till this heart is unfit to join the happy throng that are now ready and willing to receive me? My father, with outstretched arms is calling me home. Dear mother, unsay that cruel prayer and let me go." The mother complied, and the child died. She never regretted her decision.[44]

A reversal of this theme appeared in *Godey's* under the title "The Child and the Angels." In this story a sleeping baby, being tended by both its mother and its guardian angel, awoke from a nap in extreme pain. Frightened, the mother pleaded with God to spare her child. He granted her wish. But as the infant matured and grew out of its sinless state, the mother came to regret that she had asked God to preserve its life.[45]

In their portrayal of the self-sacrificing mother, the authors of these stories and poems testified to the degree to which people had come to recognize the separation of spheres and the increasing influence of mothers over the spiritual state and eternal future of their children. They suggested that mothers could act as agents of redemption. These mothers did not merely submit to the deaths of their babies. They chose (or, as in the last example, did not choose) to give their children up in order to preserve their infant purity and save their souls. They acted as God's agents and worked with him to secure eternal life for their babies. At the same time, however, by portraying mothers as willing to give up their children, popular authors also suggested that mother love and ambivalence toward the maternal role were not mutually exclusive. While these authors confirmed the love that a mother had for her children and the importance of a mother's role in their moral nurture, they reminded their readers that whatever the influence of mothers over infants, it could not guarantee the salvation of a child who grew to adulthood. Overwhelmed by their responsibilities and aware of the limitations of their influence, these fictional mothers gave up before they had even begun because they were terrified by the possibility that they might not be up to the job and that their children would be condemned because of their own inadequacies. For them grief for lost children was nothing compared to living with guilt for having failed them. Not being a mother was better than being a bad one.

Such stories were, however, exceptional. More often authors of popular prose and poetry extended the belief in infant innocence in such a way as to propose that infants, not mothers, were redemptive agents. In the literature that they produced and published between 1840 and 1860, these authors used sentimental rhetoric to suggest that living infants established a direct connection between earthly mortals and the spiritual world and acted to enhance the moral sensibilities of those around them. They assured bereaved parents that children who died in infancy were preparing a place in heaven for family members who had been receptive to their purifying influence and that in death they would once more be reunited as a family.

One of the ways that writers did this was to employ the image of angels as a metaphor to dramatize the idea that babies remained close to heaven and were surrounded with an aura of purity after birth. A poem appearing in the *Christian Observer* described infants as "ye tiny angels of my house."[46] Another poet spoke of an infant as "an angel visitant from heaven."[47] In an 1844 editorial Hale argued that "a blessed doctrine, in the maternal creed," held that "angelic beings" surrounded infants in order to "guard with peculiar tenderness and care the opening buds of human life."[48]

Novelists used the same metaphor when referring to infants. Elizabeth Oakes Smith wrote in *The Newsboy* that "children are nearest heaven . . . the angels come wherever the child is."[49] T. S. Arthur developed the image in his books. In "The Wife," for example, he pictured Anna Hartley as saying to her husband, "When our babe is in my arms, and especially when it lies at my bosom, it seems as if angels were near me." "And angels are near you," replied her husband. "Angels love innocence, and especially infants, that are forms of innocence. They are present with them, and the mother shares the blessed company."[50]

Ordinary people, already convinced that babies were pure and innocent, found the metaphor a useful way to refer to their own children. In 1842 a friend assured Mary Pierce Poor that "celestial angels who stand in the immediate presence of God, watch over infants." Comforted by that thought, Poor was hopeful that "their benign influence may in some measure extend to the parents of our little one and enable us to become in spirit like a little child, that our hearts may be fitted for the reception of the kingdom of Heaven."[51]

While they remained innocent, metaphorically surrounded by angels, babies could, according to the popular authors of the day, provide a direct link between heaven and earth. Children, argued Hale in *Godey's* in 1851, stand nearer to heaven than adults.[52] Infants are a "link of life eternal, reaching from earth to heaven," wrote another.[53]

According to popular authors a baby also acted as a "messenger of peace and love" sent to earth to purify the worldly and prepare them to take their own place in heaven. "He came," wrote poet James H. Perkins of a baby, "an herald from above / Pure from his God he came to them, / Teaching new duties, deeper love."[54] Harriet Beecher Stowe pictured infants explicitly as a surrogate for the great Redeemer. In the form of a baby, she wrote, the "gentle teacher still remains to us. By every hearth and fireside, Jesus still *sets* the little child in the midst of us" to "awaken a mother from worldliness and egotism to a world of new and higher feeling!"[55] Babies described in this way served as emissaries from heaven, like Jesus, sent to earth to purify the worldly.

The baby Grace in T. S. Arthur's *Angel of the Household* played a role similar to that described by Stowe and others. Arthur's story was intended to demonstrate the redemptive influence of an innocent infant and her guardian angels on the family of Jacob and Mary Harding and their willful, defiant, and rebellious children. One evening after a particularly heated domestic quarrel, the Hardings found a baby that had been left at their cottage door. The presence of this child, whom they called Grace, had a profound effect on every member of the family. The sight of the child called forth all of the long-forgotten nurturing instincts of Mary. Even the ill-tempered Jacob fell under the infant's spell, feeling himself "within the circle of some strange power that stilled the waves of passion in his heart." The influence of celestial and infant purity helped every member of the family modify his behavior. The Hardings's son became more honest and self-controlled, and their other children became more polite and affectionate.[56]

Infants could play an important role in rescuing the souls of others it seemed. Children, argued Hale in *Godey's*, save us from our own sin.[57] "How many spirits have been purified and upborne by the presence of infant innocence?" asked S. D. Robbins.[58] Lydia Sigourney described the influence of a baby on a mother in these terms: "The feeble hand of the babe that she nourished, led her through more profound depths of humility, to higher aspirations of faith . . . guiding her to a higher seat among the 'just made perfect.'"[59] By serving as messengers from God, as sources of inspiration, babies could lead those around them through the first step in the redemptive process—purification.

If purification could be achieved through the agency of living infants, salvation could be ensured through the agency of dying ones. In their writings popular authors suggested that this was the reason why children died in infancy. Lydia Sigourney claimed that "the glorified spirit of the infant is a star to guide the mother to its own blissful clime."[60] R. C. Waterston wrote that when a baby dies, "it throws a degree of sanctity around those who remain. They are not simply connected with this world, but with another. . . . This idea makes every child a monitor pointing to the spiritual world."[61] This image was similar to the one used by Fanny Longfellow when she sadly noted after the death of her namesake, "I feel as if my lost darling were drawing me to her—as I controlled her before birth so does she me now."[62] T. S. Arthur described a mother whose two children in heaven provided "invisible cords" that drew her "soul upwards."[63] S. D. Robbins, a minister writing in the *Monthly Religious Magazine*, claimed that infants and children brought others close to God and gave them "a new bond to heaven. . . . We are indebted to them all," he continued, "for the heaven they prepare us to reach when they go away."[64] Dying babies had an important role to play on earth. By directing the attention of family members toward heaven, they helped to redeem the souls of others and in that way guarantee the reunification of the family in heaven. No longer was the death of children viewed as a rebuke to survivors, a way of reprimanding them for their sins. The death of a child carried with it the promise of redemption for every member of the family.

Popular writers assured parents that their children would wait for them in heaven and that the death of one member of the family was but a temporary absence, not an eternal separation. T. S. Arthur pictured James Hartley comforting his bereaved wife with the words, "she cannot return to us, but we will go to her. Our real home is not here."[65] A writer for the *Ladies' Garland* deprecated excessive grief expressed over the loss of a child on the grounds that parents should find comfort in the conviction that they and their children would be reunited in heaven.[66] Another author wrote of the comfort offered by the angel of death who appeared before an anxious and fearful mother intending to transport her infant into the arms of God. He assured her that her separation from the child would be temporary and that he would return soon to convey her to "the same blissful shore."[67]

The belief that death did not mean permanent separation from their children was a great comfort to grieving mothers. Lucy Lovell wrote after the death of two of her children: "We are left childless. . . . But if Earth is losing, I trust heaven is increasing its attractions. We feel that, though taken from us, our children still live, and that in a peculiar and most endearing relation, they are united to us, and we may yet call them ours." Lovell added that she and her husband hoped their children were redeemed, "and that we shall one day stand before the throne with the children God has given us."[68] Peggy Dow had similar hopes for the future. Writing of her dead daughter, she hoped that "when life should end, I should meet her to part no more!"[69]

Popular authors did not consciously set out to create an infant-as-redeemer ideology in order to comfort bereaved parents. Through the use of romantic rhetoric, they merely expanded upon a belief in infant innocence that had been thrashed out by generations of theologians and that was by this time widely accepted by their contemporaries. By stressing the purifying influence of living babies and the redemptive influence of dying ones, they were able to provide an explanation for the seemingly meaningless deaths of small children. They provided parents with reason to believe that their children's lives, however short, had some purpose, performed some valuable service. Mourning the loss of a beloved child, parents could find comfort in the thoughts that their children were happy in paradise, that there was some justification for the grief they were experiencing, and that when their family was reunited in heaven, they would be rewarded for suffering.

Besides offering comfort to bereaved parents and an explanation for infant death, the ideas of popular authors also suggested an alternative to traditional methods of preserving a sense of family unity. In the urban environment of the early nineteenth century among the middle and upper classes, the workplace was often separated from the home, and fathers were likely to spend less time with their families. Some social critics were so concerned about this situation that they were beginning to charge that middle-class husbands were abdicating their paternal responsibilities, that they were becoming "almost strangers to their own children."[70] As middle-class men accepted more and more responsibility for the economic support of their families, the assumption that their wives and children would significantly contribute to the family income declined. Children, while regarded as a source of pride and pleasure, became temporary economic liabilities whose need for food, clothing, shelter, and education placed a drain on the economic resources of their families.

Depicting infants as redeeming agents was a way of accommodating these changes by measuring their value in moral and spiritual rather than economic terms. Viewed in this way, babies became a part of the sacred rather than the profane world and performed a unique service for the family and society. Innocent and pure like T. S. Arthur's Grace, their birth and subsequent presence in the household could help to modify the strains that the modern world placed on family members. Babies could awaken moral sensibilities in others and serve as a reminder of the need to preserve and perpetuate traditional ethical values that were deemed important to the survival of the American republic. By acting as a purifying influence in this world, by preparing the way to heaven for others, the lives and deaths of infants also established a spiritual basis for family unity. This basis could ensure that the separation caused by their deaths was only temporary and that the family would live together in eternity.

## Notes

1. Christiana B. Cowell, *Life and Writings of Mrs. Christiana B. Cowell, Consort of Rev. D. B. Cowell, Who Died in Lebanon, Maine, Oct. 8, 1862, Aged 41 Years* (Biddleford, Maine: John E. Butler, 1872), 140.

2. Samuel Longfellow, ed., *The Life of Henry Wadsworth Longfellow with Extracts from His Journals and Correspondence*, 3 vols. (Boston: Houghton Mifflin, 1891), 2:136.

3. Nehemiah Adams, *Agnes and the Little Key; or, Bereaved Parents Instructed and Comforted* (Boston: S. K. Whipple, 1857), 30.

4. Saccharine and sentimental, bereavement literature during this period also served a number of other functions. In her discussion of the domestication of death, Ann Douglas suggests that it provided its authors an opportunity to make a place for themselves as arbiters of American social values (*The Feminization of American Culture* [New York: Knopf, 1977], 240–72). According to James Farrell the sentimentalization of death in the early nineteenth century also allowed people to avoid facing the terrors of death's finality (*Inventing the American Way of Death, 1830–1920* [Philadelphia: Temple University Press, 1980], 34).

5. Mary Wilder Tileston, ed., *Memorials of Mary Wilder White: A Century Ago in New England* (Boston: Everett Press, 1903), 327.

6. Abigail and Lavius Hyde to Mr. and Mrs. Asahel I. Bradley, Mar. 28, 1832, box 1, folder 4, Abigail and Lavius Hyde Letters, Bradley-Hyde Collection, Schlesinger Library, Radcliffe College, Cambridge, Mass.

7. William Lloyd Garrison, *The Letters of William Lloyd Garrison: No Union with Slave-Holders, 1841–1849*, ed. Walter Merrill (Cambridge, Mass.: Belknap Press, 1973), 556.

8. According to Pheobe Lloyd this practice was particularly popular from 1830 to 1860 ("Posthumous Mourning Portraiture," in *A Time to Mourn: Expressions of Grief in Nineteenth Century America*, ed. Martha V. Pike and Janice Gray Armstrong [Stony Brook, N.Y.: Museums at Stony Brook, 1980], 85). For further discussion of posthumous mourning portraits of children, see Phoebe Lloyd, "A Young Boy in His First and Last Suit," *Minneapolis Institute of Arts Bulletin* 64 (1978–80): 104–11.

9. Edward Wagenknecht, ed., *Mrs. Longfellow: Selected Letters and Journals of Fanny Appleton Longfellow (1817–1861)* (New York: Longmans, Green, 1956), 142.

10. Abigail and Lavius Hyde to Mrs. Asahel I. Bradley, Mar. 28, 1832, box 1, folder 4, Abigail and Lavius Hyde Letters.

11. Elizabeth Ellery Sedgwick journal, 1827, Houghton Library, Harvard University, Cambridge, Mass.

12. This view is consistent with that first proposed by Freud in 1915 and discussed in Richard Schulz, *The Psychology of Death, Dying, and Bereavement* (Reading, Mass.: Addison-Wesley, 1978), 137.

13. Frances Miriam Berry Whitcher to William Whitcher, May 25, 1849, Frances Miriam Berry Whitcher Letters, Whitcher Collection, New-York Historical Society, N.Y.

14. Erich Lindemann, "Symptomatology and Management of Acute Grief," in *Death and Identity*, ed. Robert Fulton (New York: John Wiley, 1965), 187–89. For more recent discussions of the symptoms of grief, see John Bowlby, *Attachment and Loss*, 3 vols. (New York: Basic, 1969–80), 3:122–24; Elisabeth Kubler-Ross, *On Death and Dying* (New York: Macmillan, 1969), 142, 149, 159; Schulz, *Psychology of Death*, 142–48.

15. Malcolm R. Lovell, ed., *Two Quaker Sisters: From the Original Diaries of Elizabeth Buffum Chace and Lucy Buffum Lovell* (New York: Liveright, 1937), 109.

16. Wagenknecht, ed., *Mrs. Longfellow*, 142–43, 145, 147, 175; Longfellow, ed., *Life of Henry Wadsworth Longfellow*, 130.

17. Jane Harris to Mary Harris, June 1, 1828, Mary Harris Letters, George B. Harris Papers, Historical Society of Pennsylvania, Philadelphia.

18. Benjamin B. Wisner, ed., *Memoirs of the Late Mrs. Susan Huntington, of Boston, Mass.* (Boston: Crocker and Brewster, 1826), 117.

19. Wagenknecht, ed., *Mrs. Longfellow*, 126.

20. Frances Rollins Morse, ed., *Henry and Mary Lee: Letters and Journals with Other Family Letters, 1802–1860* (Boston: T. Todd, 1926), 103.

21. Adams, *Agnes*, 31.

22. Peggy Dow, *Vicissitudes; or, The Journey of Life* (Philadelphia: Joseph Rakestraw, 1816), 611. For similar comments, see Jane Harris to Mary Harris, Jan. 29, 1828, Mary Harris Letters; Sally Hughes to George Hughes, Aug. 23, 1847, folder 6; and July 8, 1848, folder 7, Sally Hughes Letters, Maxcy-Markoe-Hughes Collection, Historical Society of Pennsylvania; Wagenknecht, ed., *Mrs. Longfellow*, 143; a friend to Jeannie McCall, [1840s or early 1850s,] Jeannie McCall Letters, McCall Section, Cadwallader Collection, Historical Society of Pennsylvania; Sarah Connell Ayer, *Diary of Sarah Connell Ayer* (Portland, Maine: Lefavor-Tower, 1910), 209; Garrison, *Letters*, ed. Merrill, 556.

23. Dow, *Vicissitudes*, 612.

24. Mehetable May Dawes Goddard to Ann Goddard, Mar. 7, 1826, box 1, folder 16, Mehetable May Dawes Goddard Letters, May-Goddard Collection, Schlesinger Library. For similar comments, see also Mary Rodman Fisher Fox diary, Jan. 30, 1853, box 13, folder 30, Logan-Fisher-Fox Papers,

Historical Society of Pennsylvania; Cowell, *Life and Writings*, 141; Wagen-knecht, ed., *Mrs. Longfellow*, 143.

25. Peter Gregg Slater, *Children in the New England Mind: In Death and in Life* (Hamden, Conn.: Archon, 1977), 39–41.

26. Anne Bradstreet, *The Complete Works of Anne Bradstreet*, ed. Joseph R. McElrath and Allan P. Robb (Boston: Twayne, 1981), 187, 188.

27. Philip Greven, *The Protestant Temperament: Patterns of Child-Rearing, Religious Experience, and the Self in Early America* (New York: New American Library, 1977), 30.

28. "On the Education of Children," *Panoplist and Missionary Magazine* 10 (Sept. 1814): 394.

29. For a more detailed discussion of this change in doctrine, see Slater, *Children*, 26–32, 52–88; H. Shelton Smith, *Changing Conceptions of Original Sin: A Study in American Theology since 1750* (New York: Scribner's, 1955).

30. Sarah Ripley Stearns diary, Apr. 25, 1813, Stearns Collection, Schlesinger Library.

31. Robert W. Lynn and Elliott Wright, *The Big Little School: Sunday Child of American Protestantism* (New York: Harper and Row, 1971), 44; William G. McLoughlin, ed., *The American Evangelicals, 1800–1900: An Anthology* (New York: Harper and Row, 1968), 5, 26; Horace Bushnell, *Christian Nurture* (New Haven: Yale University Press, 1967), 4.

32. William Wordsworth, "Ode: Intimations of Immortality from Recollections of Early Childhood," in *The Complete Poetical Works of William Wordsworth* (Boston: Houghton Mifflin, 1904), 354. For a discussion of this poem and its influence on nineteenth-century thought in England and America, see Barbara Garlitz, "The Immortality Ode: Its Cultural Progeny," *Studies in English Literature* 6 (Autumn 1966): 639–49. It should be noted that Wordsworth was not the first to make this suggestion. In his poem "The Retreate," Henry Vaughan, a seventeenth-century mystic, wrote of infants in similar terms. "Happy those early dayes! when I / Shin'd in my Angell-infancy" (*The Complete Poetry of Henry Vaughan*, ed. French Fogel [New York: W. W. Norton, 1969], 169).

33. "Editor's Table," *Godey's Lady's Book* 28 (Jan. 1844): 53.

34. Mary Pierce Poor to Feroline Pierce Fox, July 13, 1844, box 12, folder 168, Mary Pierce Poor Letters, Poor Family Collection, Schlesinger Library.

35. S. F. Clapp, "Infancy," *Christian Examiner and Theological Review* 56 (Jan. 1854): 129–30.

36. Slater, *Children*, 90.

37. Mary P. Ryan, *Cradle of the Middle Class: The Family in Oneida County, New York, 1790–1865* (Cambridge: Cambridge University Press, 1981), 232; Greven, *Protestant Temperament*, 157–70.

38. Timothy Shay Arthur, *The Mother* (Philadelphia: E. Ferrett, 1846), 126.

39. E. L. Follen, *Sketches of Married Life* (Boston: Hilliard, Gray, 1838), 289. See also Timothy Shay Arthur, *Married and Single; or, Marriage and Celibacy Contrasted in a Series of Domestic Pictures* (New York: Harper and Bros., 1845), 53.

40. "The Empty Cradle," *Godey's Lady's Book* 34 (Jan. 1847): 12. See also D. W. Belisle, "A Mother's Grief," *Godey's Lady's Book* 36 (June 1848): 349; Arthur, *Married and Single*, 49.

41. "Lines to an Infant Child," *Godey's Lady's Book* 3 (Sept. 1831): 145.

42. Ella, "A Mother's Prayer," *Friend* 10 (Nov. 12, 1836): 44.

43. "The Mother's Prayer: A Sketch," *Lady's Pearl* 1 (Sept. 1840): 84–85.

44. M. J. Shrouds, "The Young Mother's Dream," *Ladies' Repository* 14 (July 1854): 302–3.

45. M. A. E., "The Child and the Angels," *Godey's Lady's Book* 39 (Sept. 1849): 173.

46. "The Angels in the House," *Christian Observer*, May 8, 1856, 76.

47. Helen Bruce, "Our Little Sleeper," *Ladies' Wreath* 9 ([1855]): 167.

48. "Editor's Table," *Godey's Lady's Book* 28 (Jan. 1844): 53; see also "The Guardian Angels," *United States Catholic Magazine* 3 (Oct. 1844): 660.

49. Elizabeth Oakes Smith, *The Newsboy* (New York: J. C. Derby, 1854), 163.

50. Timothy Shay Arthur, "The Wife: A Story for My Young Countrywomen," in *Three Eras of a Woman's Life: The Maiden, Wife, and Mother* (Philadelphia: Henry F. Anners, 1848), 158. See also Timothy Shay Arthur, *The Angel of the Household* (Philadelphia: J. W. Bradley, 1854), 25.

51. Mary Pierce Poor to Feroline Pierce Fox, Dec. 4, 1842, box 12, folder 167, Mary Pierce Poor Letters. For a similar comment, see Longfellow, ed., *Life of Henry Wadsworth Longfellow* 2:130.

52. "Editor's Table," *Godey's Lady's Book* 43 (Nov. 1851): 310.

53. Spencer W. Cone, "A Curious Question," newspaper clipping in Julia Ann Hartness Lay diary, 1855–57, Rare Books and Manuscripts Division, Astor, Lenox and Tilden Foundations, New York Public Library. See also "Infancy," *Ladies' Wreath* 1 (1847): 145; S. D. Robbins, "Childhood's Mission," *Monthly Religious Magazine* 4 (Feb. 1847): 64.

54. "Infancy," 145; James H. Perkins, "On the Death of a Young Child," *Godey's Lady's Book* 32 (June 1846): 251. See also Seba Smith, "The Ministry of Childhood," *Ladies Companion and Literary Expositor* 10 (Apr. 1839): 269.

55. Harriet Beecher Stowe, "A Little Child Shall Lead Them," *Christian Parlor Book* 7 (1851): 248–49.

56. Arthur, *Angel of the Household*.

57. "Editor's Table," *Godey's Lady's Book* 43 (Nov. 1851): 310.

58. Robbins, "Childhood's Mission," 64.

59. Lydia H. Sigourney, *Letters to Mothers* (New York: Harper and Bros., 1840), 25. See also R. C. Waterston, *Thoughts on Moral and Spiritual Culture* (Boston: Crocker and Ruggles, 1842), 26–27.

60. Sigourney, *Letters*, 262.

61. Waterston, *Thoughts*, 289. See also Frances S. Osgood, "The Child and Its Angel-Playmate," *Ladies Companion and Literary Expositor* 17 (July 1842): 157.

62. Wagenknecht, ed., *Mrs. Longfellow*, 144.

63. Timothy Shay Arthur, *The Mother's Rule; or, The Right Way and the Wrong Way* (Rochester: E. Darrow and Bro., 1856), 215.

64. Robbins, "Childhood's Mission," 64, 66. See also "The Infant's Mission," *Christian Parlor Magazine* 1 (Oct. 1844): 179.

65. Arthur, *Mother*, 126.

66. B. B. H., "Death of the Young," *Ladies' Garland* 6 (June 1846): 283.

67. "An Angel's Visit," *Christian Parlor Book* 7 (1851): 349. See also "The Cherub Brothers," *Ladies' Wreath* 2 (1848–49): 84–85.

68. Lovell, ed., *Two Quaker Sisters*, 76.

69. Dow, *Vicissitudes*, 612. See also Fox diary, Jan. 30, 1853, box 13, folder 30, Logan-Fisher-Fox Papers; Sally Hughes to George Hughes, Aug. 23, 1847, folder 6, Sally Hughes Letters.

70. Bushnell, *Christian Nurture*, xxxviii. For similar observations, see Arthur, *Mother*, 18; Samuel K. Jennings, *The Married Lady's Companion; or, Poor Man's Friend* (New York: Lorenzo Dow, 1808), 163; "Parental Duty," *Christian Observer*, Dec. 9, 1854, 193.

# Conclusion

IN THE EARLY nineteenth century concern for privacy, the ideology of motherhood, the increasing availability of birth control information, geographic mobility, the growth of cities, the rise of the publishing industry, the anonymity of urban life, opportunities for social mobility, advances in technology and medical knowledge, and the availability of doctors and private nurses combined to alter the context in which middle- and upper-class couples in the towns and cities of the North conducted family life. These factors tended to undermine or at least encourage some to reexamine traditional attitudes and practices associated with bearing and rearing children and gave them the opportunity to make new choices regarding the fulfillment of their parental responsibilities.

Convinced that it was to their advantage to bear fewer children, these young wives in ever-increasing numbers decided, sometimes on their own and sometimes in collaboration with their husbands, to try to limit the size of their families and space the births of their children. They were not always successful, but in trying to limit their fertility, they made an attempt to control at least one aspect of their lives. When they did become pregnant, they were not inclined to accept the notion that pregnancy was a disease. Despite the determination of some doctors to define the physical and emotional symptoms of pregnancy as medical problems, women did not routinely consult physicians during pregnancy either because they did not believe that doctors would not take their complaints seriously and treat them effectively or because they were too modest to discuss them. Instead they tended to combine the advice of friends and relatives with that offered by health manuals and lecturers in their efforts to cope with the physical discomforts and emotional stress that sometimes preceded the birth of a child.

Before the Civil War the belief that maternal responsibility began before birth encouraged women to take precautions to ensure the well-being of their unborn children. But the conviction that pregnant women should limit their public activities and remove themselves from polite society during the last months of pregnancy was not yet strong enough to force women to withdraw totally from public life. As long as they were so inclined and did not suffer from ill health, childbearing women remained active during pregnancy and adjusted their wardrobes to make themselves presentable. Nevertheless, concern with prenatal care was increasing, and in some areas considerable pressure was placed on expectant mothers to withdraw from society weeks before the baby was actually born.

As opportunities presented themselves, childbearing women began to change some of the rituals of birth and recovery and to modify others. They chose the people who they wanted to attend them on the basis of who was available, what services they thought they required, and who they thought was best suited to deliver those services. Deferring to the medical definition of birth as an illness, to their fear that childbirth was likely to be accompanied by pain, debility, or death, and to the assurance of doctors that the application of medical technology could reduce danger and help alleviate pain, many began to engage physicians rather than midwives to attend them during normal as well as difficult deliveries. Some wives began to request the presence of their husbands during the birth of their children and to depend on their emotional support during labor and delivery. They began to replace the coterie of female friends and relatives that had traditionally attended parturient women during confinement with private nurses, contracted to assist the doctor during delivery and to assume primary responsibility for the care of mother and infant for a month after birth. Close relatives like mothers or sisters continued to be welcome in the lying-in chamber, but as the century progressed, groups of friends and neighbors were less likely to be asked to assist during parturition or to take over the child care and household duties of a woman recently delivered. Instead they were more likely to pay formal calls to express their congratulations and good wishes after the baby was born. The support they were expected to provide was becoming increasingly ceremonial and less practical. Childbearing women typically convalesced for a month after the birth of their children to regain their health as well as to establish or maintain reputations for being respectably genteel. During that period they depended on their monthly nurses to manage their recovery and to teach them how to care for their babies.

Like their mothers and grandmothers, childbearing women in the early nineteenth century were aware that despite their attentiveness and concern for the welfare of their babies, their children were liable to die in infancy. Like their forebears, their fear of death did not necessarily diminish the emotional investment they made in their babies. As they cared for their children, they anticipated grief. And when their babies died, they expressed the kind of passive acceptance that had characterized response to infant death in the past. Unlike those in earlier generations, however, they were increasingly convinced that young children died in a state of innocence and were untroubled by the idea that their babies might be any place but heaven. Emotionally and ideologically, they were prepared to find reassuring the idea that small children could purify and redeem other family members and thereby ensure a sense of family unity and perpetuate traditional moral values. Implicit in the infant-as-redeemer ideology was the suggestion that the deaths as well as the births of babies helped them to fulfill the demands made upon them by the ideology of motherhood.

The changes that childbearing women made in the conduct of pregnancy, birth, recovery, and infant nurture had a number of consequences. Hiring doctors to attend normal as well as complicated deliveries brought new sources of tension into the delivery room as doctors, nurses, attendants, and patients all vied for control over how birth and recovery were to be conducted. The application of technology eventually gave physicians the upper hand, but between 1800 and 1860 childbearing women and their attendants maintained some control over the practice of obstetrics by demanding that physicians defer to rigid standards of modesty and by assuming the right to demand that doctors speed delivery or attempt to alleviate pain. In the process of attempting to gain clinical control over obstetrics cases, doctors found it necessary to refine and articulate their attitudes about the women they were most likely to treat, the social responsibilities of mothers, and the function of parturient pain. While they recognized that the use of forceps, ergot, and anesthesia helped to legitimize their presence in the lying-in chamber, the most conscientious also struggled to define those clinical circumstances that warranted the application of medical technology in obstetrics cases.

The conduct of pregnancy and childbirth became a way for women to testify to their position in society. Hiring a doctor rather than a midwife demonstrated a certain degree of affluence and served to separate those women for whom the whole process of childbearing could be expected to be difficult and dangerous from those in uncivilized lands or the lower classes for whom childbearing was believed to pose little or no threat. Obliging medical practitioners to defer to the demands of modesty in order to protect the refined sensibilities of middle- and upper-class obstetrics patients helped childbearing women validate their claim to respectability. The rhetorical use of the term *ill* to describe being in labor served to indicate that the social position of the woman in question did not require her to perform physical work. Seeking the services of a monthly nurse to assist a physician and to supervise the care of a newborn and maternal recovery provided additional evidence of economic ability to bear extra expense. It also implied that while it was appropriate to expect family members and friends to provide moral support, they could not necessarily be expected to assume primary responsibility for performing practical services in another woman's home for an extended period of time. Demanding the right to reduce one's domestic and social obligations during pregnancy because of ill health and the right to convalesce for as long as a month after delivery testified to the delicate nature of a woman's health in an age when some people correlated physical weakness with social refinement.

Women were beginning to believe not only that they had a right to protect themselves but also that they had the power to do so. Their concerns, however, tended to be narrow and personal rather than broad and public. While they were not totally oblivious to the social and political implications of their maternal responsibilities, they were more immediately concerned with the private consequences of their behavior. When they wrote about their childbearing experiences and maternal duties, they did so with a conspicuous lack of sentimentality or sense of patriotism. During their children's infancy they tended to focus more on the practical than on the ideological aspects of mothering and were relatively unconcerned with the impact their performance of maternal duties had on the fate of the nation and the world. The political implications of the ideology of motherhood may have complicated but did not dictate the way they conducted themselves as the mothers of infant children. It is not surprising to find, then, that when they sought advice about the conduct of pregnancy, confinement, recovery, and infant care or sought solace after the death of a baby, mothers were likely to implement those suggestions that were most consistent with their desire to avoid illness, pain, and death, to assure emotional and material comfort, and to establish or maintain a respectable position in society.

Making conscious decisions about the conduct of childbearing and infant nurture rather than deferring to tradition meant that women had to accept responsibility for their actions. It exposed them to the scrutiny of those who, sensitive to the inherent conflict between private needs and public responsibilities and convinced that the conduct of family life had profound implications for society as a whole, were concerned about the willingness or ability of American mothers to carry out the obligations of motherhood. Critics often charged that mothers whose attitudes and behavior patterns did not conform to ideal standards were selfish and irresponsible. They accused women of being self-indulgent who, ignoring the important role babies had in strengthening the bonds of affection within the family, practiced birth control to ensure their own personal comfort or economic security. They began to criticize women who continued to enjoy their normal activities during pregnancy on the grounds that they were unnecessarily risking their health and that of their unborn children merely to gratify themselves. They characterized as irresponsible women whose vanity demanded that they wear tight clothing during pregnancy. They accused women who chose doctors rather than midwives to attend them during labor and delivery of capriciously bowing to the demands of fashion. Women who demanded anesthesia in order to avoid the pain of labor were censured for risking their respectability as well as for abdicating their responsibility for cultivating strong bonds of affection between themselves and their babies. And for refusing to subordinate themselves to their male midwives during delivery the critics berated women for placing their own autonomy above the welfare of their infants. They characterized mothers who, for the sake of convenience, refused to nurse as unworthy and unfit for placing in jeopardy the health and emotional development of their children. They accused women who mourned excessively the loss of their babies of placing their own emotional comfort above the spiritual welfare of their children. They judged mothers not just on the quality of their work but also on the degree to which they were willing to sacrifice their own comfort and personal interests without complaint. Sometimes their criticism was justified as in the case of wearing restrictive clothing during pregnancy. Sometimes it was not. Nevertheless, the message was that private behavior should serve the public good and that for women to make choices which took self-interest into account was an abuse of power that could lead to the disruption of the social order. Despite the emergence of modern family patterns with their emphasis on privacy, very little associated with the conduct of childbearing and child rearing was removed from public scrutiny. Whether because of concern for public health or the desire to ensure social and political stability, many in the medical, religious, and literary communities, as well as friends, neighbors, and family members, had a vested interest in such private matters as family formation and the conduct of family life.

The very factors that allowed women more choices in the conduct of their maternal responsibilities could also undermine their confidence in their ability to fulfill them. Implicit in the advice offered to them by doctors and popular authors were both a recognition of the importance of their obligations and a suggestion that they needed assistance in carrying them out. Medical knowledge and technology were advanced enough to suggest that mothers should protect their health and that of their children but were not advanced enough to provide them the means to do so. The tendency of young married women to move away from their families to set up households with their husbands helped to liberate them from traditional community controls over matters relating to the conduct of childbearing and rearing while at the same time it sometimes deprived them of immediate and easy access to traditional sources of information and support. The opportunities for social mobility that produced the need to establish or maintain positions for themselves and their families limited the choices they could make as individuals about the conduct of pregnancy, childbirth, recovery, and infant care by forcing them to conform to standards of genteel behavior imposed by anonymous social arbiters. The more mothers became convinced that careful management was the determining factor in ensuring the physical, emotional, and moral well-being of their children, the less confident they were likely to be in their ability to provide it and the more inadequate they felt.

Despite the glorification of motherhood, childbearing women had good reason to be ambivalent about their maternal role. They were convinced that bearing children was likely to damage their health if not threaten their lives. They frequently found the demands of maternity frustrating, time-consuming, exhausting, and tedious. Caring for young children usually temporarily suspended their participation in all but the most perfunctory public activities. And they were very much aware that the more time and affection they invested in their babies, the more they were likely to suffer if they lost them.

Nevertheless, they were convinced that their maternal duties were important and that the time they devoted to them was time well spent. They viewed the safe birth of a healthy child with great pleasure and pride. They enjoyed watching their children develop physically, emotionally, and spiritually. And they found in their maternal role an important source of personal fulfillment. During much of their early married lives, the nursery was the one place where they were subordinate to no one.

# *Appendix*

This appendix includes information on forty of the
women in this study; the other women in the study
have been excluded because there was insufficient biographical information on them. The appendix is arranged chronologically by date of marriage.

Biographical Information on Women in This Study

| Name | Year of Marriage | Age at Marriage[1] | Number of Known Births | Span of Childbearing Years[3] | Years of Birth of Children | Year of Death | Husband's Occupation | Married Residence |
|---|---|---|---|---|---|---|---|---|
| Lucy Tappan Pierce | ca. 1802[2] | — | 7 | 18 | 1803 1804 1806 1808 1811 1813 1820 | — | minister | Brookline, Mass. |
| Peggy Holcomb Dow[4] | 1804 | 24 | 1 | 1 | 1806 | 1820 | minister | no permanent residence |
| Mary Guion | 1807 | 25 | 2 | 4 | 1811 1814 | — | — | Northcastle, N.Y. |
| Mary Wilder White[4] | 1807 | 27 | 3 | 2.5 | 1808 1809 1810 | 1811 | lawyer | Newburyport, Mass. |
| Mary Jackson Lee[4] | 1809 | 26 | 6 | 17 | 1810 1811 1817 | 1860 | merchant | Boston |

| | | | | | Births | | | | Residence |
|---|---|---|---|---|---|---|---|---|---|
| Susan Mansfield Huntington[4] | 1809 | 18 | 6 | 9 | 1811, 1812, 1813, —, —, 1819 | 1819, 1823, 1826 | 1823 | minister | Boston |
| Sarah Connell Ayer[4] | 1810 | 19 | 7 | 13 | 1811, 1812, 1813, 1814, 1817, 1819, 1823 | | 1835 | doctor | Bow, N.H.; Portland, Maine; Eastport, Maine |

[1] Age is accurate to within one year since information about month of marriage and birth is often unavailable.
[2] Marriage date unknown; estimated to be one year previous to birth of first child.
[3] Length of time between first known birth and last known birth, accurate to within one year.
[4] Lost a child prematurely, at birth, in infancy.

*Biographical Information on Women in This Study (cont.)*

| Name | Year of Marriage | Age at Marriage[1] | Number of Known Births | Span of Childbearing Years[3] | Years of Birth of Children | Year of Death | Husband's Occupation | Married Residence |
|---|---|---|---|---|---|---|---|---|
| Eliza Fenwick Rutherford | 1812 | 23 | 4 | 7 | 1813 1815 1817 1819 | — | teacher | Bridgetown, Barbados; New Haven, Conn.; New York |
| Sarah Ripley Stearns | 1812 | 27 | 4 | 7 | 1813 1815 1816 1819 | — | merchant | Shelburne, Mass. |
| Mehetable May Dawes Goddard[4] | 1818 | 22 | 10 | 22 | 1819 1821 1823 1825 1827 1829 1832 1834 1837 1840 | 1882 | merchant | Manchester, England; Brookline, Mass. |

| Name | | | | | | | | |
|---|---|---|---|---|---|---|---|---|
| Sarah Hill Fletcher | 1821 | 19 | 11 | 24 | 1823 1824 1826 1828 1831 1833 1835 1837 1840 1842 1846 | 1854 | lawyer | Indianapolis |
| Mary Ann Hammond Palfrey[4] | 1823 | 23 | 6 | 15 | 1824 1825 1828 1831 1833 1838 | 1898 | minister | Cambridge, Mass. |
| Elizabeth Ellery Sedgwick[4] | ca. 1823[2] | 24 | 4 | 5 | 1824 1825 1826 1828 | — | lawyer | New York |

205

## Biographical Information on Women in This Study (cont.)

| Name | Year of Marriage | Age at Marriage[1] | Number of Known Births | Span of Childbearing Years[3] | Years of Birth of Children | Year of Death | Husband's Occupation | Married Residence |
|---|---|---|---|---|---|---|---|---|
| Millicent Hunt | 1824 | — | 5 | 7 | 1826 1827 1828–29 1830 1832 | — | — | Detroit |
| Parke Lewis Butler[4] | 1826 | 27 | 5 | 7 | 1826 1828 (twins) 1829 1832 | — | soldier | no permanent residence |
| Mary Lovell Pickard Ware | 1827 | 28 | 6 | 13 | 1828 1830 1832 1834 1838 1840 | 1849 | minister, teacher | Boston; Cambridge, Mass.; Framingham, Mass. |
| Abigail May Alcott[4] | 1830 | 30 | 5 | 10 | 1831 1832 1835 1839 1840 | 1877 | teacher, philosopher | Germantown, Pa.; Concord, Mass.; Boston; Walpole, N.H. |

| | | | | | | 1876 | publisher, reformer | Boston |
|---|---|---|---|---|---|---|---|---|
| Helen Benson Garrison[4] | 1834 | 23 | 7 | 13 | 1836 1838 1840 1842 1844 1846 1848 | 1876 | publisher, reformer | Boston |
| Agnes Treat Lamb Richards | 1835 | 24 | 1 | 1 | 1839 | — | — | Newburgh, N.Y. |
| Kate Ross | 1835 | — | 1 | 1 | 1836 | — | soldier | Fort Hamilton, N.Y. |
| Lucy Buffum Lovell[4] | 1835 | 26 | 7 | — | 1837 1839 1841 — — — — | — | minister | Amherst, Mass.; Bellingham, Mass. |

207

## Biographical Information on Women in This Study (cont.)

| Name | Year of Marriage | Age at Marriage[1] | Number of Known Births | Span of Childbearing Years[3] | Years of Birth of Children | Year of Death | Husband's Occupation | Married Residence |
|---|---|---|---|---|---|---|---|---|
| Harriet Beecher Stowe[4] | 1836 | 24 | 7 | 15 | 1836 (twins) 1838 1840 1843 1849 1850 | 1896 | teacher | Cincinnati; Brunswick, Maine; Hartford, Conn.; Andover, Mass. |
| Elizabeth Cady Stanton | 1840 | 24 | 7 | 18 | 1842 1844 1845 1851 1852 1856 1859 | 1899 | lawyer | Johnstown, N.Y.; Boston; Seneca Falls, N.Y.; New York; Tenafly, N.J. |
| Mary Pierce Poor | 1841 | 21 | 7 | — | 1842 1844 1848 1853 1855–56 — — | 1912 | journalist, economist | Bangor, Maine; New York |

| Julia Ann Hartness Lay | 1841 | 22 | 5 | 11 | 1845<br>1847<br>1850<br>1853<br>1855 | 1878 | bank<br>bookkeeper | New York |
|---|---|---|---|---|---|---|---|---|
| Sarah Watson Dana | 1841 | 27 | 6 | 16 | 1842<br>1844<br>1846<br>1848<br>1851<br>1857 | 1907 | writer,<br>lawyer | Cambridge,<br>Mass.; Boston |
| Christiana B. Cowell[4] | 1841 | 19 | 5 | 15 | 1842–43<br>—<br>—<br>1853<br>1856 | 1862 | minister | Lebanon, Maine |

## Biographical Information on Women in This Study *(cont.)*

| Name | Year of Marriage | Age at Marriage[1] | Number of Known Births | Span of Childbearing Years[3] | Years of Birth of Children | Year of Death | Husband's Occupation | Married Residence |
|---|---|---|---|---|---|---|---|---|
| Fanny Appleton Longfellow[4] | 1843 | 26 | 6 | 12 | 1844 1845 1847 1850 1853 1855 | 1861 | writer, teacher | Cambridge, Mass. |
| Rachel B. Gleason | 1844 | 23 | 2 | 6 | 1850 1855 | 1905 | doctor | Carlisle, N.Y.; Cuba, N.Y.; Cortland County, N.Y.; Ithaca, N.Y.: Elmira, N.Y. |
| Maria D. Brown[4] | 1845 | 18 | 8 | 25 | 1846 1848 1852 1854 1860 — — 1870 | 1927 | paper manufacturer, farmer | Amesville, Ohio; Iowa farm, Fort Madison, Iowa |

| Name | | | | | | | | |
|---|---|---|---|---|---|---|---|---|
| Jeannie Mercer McCall[4] | ca. 1846[2] | — | 2 | 3 | 1847 1849 | — | teacher | Philadelphia |
| Sarah Edgarton Mayo | 1846 | 27 | 1 | 1 | 1847 | 1848 | minister | Gloucester, Mass. |
| Anna Colton Clayton | ca. 1846[2] | 26 | 2 | 4 | 1847 1850 | — | lawyer | West Chester, Pa.; Cape May, N.J. |
| Frances Miriam Berry Whitcher[4] | 1847 | 35 | 2 | 2 | 1848 1849 | 1852 | minister | Elmira, N.Y.: Whitesboro, N.Y. |
| Mary Harris Lester | 1847 | — | 1 | 1 | 1848 | — | merchant | New York |
| Harriet Hanson Robinson | 1848 | 23 | 4 | 10 | 1850 1852 1854 1859 | 1911 | journalist | Lowell, Mass.; Concord, Mass.; Malden, Mass. |
| Ellen Ruggles Strong[4] | 1848 | 22 | 4 | 12 | 1849 1851 1856 1860 | 1891 | lawyer | New York |

## Biographical Information on Women in This Study *(cont.)*

| Name | Year of Marriage | Age at Marriage[1] | Number of Known Births | Span of Childbearing Years[3] | Years of Birth of Children | Year of Death | Husband's Occupation | Married Residence |
|---|---|---|---|---|---|---|---|---|
| Mary Rodman Fisher Fox | 1849 | 27 | 5 | 9 | 1850<br>1851<br>1853<br>1855<br>1858 | 1903 | — | Philadelphia |
| Elizabeth Dwight Cabot[4] | 1857 | 27 | 8 | 14 | 1859<br>1861<br>1864<br>1866<br>1868<br>1871<br>1872 (twins) | 1901 | lawyer, philosopher | Brookline, Mass. |
| Bessie Huntting Rudd | 1859 | 28 | 2 | 3 | 1860<br>1862 | 1862 | publisher | Bloomfield, N.J.; New York |

# Bibliography of Primary Sources

LETTERS, DIARIES, AND MEMOIRS —UNPUBLISHED

Chester County Historical Society, West Chester, Pa.
    Ann Jefferis Sheppard Letters, Jefferis Family Letters.
    Gleason, Rachel Brooks, "Reminiscences of Early Life," privately held.
Historical Society of Pennsylvania, Philadelphia.
    Mary Brown Askew diary.
    Anna Colton Clayton Letters, John Clayton Papers.
    Sally Logan Fisher diary.
    Mary Rodman Fisher Fox diary, Logan-Fisher-Fox Papers.
    Cornelia Hand Letters, Hand Family Correspondence.
    Mary Harris Letters, George B. Harris Papers.
    Sally Hughes Letters, Maxcy-Markoe-Hughes Collection.
    Eleanor Parke Custis Lewis Letters.
    Jeannie McCall Letters, McCall Section, Cadwallader Collection.
    Gertrude Meredith Letters, Meredith Papers.
    Elizabeth Parker Letters, Parker-Brinley Papers.
Houghton Library, Harvard University, Cambridge, Mass.
    Abigail May Alcott Letters, Alcott Family Papers.
    A. Bronson Alcott Papers, Alcott Family Papers.
    Sarah Snell Bryant diary.
    Henry Wadsworth Longfellow journal.
    Elizabeth Ellery Sedgwick journal.
Longfellow National Historic Site, National Park Service, Cambridge, Mass.
    Frances Elizabeth Appleton Longfellow Papers.
Maine Historical Society, Portland.
    Timothy Carter Papers.
New-York Historical Society, N.Y.
    Mary Guion diary.
    Susan Kitteridge Osgood Field Papers.
    Agnes Treat Lamb Letters, Lamb Papers.
    Mary Harris Lester diary, Andrew Lester Papers.
    Edward C. Ross Letters, Chrystie Family Papers.
    George Templeton Strong diary, George Templeton Strong Papers.
    Frances Miriam Berry Whitcher Letters, Whitcher Collection.

New York Public Library, Rare Books and Manuscripts Division, Astor, Lenox and Tilden Foundations.
>   Benjamin Drake Letters, Benjamin Drake Papers.
>   Julia Ann Hartness Lay diary.
Schlesinger Library, Radcliffe College, Cambridge, Mass.
>   Elizabeth Dwight Cabot diary, Hugh Cabot Family Collection.
>   Elizabeth Dwight Cabot Letters, Hugh Cabot Family Collection.
>   Sarah Watson Dana diary, Dana Family Papers.
>   Sarah Watson Dana Letters, Dana Family Papers.
>   Mehetable May Dawes Goddard Letters, May-Goddard Collection.
>   Hooker Collection of Miscellaneous Letters.
>   Abigail and Lavius Hyde Letters, Bradley-Hyde Collection.
>   Lucy Tappan Pierce Letters, Poor Family Collection.
>   Mary Pierce Poor diary, Poor Family Collection.
>   Mary Pierce Poor Letters, Poor Family Collection.
>   Harriet Hanson Robinson diary, Robinson-Shattuck Papers.
>   Harriet Hanson Robinson Letters, Robinson-Shattuck Papers.
>   Bessie Huntting Rudd Letters, Huntting-Rudd Family Papers.
>   Sarah Ripley Stearns diary, Stearns Collection.
>   Harriet Beecher Stowe Letters, Beecher-Stowe Collection.

LETTERS, DIARIES, AND MEMOIRS—PUBLISHED

Adams, Abigail. *New Letters of Abigail Adams, 1788–1801.* Edited by Stewart Mitchell. Boston: Houghton Mifflin, 1947.

Adams, Horace. "A Puritan Wife on the Frontier." *Mississippi Valley Historical Review* 27 (June 1940): 67–84.

Ayer, Hannah Palfrey, ed. *A Legacy of New England: Letters of the Palfrey Family.* 2 vols. Portland, Maine: Anthoensen, 1950.

Ayer, Sarah Connell, *Diary of Sarah Connell Ayer.* Portland, Maine: Lefavor-Tower, 1910.

Brown, Harriet Conner. *Grandmother Brown's Hundred Years, 1827–1927.* Boston: Little, Brown, 1929.

Cabot, Elizabeth. *Letters of Elizabeth Cabot.* 2 vols. Boston: privately printed, 1905.

Channing, Katherine Minot, ed. *Minot Family Letters: 1773–1871.* Sherborn, Mass.: privately printed, 1957.

Cowell, Christiana B. *Life and Writings of Mrs. Christiana B. Cowell, Consort of Rev. D. B. Cowell, Who Died in Lebanon, Maine, Oct. 8, 1862, Aged 41 Years.* Biddleford, Maine: John E. Butler, 1872.

Dana, Richard Henry, Jr. *The Journal of Richard Henry Dana, Jr.* Edited by Robert F. Lucid. 3 vols. Cambridge, Mass.: Belknap Press, 1968.

Dobkin, Marjorie Housepian, ed. *The Making of a Feminist: Early Journals and Letters of M. Carey Thomas.* Kent, Ohio: Kent State University Press, 1979.

Dow, Peggy. *Vicissitudes; or, The Journey of Life.* Philadelphia: Joseph Rakestraw, 1816.

Drinker, Cecil K. *Not So Long Ago: A Chronicle of Medicine and Doctors in Colonial Philadelphia.* New York: Oxford University Press, 1937.

Fletcher, Calvin. *The Diary of Calvin Fletcher, Including Letters to and from Calvin Fletcher: 1838–1843.* Edited by Gayle Thornbrough. Indianapolis: Indiana Historical Society, 1973.

———. *The Diary of Calvin Fletcher, 1817–1838, Including Letters of Calvin Fletcher and Diaries and Letters of His Wife Sarah Hill Fletcher.* Edited by Gayle Thornbrough. Indianapolis: Indiana Historical Society, 1972.

Garrison, William Lloyd. *The Letters of William Lloyd Garrison: A House Divided against Itself, 1836–1840.* Edited by Louis Ruchames. Cambridge, Mass.: Belknap Press, 1971.

———. *The Letters of William Lloyd Garrison: No Union with Slave-Holders, 1841–1849.* Edited by Walter Merrill. Cambridge, Mass.: Belknap Press, 1973.

Hellerstein, Erna Olafson, Leslie Parker Hume, and Karen M. Offen, eds. *Victorian Women: A Documentary Account of Women's Lives in Nineteenth-Century England, France, and the United States.* Stanford: Stanford University Press, 1981.

Huntington, Susan. *Memoirs of the Late Mrs. Susan Huntington, of Boston, Mass.* Edited by Benjamin Wisner. Boston: Crocker and Brewster, 1826.

Lawrence, Jenny. "Miriam Berry Whitcher Speaks Her Mind: Letters Home, 1846–1852." *New-York Historical Society Quarterly* 63 (Jan. 1979): 25–53.

Lerner, Gerda, ed. *The Female Experience: An American Documentary.* Indianapolis: Bobbs-Merrill, 1977.

Longfellow, Frances Appleton. *Mrs. Longfellow: Selected Letters and Journals of Fanny Appleton Longfellow (1817–1861).* Edited by Edward Wagenknecht. New York: Longmans, Green, 1956.

Longfellow, Henry Wadsworth. *The Letters of Henry Wadsworth Longfellow.* Edited by Andrew Hilen. 4 vols. Cambridge: Harvard University Press, 1972.

Longfellow, Samuel, ed. *Life of Henry Wadsworth Longfellow with Extracts from His Journals and Correspondence.* 3 vols. Boston: Houghton Mifflin, 1891.

Lovell, Malcolm R., ed. *Two Quaker Sisters: From the Original Diaries of Elizabeth Buffum Chace and Lucy Buffum Lovell*. New York: Liveright, 1937.

Mayo, A. D. *Selections and Writings of Mrs. Sarah C. Edgarton Mayo: With a Memoir, by Her Husband*. Boston: A. Tomkins, 1849.

Morse, Frances Rollins, ed. *Henry and Mary Lee: Letters and Journals with Other Family Letters, 1802–1860*. Boston: T. Todd, 1926.

Nash, Charles Elventon. *The History of Augusta: First Settlements and Early Days as a Town Including the Diary of Mrs. Martha Moore Ballard (1785–1812)*. Augusta, Maine: Charles E. Nash, 1904.

Stanton, Theodore, and Harriot Stanton Blatch, eds. *Elizabeth Cady Stanton As Revealed in Her Letters, Diary, and Reminiscences*. 2 vols. New York: Harper, 1922.

Strong, George Templeton. *The Diary of George Templeton Strong: The Turbulent Fifties, 1850–1859*. Edited by Allan Nevins and Milton Halsey Thomas. New York: Macmillan, 1952.

———. *The Diary of George Templeton Strong: Young Man in New York, 1835–1849*. Edited by Allan Nevins and Milton Halsey Thomas. New York: Macmillan, 1952.

Tileston, Mary Wilder, ed. *Memorials of Mary Wilder White: A Century Ago in New England*. Boston: Everett Press, 1903.

Ware, Mary L. *Memoir of Mary L. Ware, Wife of Henry Ware, Jr.*. Edited by Edward B. Hall. Boston: Crosby, Nichols, 1853.

Wedd, A. F., ed. *The Fate of the Fenwicks: Letters to Mary Hays*. London: Methuen, 1927.

NOVELS

Arthur, Timothy Shay. *The Angel of the Household*. Philadelphia: J. W. Bradley, 1854.

———. *Married and Single; or, Marriage and Celibacy Contrasted in a Series of Domestic Pictures*. New York: Harper and Bros., 1845.

———. *The Mother*. Philadelphia: E. Ferrett, 1846.

———. *The Mother's Rule; or, The Right Way and the Wrong Way*. Rochester: E. Darrow and Bro., 1856.

———. *Our Children: How Shall We Save Them?* New York: Brognard, 1850.

———. *Three Eras of a Woman's Life: The Maiden, Wife and Mother*. Philadelphia: Henry F. Anners, 1848.

Fern, Fanny [Sarah Payson Parton]. *Fresh Leaves*. New York: Mason and Bros., 1857.

———. *Ruth Hall: A Domestic Tale of the Present Time*. New York: Mason Bros., 1855.

Follen, E. L. *Sketches of Married Life*. Boston: Hilliard, Gray, 1838.

Foster, Hannah Webster. *The Coquette; or, The History of Eliza Wharton*. Boston: E. Larkin, 1797.

Hentz, Caroline Lee. *Ernest Linwood: A Novel*. Boston: John P. Jewett, 1856.

———. *Ugly Effie; or, The Neglected One and the Pet Beauty and Other Tales*. Philadelphia: T. B. Peterson, [1850].

McIntosh, Maria J. *Charms and Counter-charms*. New York: D. Appleton, 1848.

Manvill, P. D. *Lucinda; or, The Mountain Mourner*. Johnstown: n.p., 1807.

Rowson, Susanna. *Charlotte, a Tale of Truth*. 2 vols. Philadelphia: Mathew Carey, 1794.

Rush, Caroline. *The North and the South; or, Slavery and Its Contrasts, a Tale of Real Life*. Philadelphia: Crissy and Markley, 1852.

Sedgwick, C. M. *Home*. Boston: James Munroe, 1835.

Smith, Elizabeth Oakes. *The Newsboy*. New York: J. C. Derby, 1854.

Thayer, J. *The Drunkard's Daughter*. Boston: William S. Damrell, 1842.

Williams, Catharine Read Arnold. *Religion at Home, a Story, Founded on Facts*. Providence: Marshall and Hammond, 1829.

Wood, S. S. B. K. *Amelia; or, The Influence of Virtue: An Old Man's Story*. Portsmouth: William Treadwell, 1802.

## MEDICAL TEXTS AND HEALTH MANUALS

Alcott, William A. *The Physiology of Marriage*. Boston: John P. Jewett, 1956.

Aristotle. *The Works of Aristotle, the Famous Philosopher, in Four Parts*. New England: n.p., 1813.

Bard, Samuel. *A Compendium of the Theory and Practice of Midwifery*. New York: Collins and Perkins, 1807.

Blundell, James. *The Principles and Practice of Obstetricy*. Washington, D.C.: Duff Green, 1834.

Bright, John W. *The Mother's Medical Guide*. Louisville: A. S. Tilden, 1844.

Buchan, William. *Advice to Mothers on the Subject of Their Own Health; and on the Means of Promoting the Health, Strength, and Beauty of Their Offspring*. Philadelphia: John Bioren, 1804.

———. *Domestic Medicine; or, A Valuable Treatise on the Prevention and Cure of Diseases*. Leominster: Adams and Wilder, 1804.

Bull, Thomas. *The Maternal Management of Children, in Health and Disease*. Philadelphia: Lindsay and Blakiston, 1853.

Burns, John. *The Principles of Midwifery, Including the Diseases of Women and Children*. Philadelphia: Hopkins and Earle, 1810.

Channing, Walter. *Remarks on the Employment of Females as Practitioners in Midwifery*. Boston: Cummings and Hilliard, 1820.

————. *A Treatise on Etherization in Childbirth Illustrated by Five Hundred and Eighty-one Cases*. Boston: William D. Ticknor, 1848.

Chavasse, Pye Henry. *Advice to Wives on the Management of Themselves during the Periods of Pregnancy, Labour, and Suckling*. New York: D. Appleton, 1844.

Churchill, Fleetwood. *On the Theory and Practice of Midwifery*. Philadelphia: Lea and Blanchard, 1843.

Combe, Andrew. *Treatise on the Physiological and Moral Management of Infancy*. Boston: Saxton and Kelt, 1846.

Condie, D. Francis. *A Practical Treatise on the Diseases of Children*. Philadelphia: Lea and Blanchard, 1847.

Croserio, C. *Homoeopathic Manual of Obstetrics; or, A Treatise on the Aid the Art of Midwifery May Derive from Homoeopathy*. Translated by H. Cote. Cincinnati: More, Anderson, Wilstack and Keys, 1853.

Culverwell, R. J. *The Institutes of Marriage*. New York: n.p., 1846.

Curtis, A. *Lectures on Midwifery and the Forms of Disease Peculiar to Women and Children Delivered to the Members of the Botanico-Medical College of the State of Ohio*. Cincinnati: C. Nagle, 1846.

Denman, Thomas. *An Introduction to the Practice of Midwifery*. Brattleborough, Vt.: William Fessenden, 1807.

Dewees, William P. *A Compendious System of Midwifery, Chiefly Designed to Facilitate the Inquiries of Those Who May Be Pursuing This Branch of Study*. Philadelphia: Carey and Lea, 1826.

————. *An Essay on the Means of Lessening Pain, and Facilitating Certain Cases of Difficult Parturition*. Philadelphia: John H. Oswald, 1806.

————. *Treatise on the Physical and Medical Treatment of Children*. Philadelphia: Carey and Lea, 1825.

Dickson, Samuel Henry. *Essays on Life, Sleep, Pain, Etc*. Philadelphia: Blanchard and Lea, 1852.

Duncan, J. Matthews. *On the Mortality of Childbed and Maternity Hospitals*. Edinburgh: Adam and Charles Black, 1870.

Eberle, John. *A Treatise on the Mental and Physical Education of Children*. Cincinnati: Corey and Fairbank, 1833.

Ewell, Thomas. *Letters to Ladies, Including Important Information concerning Themselves and Infants*. Philadelphia: W. Brown, 1817.

Gardner, Augustus K. *A History of the Art of Midwifery: A Lecture Delivered at the College of Physicians and Surgeons, November 11, 1851*. New York: Stringer and Townsend, 1852.

Guillimeau, James. *Child-birth; or, The Happy Deliverie of Women*. London: A. Hatfield, 1612.

Hamilton, Alexander. *Outline of the Theory and Practice of Midwifery*. Northhampton, Mass.: Thomas and Andrews, 1797.

Hamilton, James. *Practical Observations on Various Subjects Relating to Midwifery*. 2 vols. Philadelphia: A. Waldie, 1837–38.

Hersey, Thomas. *The Midwife's Practical Directory; or, Woman's Confidential Friend*. Baltimore: Hersey, 1836.

Hodge, Hugh L. *An Eulogium of William P. Dewees, M.D., Delivered before the Medical Students of the University of Pennsylvania, November 5, 1842*. Philadelphia: Merrihew and Thompson, 1842.

Hollick, Frederick. *The Marriage Guide; or, Natural History of Generation*. New York: T. W. Strong, 1850.

———. *The Matron's Manual of Midwifery, and the Diseases of Women during Pregnancy and in Child Bed*. New York: T. W. Strong, 1848.

Holmes, Oliver Wendell. *Puerperal Fever, as a Private Pestilence*. Boston: Ticknor and Fields, 1855.

Hooker, Worthington. *Physician and Patient; or, A Practical View of Mutual Duties, Relations and Interests of the Medical Profession and the Community*. New York: Baker and Scribner, 1849.

Howard, Horton. *A Treatise on the Complaints Peculiar to Females: Embracing a System of Midwifery, the Whole in Conformity with the Improved System of Botanic Medicine*. Columbus, Ohio: Horton, 1832.

Jennings, Samuel K. *The Married Lady's Companion; or, Poor Man's Friend*. New York: Lorenzo Dow, 1808.

Lee, Robert. *Lectures on the Theory and Practice of Midwifery*. Philadelphia: Ed. Barrington and Geo. D. Haswell, 1844.

McNair, Alexander H. *Suggestions to Parents and Others, on the Physical and Medical Treatment of Children; Also, Diseases of Females*. Philadelphia: McNair, 1842.

Mauriceau, A. M. *The Married Woman's Private Medical Companion*. New York: Joseph Trow, 1847.

Meigs, Charles D. *Introductory Lecture to a Course on Obstetrics, Delivered in Jefferson Medical College, November 4, 1841*. Philadelphia: Merrihew and Thompson, 1841.

———. *A Lecture Introductory to the Course of Obstetrics in Jefferson Medical College of Philadelphia, Delivered November 5, 1842*. Philadelphia: Merrihew and Thompson, 1842.

———. *Lecture on Some of the Distinctive Characteristics of the Female, Delivered before the Class of the Jefferson Medical College, January 5, 1847*. T. K. and P. G. Collins, 1847.

————. *Obstetrics: The Science and the Art*. Philadelphia: Blanchard and Lea, 1856.

————. *On the Nature, Signs, and Treatment of Childbed Fever in a Series of Letters Addressed to the Students of His Class*. Philadelphia: Blanchard and Lea, 1854.

————. *The Philadelphia Practice of Midwifery*. Philadelphia: James Kay, 1838.

————, ed. *The History, Pathology, and Treatment of Puerperal Fever and Crural Phlebitis*. Philadelphia: Ed. Barrington and Geo. D. Haswell, 1842.

Merriman, Samuel. *A Synopsis of the Various Kinds of Difficult Parturition*. Philadelphia: Thomas Dobson, 1816.

Miller, Henry. *Report of the Obstetric Committee on Anaesthesia in Midwifery, and the Speculum Uteri*. Louisville: Webb and Levering, 1853.

Pendleton, Mrs. [Hester]. *Parents' Guide for the Transmission of Desired Qualities to Offspring, and Childbirth Made Easy*. New York: Fowler and Wells, 1856.

Raynalde, Thomas. *The Birth of Man-kinde, Otherwise Named, the Womans Booke Set Forth in English by Thomas Raynalde Physician, and by Him Corrected and Augmented*. London: A. H., 1634.

*Reproductive Control; or, A Rational Guide to Matrimonial Happiness*. Cincinnati: n.p., 1855.

Rush, Benjamin. *Medical Inquiries and Observations upon the Diseases of the Mind*. Philadelphia: Kimber and Richardson, 1812.

Ryan, Michael. *The Philosophy of Marriage in Its Social, Moral, and Physical Relations*. London: H. Bailliere, 1839.

Seaman, Valentine. *The Midwives Monitor and Mothers Mirror*. New York: Isaac Collins, 1800.

Simpson, James Y. *The Obstetric Memoirs and Contributions of James Y. Simpson, M.D., F.R.S.E.* Edited by W. O. Priestly and Horatio R. Storer. 2 vols. Philadelphia: Lippincott, 1855–56.

Skinner, H. B. *The Female's Medical Guide and Married Woman's Advisor*. Boston: Skinner, 1849.

Smellie, W. *A Treatise on the Theory and Practice of Midwifery*. London: D. Wilson and T. Durham, 1752.

White, Charles. *A Treatise on the Management of Pregnant and Lying-in Women*. London: Edward and Charles Dilly, 1773.

Whitney, Daniel H. *The Family Physician and Guide to Health*. New York: H. Gilbert, 1833.

PERIODICALS CONSULTED FOR MATERIALS USED IN THIS STUDY

LADIES' MAGAZINES
*Godey's Lady's Book*, 1830–60.
*Graham's Magazine*, 1841–58.
*Ladies Companion and Literary Expositor*, 1834–44.
*Ladies' Garland*, 1837–50.
*Ladies' Literary Cabinet*, 1819–22.
*Ladies' Wreath*, 1847–59.
*Lady's Monitor*, 1801–2.
*Lady's Pearl*, 1840–43.
*Weekly Visitor; or, Ladies Miscellany*, 1802–12.

RELIGIOUS PERIODICALS
*Christian Examiner and Theological Review*, 1824–60.
*Christian Observer*, 1840–60.
*Christian Parlor Magazine*, 1844–55.
*Christian Review*, 1840–60.
*Friend*, 1827–60.
*Literary and Theological Review*, 1834–39.
*Monthly Religious Magazine*, 1844–60.
*United States Catholic Magazine*, 1842–49.

MEDICAL JOURNALS
*American Journal of Insanity*, 1844–61.
*American Journal of the Medical Sciences*, 1827–59.
*Boston Medical and Surgical Journal*, 1828–60.
*Eclectic Journal of Medicine*, 1836–40.
*Medical Examiner, and Record of Medical Science*, 1836–56.
*Medical Repository*, 1799–1823.
*Transactions of the American Medical Association*, 1848–60.

MISCELLANEOUS PRIMARY SOURCES

Adams, Nehemiah. *Agnes and the Little Key; or, Bereaved Parents Instructed and Comforted*. Boston: S. K. Whipple, 1857.
*Annual Reports of the Managers of the New York Asylum for Lying-in Women*. New York Hospital–Cornell Medical Center Archives, N.Y.
Barwell, Louisa Mary. *Advice to Mothers on the Treatment of Infants*. Philadelphia: Leary and Getz, 1853.

Bradstreet, Anne. *The Complete Works of Anne Bradstreet*. Edited by Joseph R. McElrath and Allan P. Robb. Boston: Twayne, 1981.

Brown, Helen E. *The Mother and Her Work*. Boston: American Tract Society, 1862.

Carey, Mathew. *Philosophy of Common Sense*. Philadelphia: Blanchard, 1838.

DeBow, J. D. B. *Statistical View of the United States*. Washington, D.C.: Beverley Tucker, 1854.

Gregory, Samuel. *Man-Midwifery Exposed and Corrected*. Boston: George Gregory, 1848.

Massachusetts General Hospital. *The Semi-Centennial of Anaesthesia Oct. 16, 1846–Oct. 16, 1896*. Boston: Massachusetts General Hospital, 1897.

Merritt, M. Angeline. *Dress Reform Practically and Physiologically Considered*. Buffalo: Jewett, Thomas, 1852.

Miller, Peter. "An Essay on the Means of Lessening the Pains of Parturition." In *Medical Theses, Selected from among the Inaugural Dissertations, Published and Defended by the Graduates in Medicine of the University of Pennsylvania and Other Medical Schools in the United States*. Edited by Charles Caldwell. Philadelpia: Thomas and William Bradford, 1805.

"Notes on the Lectures on Midwifery in the University of Pa. Delivered by Doctors James and Dewees," 1826. Manuscript Collections. College of Physicians of Philadelphia.

Rauch, Frederick A. *Psychology; or, A View of the Human Soul, Including Anthropology*. New York: M. W. Dodd, 1841.

Sigourney, Lydia H. *Letters to Mothers*. New York: Harper and Bros., 1840.

Sims, J. Marion. *The Story of My Life*. New York: D. Appleton, 1884.

Throckmorton, John. "Notebook of Medical School Lectures, 1815–1816." Monmouth County Historical Association, Freehold, N.J.

Vaughan, Henry. *The Complete Poetry of Henry Vaughan*. Edited by French Fogel. New York: W. W. Norton, 1969.

Warren, Edward. *The Life of John Collins Warren, M.D., Compiled from His Autobiography and Journals*. 2 vols. Boston: Ticknor and Fields, 1860.

Waterston, R. C. *Thoughts on Moral and Spiritual Culture*. Boston: Crocker and Ruggles, 1842.

Wordsworth, William. *The Complete Poetical Works of William Wordsworth*. Boston: Houghton Mifflin, 1904.

Wright, Henry C. *Marriage and Parentage*. Boston: Bela Marsh, 1855.

———. *The Unwelcome Child; or, The Crime of an Undesigned and Undesired Maternity*. Boston: Bela Marsh, 1858.

# Index

229